IMAGINATION AN

OR, SELECTIONS

FROM THE ENGLISH POETS,

ILLUSTRATIVE OF THOSE FIRST REQUISITES OF THEIR ART; WITH MARKINGS
OF THE BEST PASSAGES, CRITICAL NOTICES OF THE WRITERS,
AND AN ESSAY IN ANSWER TO THE QUESTION

"WHAT IS POETRY?"

BY LEIGH HUNT.

A NEW EDITION.

1883.

British Library Cataloguing-in-Publication Data
A catalogue record for this book is available from the
British Library

Leigh Hunt

James Henry Leigh Hunt – better-known by his pen name, Leigh Hunt – was born in London, England in 1784. He was educated at Christ's Hospital, entering the school shortly after Samuel Taylor Coleridge and Charles Lamb had both left. Hunt published his first volume of poetry, *Juvenilia* (1801), at the age of just seventeen, and for the rest of his life was immersed in the literary and theatrical worlds.

Hunt began to write for the newspapers, and in 1807 published a volume of theatre criticism. From 1808 onwards, he worked for the *Examiner,* a popular and often vitriolic paper which earned Hunt a two-year stint in prison for an attack he penned on the Prince Regent. Upon his release form prison, he spent a year editing *The Reflector,* before focussing again on his poetry. In 1816, he published his most significant work, *Story of Rimini,* and followed this with *Foliage* (1818), *Hero and Leander* (1819) and *Bacchies and Ariadne* (1819). Together, these works established him as a talented and important poet.

Hunt's newfound literary fame saw him make the acquaintance of John Keats, Percy Shelley and others. However, he gradually fell into deep financial trouble. His newspaper, *The Examiner,* folded, and he troubled to make ends meet. For the rest of his life, he struggled with poverty and sickness. In spite of this, Hunt did produce some of his best poems during the 1830s, including *Captain Sword and Captain Pen* (1835). He died in 1859, aged 74.

PREFACE.

----◦◦----

THIS book is intended for all lovers of poetry and the sister arts, but more especially for those of the most poetical sort, and most especially for the youngest and the oldest: for as the former may incline to it for information's sake, the latter will perhaps not refuse it their good-will for the sake of old favourites. The Editor has often wished for such a book himself; and as nobody will make it for him, he has made it for others.

It was suggested by the approbation which the readers of a periodical work bestowed on some extracts from the poets, *commented, and marked with italics, on a principle of co-perusal,* as though the Editor were reading the passages in their company. Those readers wished to have more such extracts; and here, if they are still in the mind, they now possess them. The remarks on one of the poems that formed a portion of the extracts (*The Eve of Saint Agnes*) are repeated in the present volume. All

the rest of the matter contributed by him is new. He
does not expect, of course, that every reader will agree
with the preferences of particular lines or passages,
intimated by the italics. Some will think them too
numerous; some perhaps too few; many who chance to
take up the book, may wish there had been none at all;
but these will have the goodness to recollect what has just
been stated,—that the plan was suggested by others who
desired them. The Editor, at any rate, begs to be con-
sidered as having marked the passages in no spirit of
dictation to any one, much less of disparagement to all
the admirable passages not marked. If he assumed any-
thing at all (beyond what is implied in the fact of
imparting experience), it was the probable mutual pleasure
of the reader his companion; just as in reading out loud,
one instinctively increases one's emphasis here and there,
and implies a certain accordance of enjoyment on the part
of the hearers. In short, all poetic readers are expected
to have a more than ordinary portion of sympathy,
especially with those who take pains to please them; and
the Editor desires no larger amount of it than he grate-
fully gives to any friend who is good enough to read out
similar passages to himself.

The object of the book is threefold;—to present
the public with some of the finest passages in English

poetry, *so marked and commented;*—to furnish such an account, in an Essay, of the nature and requirements of poetry, *as may enable readers in general to give an answer on those points to themselves and others;*—and to show, throughout the greater part of the volume, what sort of poetry is to be considered *as poetry of the most poetical kind*, or such as exhibits the imagination and fancy in a state of predominance, undisputed by interests of another sort.   Poetry, therefore, is not here in its compound state, great or otherwise (except incidentally in the Essay), but in its element, like an essence distilled.   All the greatest poetry includes that essence, but the essence does not present itself in exclusive combination with the greatest *form* of poetry.   It varies in that respect from the most tremendous to the most playful effusions, and from imagination to fancy through all their degrees;—from Homer and Dante, to Coleridge and Keats; from Shakspeare in *King Lear*, to Shakspeare himself in the *Midsummer Night's Dream;* from Spenser's *Fairy Queen* to the *Castle of Indolence;* nay, from Ariel in the *Tempest*, to his somewhat presumptuous namesake in the *Rape of the Lock.*   And passages, both from Thomson's delightful allegory, and Pope's paragon of mock-heroics, would have been found in this volume, but for that intentional, artificial imitation, even in the former, which removes

a 3

them at too great a distance from the highest sources of inspiration.

With the great poet of the *Fairy Queen* the Editor has taken special pains to make readers in general better acquainted; and in furtherance of this purpose he has exhibited many of his best passages in remarkable relation to the art of the Painter.

For obvious reasons no living writer is included; and some, lately deceased, do not come within the plan. The omission will not be thought invidious in an Editor, who has said more of his contemporaries than most men; and who would gladly give specimens of the latter poets in future volumes.

One of the objects indeed of this preface is to state that should the public evince a willingness to have more such books, the Editor would propose to give them, in succession, corresponding volumes of the Poetry of Action and Passion (Narrative and Dramatic Poetry), from Chaucer to Campbell (here mentioned because he is the latest deceased poet);—the Poetry of Contemplation, from Surrey to Campbell;—the Poetry of Wit and Humour, from Chaucer to Byron; and the Poetry of Song, or Lyrical Poetry, from Chaucer again (see in his Works his admirable and only song, beginning

Hide, Absalom, thy gilded tresses clear),

to Campbell again, and Burns, and O'Keefe. These volumes, if he is not mistaken, would present the Public with the *only selection*, hitherto made, *of none but genuine poetry ;* and he would take care, that it should be unobjectionable in every other respect. *

Kensington, Sept. 10, 1844.

* While closing the Essay on Poetry, a friend lent me Coleridge's *Biographia Literaria*, which I had not seen for many years, and which I mention, partly to notice a coincidence at page 38 of the Essay, not otherwise worth observation; and partly to do what I can towards extending the acquaintance of the public with a book containing masterly expositions of the art of poetry.

Note.—It is much to be regretted that the Author's ill-health prevented him from completing his design; *Wit and Humour* being the only other volume of the intended series.

CONTENTS.

AN ANSWER TO THE QUESTION

WHAT IS POETRY?

INCLUDING

REMARKS ON VERSIFICATION.

POETRY, strictly and artistically so called, that is to say, considered not merely as poetic feeling, which is more or less shared by all the world, but as the operation of that feeling, such as we see it in the poet's book, is the utterance of a passion for truth, beauty, and power, embodying and illustrating its conceptions by imagination and fancy, and modulating its language on the principle of variety in uniformity. Its means are whatever the universe contains; and its ends, pleasure and exaltation. Poetry stands between nature and convention, keeping alive among us the enjoyment of the external and the spiritual world: it has constituted the most enduring fame of nations; and, next to Love and Beauty, which are its parents, is the greatest proof to man of the pleasure to be found in all things, and of the probable riches of infinitude.

1

Poetry is a passion,* because it seeks the deepest impressions ; and because it must undergo, in order to convey them.

It is a passion for truth, because without truth the impression would be false or defective.

It is a passion for beauty, because its office is to exalt and refine by means of pleasure, and because beauty is nothing but the loveliest form of pleasure.

It is a passion for power, because power is impression triumphant, whether over the poet, as desired by himself, or over the reader, as affected by the poet.

It embodies and illustrates its impressions by imagination, or images of the objects of which it treats, and other images brought in to throw light on those objects, in order that it may enjoy and impart the feeling of their truth in its utmost conviction and affluence.

It illustrates them by fancy, which is a lighter play of imagination, or the feeling of analogy coming short of seriousness, in order that it may laugh with what it loves, and show how it can decorate it with fairy ornament.

It modulates what it utters, because in running the whole round of beauty it must needs include beauty of sound ; and because, in the height of its enjoyment, it must show the perfection of its triumph, and make difficulty itself become part of its facility and joy.

And lastly, Poetry shapes this modulation into uniformity for its outline, and variety for its parts, because it

---

* *Passio*, suffering in a good sense, —ardent subjection of one's-self to emotion.

thus realizes the last idea of beauty itself, which includes
the charm of diversity within the flowing round of habit
and ease.

Poetry is imaginative passion. The quickest and
subtlest test of the possession of its essence is in expres-
sion; the variety of things to be expressed shows the
amount of its resources; and the continuity of the song
completes the evidence of its strength and greatness. He
who has thought, feeling, expression, imagination, action,
character, and continuity, all in the largest amount and
highest degree, is the greatest poet.

Poetry includes whatsoever of painting can be made
visible to the mind's eye, and whatsoever of music can be
conveyed by sound and proportion without singing or
instrumentation. But it far surpasses those divine arts in
suggestiveness, range, and intellectual wealth ;—the first,
in expression of thought, combination of images, and the
triumph over space and time ; the second, in all that can
be done by speech, apart from the tones and modulations
of pure sound. Painting and music, however, include
all those portions of the gift of poetry that can be
expressed and heightened by the visible and melodious.
Painting, in a certain apparent manner, is things them-
selves ; music, in a certain audible manner, is their
very emotion and grace. Music and painting are proud
to be related to poetry, and poetry loves and is proud
of them.

Poetry begins where matter of fact or of science ceases
to be merely such, and to exhibit a further truth; that is
to say, the connexion it has with the world of emotion,

and its power to produce imaginative pleasure. Inquiring
of a gardener, for instance, what flower it is we see yonder,
he answers, "A lily." This is matter of fact. The botanist
pronounces it to be of the order of "Hexandria monogynia."
This is matter of science. It is tho "lady" of the garden,
says Spenser; and here we begin to have a poetical sense
of its fairness and grace. It is

The plant and flower of light,

says Ben Jonson; and poetry then shows us the beauty of
the flower in all its mystery and splendour.

If it be asked, how we know perceptions like these to
be true, the answer is, by the fact of their existence,—by
the consent and delight of poetic readers. And as feeling
is the earliest teacher, and perception the only final
proof of things the most demonstrable by science, so the
remotest imaginations of the poets may often be found to
have the closest connexion with matter of fact; perhaps
might always be so, if the subtlety of our perceptions were
a match for the causes of them. Consider this image of
Ben Jonson's—of a lily being the flower of light. Light,
undecomposed, is white; and as the lily is white, and
light is white, and whiteness itself is nothing <i>but</i> light,
the two things, so far, are not merely similar, but identical.
A poet might add, by an analogy drawn from the con-
nexion of light and colour, that there is a "golden dawn"
issuing out of the white lily, in the rich yellow of the
stamens. I have no desire to push this similarity farther
than it may be worth. Enough has been stated to show
that, in poetical as in other analogies, "the same feet of

Nature," as Bacon says, may be seen "treading in different
paths ; " and that the most scornful, that is to say, dullest
disciple of fact, should be cautious how he betrays the
shallowness of his philosophy by discerning no poetry in
its depths.

But the poet is far from dealing only with these subtle
and analogical truths. Truth of every kind belongs to
him, provided it can bud into any kind of beauty, or is
capable of being illustrated and impressed by the poetic
faculty. Nay, the simplest truth is often so beautiful
and impressive of itself, that one of the greatest proofs of
his genius consists in his leaving it to stand alone, illus-
trated by nothing but the light of its own tears or smiles,
its own wonder, might, or playfulness. Hence the com-
plete effect of many a simple passage in our old English
ballads and romances, and of the passionate sincerity
in general of the greatest early poets, such as Homer
and Chaucer, who flourished before the existence of a
"literary world," and were not perplexed by a heap of
notions and opinions, or by doubts how emotion ought
to be expressed. The greatest of their successors never
write equally to the purpose, except when they can
dismiss everything from their minds but the like simple
truth. In the beautiful poem of *Sir Eger, Sir Graham,
and Sir Gray-Steel* (see it in Ellis's *Specimens*, or
Laing's *Early Metrical Tales*), a knight thinks himself
disgraced in the eyes of his mistress :—

> Sir Eger said, "If it be so,
> Then wot I well I must forego
> Love-liking, and manhood, all clean ? "
> *The water rush'd out of his een !*

Sir Gray-Steel is killed :—

> Gray-Steel into his death thus thraws (throes ?)
> He *walters* (welters,—throws himself about) *and the*
>   *grass up draws ;*
> *   *   *   *   *
> *A little while then lay he still*
> (*Friends that him saw, liked full ill*)
> *And bled into his armour bright.*

The abode of Chaucer's *Reve*, or Steward, in the *Canterbury Tales*, is painted in two lines which nobody ever wished longer :—

> His wonning (dwelling) was full fair upon an heath,
> With greeny trees yshadowed was his place.

Every one knows the words of Lear, "most *matter-of-fact*, most melancholy : "

> Pray do not mock me :
> I am a very foolish fond old man,
> Fourscore and upward :
> Not an hour more, nor less ; and, to deal plainly,
> I fear, I am not in my perfect mind.

It is thus, by exquisite pertinence, melody, and the implied power of writing with exuberance, if need be, that beauty and truth become identical in poetry, and that pleasure, or at the very worst, a balm in our tears, is drawn out of pain.

It is a great and rare thing, and shows a lovely imagination, when the poet can write a commentary, as it were, of his own, on such sufficing passages of nature, and be thanked for the addition. There is an instance of this kind in Warner, an old Elizabethan poet, than which I know nothing sweeter in the world. He is speaking

of Fair Rosamond, and of a blow given her by Queen
Eleanor :

> With that she dash'd her on the lips,
> *So dyèd double red :*
> *Hard was the heart that gave the blow,*
> *Soft were those lips that bled.*

There are different kinds and degrees of imagination,
some of them necessary to the formation of every true
poet, and all of them possessed by the greatest. Perhaps
they may be enumerated as follows :—First, that which
presents to the mind any object or circumstance in every-
day life; as when we imagine a man holding a sword, or
looking out of a window;—Second, that which presents
real, but not every-day circumstances; as King Alfred
tending the loaves, or Sir Philip Sidney giving up the
water to the dying soldier;—Third, that which combines
character and events directly imitated from real life, with
imitative realities of its own invention; as the probable
parts of the histories of *Priam* and *Macbeth*, or what may
be called natural fiction as distinguished from super-
natural;—Fourth, that which conjures up things and
events not to be found in nature; as Homer's gods,
and Shakspeare's witches, enchanted horses and spears,
Ariosto's hippogriff, &c.;—Fifth, that which, in order to
illustrate or aggravate one image, introduces another :
sometimes in simile, as when Homer compares Apollo
descending in his wrath at noon-day to the coming of
night-time; sometimes in metaphor, or simile comprised
in a word, as in Milton's " motes that *people* the sun-
beams; " sometimes in concentrating into a word the
main history of any person or thing, past or even future,

as in the "starry Galileo" of Byron, and that ghastly
foregone conclusion of the epithet "murdered" applied to
the yet living victim in Keats's story from Boccaccio,—

> So the two brothers and their *murder'd* man
> Rode towards fair Florence ;—

sometimes in the attribution of a certain representative
quality which makes one circumstance stand for others;
as in Milton's grey-fly winding its "*sultry* horn," which
epithet contains the heat of a summer's day ;—Sixth, that
which reverses this process, and makes a variety of cir-
cumstances take colour from one, like nature seen with
jaundiced or glad eyes, or under the influence of storm or
sunshine; as when in Lycidas, or the Greek pastoral
poets, the flowers and the flocks are made to sympathize
with a man's death; or, in the Italian poet, the river
flowing by the sleeping Angelica seems talking of love—

> Parea che l' erba le fiorisse intorno,
> *E d' amor ragionasse quella riva !*—
> —*Orlando Innamorato*, canto iii.

or in the voluptuous homage paid to the sleeping Imogen
by the very light in the chamber and the reaction of her
own beauty upon itself; or in the "witch element" of the
tragedy of *Macbeth* and the May-day night of *Faust ;*—
Seventh, and last, that which by a single expression,
apparently of the vaguest kind, not only meets but sur-
passes in its effect the extremest force of the most particular
description; as in that exquisite passage of Coleridge's
Christabel, where the unsuspecting object of the witch's
malignity is bidden to go to bed :—

Quoth Christabel, So let it be !
And as the lady bade, did she.
Her gentle limbs did she undress,
And lay down in her loveliness ;—

a perfect verse surely, both for feeling and music. The
very smoothness and gentleness of the limbs is in the
series of the letter *l's*.

`. I am aware of nothing of the kind surpassing that most
lovely inclusion of physical beauty in moral, neither can
I call to mind any instances of the imagination that
turns accompaniments into accessories, superior to those I
have alluded to. Of the class of comparison, one of the
most touching (many a tear must it have drawn from
parents and lovers) is in a stanza which has been copied
into the *Friar of Orders Grey,* out of Beaumont and
Fletcher :—

Weep no more, lady, weep no more,
Thy sorrow is in vain ;
For violets pluck'd the sweetest showers
Will ne'er make grow again.

And Shakspeare and Milton abound in the very grandest ;
such as Antony's likening his changing fortunes to the
cloud-rack ; Lear's appeal to the old age of the heavens ;
Satan's appearance in the horizon, like a fleet "hanging
in the clouds;" and the comparisons of him with the
comet and the eclipse. Nor unworthy of this glorious
company, for its extraordinary combination of delicacy
and vastness, is that enchanting one of Shelley's in the
Adonais :—

Life, like a dome of many-coloured glass,
Stains the white radiance of eternity.

I multiply these particulars in order to impress upon the reader's mind the great importance of imagination in all its phases, as a constituent part of the highest poetic faculty.

The happiest instance I remember of imaginative metaphor is Shakspeare's moonlight " sleeping " on a bank ; but half his poetry may be said to be made up of it, metaphor indeed being the common coin of discourse. Of imaginary creatures none, out of the pale of mythology and the East, are equal, perhaps, in point of invention, to Shakspeare's Ariel and Caliban ; though poetry may grudge to prose the discovery of a Winged Woman, especially such as she has been described by her inventor in the story of *Peter Wilkins;* and in point of treatment, the Mammon and Jealousy of Spenser, some of the monsters in Dante, particularly his Nimrod, his interchangements of creatures into one another, and (if I am not presumptuous in anticipating what I think will be the verdict of posterity) the Witch in Coleridge's *Christabel,* may rank even with the creations of Shakspeare. It may be doubted, indeed, whether Shakspeare had bile and nightmare enough in him to have thought of such detestable horrors as those of the interchanging adversaries (now serpent, now man), or even of the huge, half-blockish enormity of Nimrod,—in Scripture, the " mighty hunter " and builder of the tower of Babel,—in Dante, a tower of a man in his own person, standing with some of his brother giants up to the middle in a pit in hell, blowing a horn to which a thunder-clap is a whisper, and hallooing after Dante and his guide in the jargon of a lost tongue ! The

transformations are too odious to quote; but of the tower-
ing giant we cannot refuse ourselves the "fearful joy" of
a specimen. It was twilight, Dante tells us, and he and
his guide Virgil were silently pacing through one of the
dreariest regions of hell, when the sound of a tremendous
horn made him turn all his attention to the spot from
which it came. He there discovered, through the dusk,
what seemed to be the towers of a city. Those are no
towers, said his guide; they are giants, standing up to the
middle in one of these circular pits :

> Come quando la nebbia si dissipa,
>> Lo sguardo a poco a poco raffigura
>> Ciò che cela il vapor, che l' aere stipa ;
> Così forando l' aura grossa e scura,
>> Più e più appressando in vêr la sponda,
>> Fuggémi errore, e giungémi paura :
> Perocchè come in su la cerchia tonda
>> Montereggion di torri si corona ;
>> Così la proda, che il pozzo circonda,
> Torreggiavan di mezza la persona
>> Gli orribili giganti, cui minaccia
>> Giove del cielo ancora, quando tuona :
> Ed io scorgeva già d' alcun la faccia,
>> Le spalle, e il petto, e del ventre gran parte,
>> E per le coste giù ambo le braccia.
>>> *   *   *   *
> La faccia sua mi parea lunga e grossa,
>> Come la pina di San Pietro a Roma :
>> E a sua proporzione eran le altr' ossa.
>>> *   *   *   *
> "Rafel maì amech zabì almi!"
>> Cominciò a gridar la fiera bocca,
>> Cui non si convenien più dolci salmi.
> E il Duca mio vêr lui : "Anima sciocca!
>> Tienti col corno, e con quel ti disfoga,
>> Quand' ira o altra passìon ti tocca.

    Cercati al collo, e troverai la soga
      Che il tien legato, o anima confusa,
      E vedi lui che il gran petto ti doga."
    Poi disse a me: " Egli stesso s' accusa:
      Questi è Nembrotto, per lo cui mal coto
      Pure un linguaggio nel mondo non s' usa.
    Lasciamlo stare, e non parliamo a voto:
      Chè così è a lui ciascun linguaggio,
      Come il suo ad altrui, ch' a nullo è noto."
                     —*Inferno*, canto xxxi. ver. 34 *et seq.*

I looked again : and as the eye makes out,
By little and little, what the mist conceal'd,
In which, till clearing up, the sky was steep'd ;
So, looming through the gross and darksome air,
As we drew nigh, those mighty bulks grew plain,
And error quitted me, and terror join'd :   •
For in like manner as all round its height
Montereggione crowns itself with towers,
So tower'd above the circuit of that pit,
Though but half out of it, and half within,
The horrible gianfs that fought Jove, and still
Are threaten'd when he thunders. As we near'd
The foremost, I discern'd his mighty face,
His shoulders, breast, and more than half his trunk,
With both the arms down hanging by the sides.
His face appear'd to me, in length and breadth,
Huge as St. Peter's pinnacle at Rome,
And of a like proportion all his bones.
He open'd, as we went, his dreadful mouth,
Fit for no sweeter psalmody ; and shouted
After us, in the words of some strange tongue,
" Ràfel ma-èe amech zabèe almee!—"
" Dull wretch ! " my leader cried, " keep to thine horn,
And so vent better whatsoever rage
Or other passion stuff thee. Feel thy throat
And find the chain upon thee, thou confusion !
Lo ! what a hoop is clench'd about thy gorge."
Then turning to myself, he said, " His howl
Is its own mockery. This is Nimrod, he

Through whose ill thought it was that humankind
Were tongue-confounded. Pass him, and say nought:
For as he speaketh language known of none,
So none can speak save jargon to himself."

Assuredly it could not have been easy to find a fiction
so uncouthly terrible as this in the hypochondria of
Hamlet. Even his father had evidently seen no such
ghost in the other world. All his phantoms were in the
world he had left. Timon, Lear, Richard, Brutus, Prospero,
Macbeth himself, none of Shakspeare's men had, in fact,
any thought but of the earth they lived on, whatever super-
natural fancy crossed them. The thing fancied was still a
thing of this world, "in its habit as it lived," or no
remoter acquaintance than a witch or a fairy. Its lowest
depths (unless Dante suggested them) were the cellars
under the stage. Caliban himself is a cross-breed between
a witch and a clown. No offence to Shakspeare : who was
not bound to be the greatest of healthy poets, and to have
every morbid inspiration besides. What he might have
done, had he set his wits to compete with Dante, I know
not : all I know is, that in the infernal line he did nothing
like him ; and it is not to be wished he had. It is far
better that, as a higher, more universal, and more bene-
ficent variety of the genus Poet, he should have been the
happier man he was, and left us the plump cheeks on his
monument, instead of the carking visage of the great,
but over-serious, and comparatively one-sided Florentine.
Even the imagination of Spenser, whom we take to have
been a " nervous gentleman " compared with Shakspeare,
was visited with no such dreams as Dante. Or, if it was,

he did not choose to make himself thinner (as Dante says
he did) with dwelling upon them. He had twenty visions
of nymphs and bowers, to one of the mud of Tartarus.
Chaucer, for all he was "a man of this world" as well as
the poets' world, and as great, perhaps a greater enemy of
oppression than Dante, besides being one of the pro-
foundest masters of pathos that ever lived, had not the
heart to conclude the story of the famished father and his
children, as finished by the inexorable anti-Pisan. But
enough of Dante in this place. Hobbes, in order to daunt
the reader from objecting to his friend Davenant's want of
invention, says of these fabulous creations in general, in
his letter prefixed to the poem of *Gondibert*, that "impe-
netrable armours, enchanted castles, invulnerable bodies,
iron men, flying horses, and a thousand other such things,
are easily feigned by them that dare." These are girds at
Spenser and Ariosto. But, with leave of Hobbes (who
translated *Homer* as if on purpose to show what execrable
verses could be written by a philosopher), enchanted castles
and flying horses are not easily feigned, as Ariosto and
Spenser feigned them ; and that just makes all the differ-
ence. For proof, see the accounts of Spenser's enchanted
castle in Book the Third, Canto Twelfth, of the *Fairy
Queen ;* and let the reader of Italian open the *Orlando
Furioso* at its first introduction of the Hippogriff
(Canto iv. st. 3), where Bradamante, coming to an inn,
hears a great noise, and sees all the people looking up at
something in the air ; upon which, looking up herself, she
sees a knight in shining armour riding towards the sunset
upon a creature with variegated wings, and then dipping

and disappearing among the hills.   Chaucer's steed of brass, that was

> So horsly and so quick of eye,

is copied from the life.   You might pat him and feel his brazen muscles.   Hobbes, in objecting to what he thought childish, made a childish mistake.   His criticism is just such as a boy might pique himself upon, who was educated on mechanical principles, and thought he had outgrown his *Goody Two-shoes*.   With a wonderful dimness of discernment in poetic matters, considering his acuteness in others, he fancies he has settled the question by pronouncing such creations " impossible ! "   To the brazier they are impossible, no doubt ; but not to the poet.   Their possibility, if the poet wills it, is to be conceded ; the problem is, the creature being given, how to square its actions with probability, according to the nature assumed of it. Hobbes did not see that the skill and beauty of these fictions lay in bringing them within those very regions of truth and likelihood in which he thought they could not exist.   Hence the serpent Python of Chaucer,

> *Sleeping against the sun upon a day,*

when Apollo slew him.   Hence the chariot-drawing dolphins of Spenser, softly swimming along the shore lest they should hurt themselves against the stones and gravel. Hence Shakspeare's Ariel, living under blossoms, and riding at evening on the bat ; and his domestic namesake in the *Rape of the Lock* (the imagination of the drawing-room) saving a lady's petticoat from the coffee with his plumes, and directing atoms of snuff into a coxcomb's nose.   In

the *Orlando Furioso* (Canto xv. st. 65) is a wild story of
a cannibal necromancer, who laughs at being cut to pieces,
coming together again like quicksilver, and picking up
his head when it is cut off, sometimes by the hair, some-
times by the nose! This, which would be purely childish
and ridiculous in the hands of an inferior poet, becomes
interesting, nay grand, in Ariosto's, from the beauties of
his style, and its conditional truth to nature. The monster
has a fated hair on his head,—a single hair,—which must
be taken from it before he can be killed. Decapitation
itself is of no consequence, without that proviso. The
Paladin Astolfo, who has fought this phenomenon on
horseback, and succeeded in getting the head and gal-
loping off with it, is therefore still at a loss what to be
at. How is he to discover such a needle in such a bottle
of hay? The trunk is spurring after him to recover it,
and he seeks for some evidence of the hair in vain. At
length he bethinks him of scalping the head. He does
so; and the moment the operation arrives at the place of
the hair, *the face of the head becomes pale, the eyes turn
in their sockets,* and the lifeless pursuer tumbles from
his horse:

> Si fece il viso allor pallido e brutto,
> Travolse gli occhi, e dimostrò all' occaso
> Per manifesti segni esser condutto :
> E 'l busto che seguia troncato al collo,
> Di sella cadde, e diè l' ultimo crollo.

> Then grew the visage pale, and deadly wet,
> The eyes turn'd in their sockets, drearily;
> And all things show'd the villain's sun was set.
> His trunk that was in chace, fell from its horse,
> And giving the last shudder, was a corse.

It is thus, and thus only, by making Nature his companion wherever he goes, even in the most supernatural region, that the poet, in the words of a very instructive phrase, takes the world along with him. It is true, he must not (as the Platonists would say) humanize weakly or mistakenly in that region ; otherwise he runs the chance of forgetting to be true to the supernatural itself, and so betraying a want of imagination from that quarter. His nymphs will have no taste of their woods and waters; his gods and goddesses be only so many fair or frowning ladies and gentlemen, such as we see in ordinary paintings; he will be in no danger of having his angels likened to a sort of wild-fowl, as Rembrandt has made them in his "Jacob's Dream." His Bacchuses will never remind us, like Titian's, of the force and fury, as well as of the graces of wine. His Jupiter will reduce no females to ashes; his fairies be nothing fantastical; his gnomes not " of the earth, earthy." And this again will be wanting to Nature ; for it will be wanting to the supernatural, as Nature would have made it, working in a supernatural direction. Nevertheless, the poet, even for imagination's sake, must not become a bigot to imaginative truth, dragging it down into the region of the mechanical and the limited, and losing sight of its paramount privilege, which is to make beauty, in a human sense, the lady and queen of the universe. He would gain nothing by making his ocean-nymphs mere fishy creatures, upon the plea that such only could live in the water : his wood-nymphs with faces of knotted oak; his angels without breath and song, because no lungs could exist between the earth's atmosphere and the empyrean. The

2

Grecian tendency in this respect is safer than the Gothic; nay, more imaginative; for it enables us to imagine *beyond* imagination, and to bring all things healthily round to their only present final ground of sympathy,—the human. When we go to heaven, we may idealize in a superhuman mode, and have altogether different notions of the beautiful; but till then we must be content with the loveliest capabilities of earth. The sea-nymphs of Greece were still beautiful women, though they lived in the water. The gills and fins of the ocean's natural inhabitants were confined to their lowest semi-human attendants; or if Triton himself was not quite human, it was because he represented the fiercer part of the vitality of the seas, as they did the fairer.

To conclude this part of my subject, I will quote from the greatest of all narrative writers two passages;—one exemplifying the imagination which brings supernatural things to bear on earthly, without confounding them; the other, that which paints events and circumstances after real life. The first is where Achilles, who has long absented himself from the conflict between his country-men and the Trojans, has had a message from heaven bidding him reappear in the enemy's sight, standing outside the camp-wall upon the trench, but doing nothing more; that is to say, taking no part in the fight. He is simply to be seen. The two armies down by the sea-side are contending which shall possess the body of Patroclus; and the mere sight of the dreadful Grecian chief—super-naturally indeed impressed upon them, in order that nothing may be wanting to the full effect of his courage and conduct upon courageous men—is to determine the question. We are to imagine a slope of ground towards the sea, in order to elevate the trench ; the camp is solitary ; the battle ("a dreadful roar of men," as Homer calls it) is raging on the sea-shore ; and the goddess Iris has just delivered her message and disappeared.—

Αὐτὰρ Ἀχιλλεὺς ὦρτο, Διΐ φίλος· ἀμφὶ δ' Ἀθήνη
"Ὤμοις ἰφθίμοισι βάλ' αἰγίδα θυσσανόεσσαν·
Ἀμφὶ δέ οἱ κεφαλῇ νέφος ἔστεφε δῖα θεάων
Χρύσεον, ἐκ δ' αὐτοῦ δαῖε φλόγα παμφανόωσαν.
Ὡς δ' ὅτε καπνὸς ἰὼν ἐξ ἄστεος αἰθέρ' ἵκηται
Τηλόθεν ἐκ νήσου, τὴν δήϊοι ἀμφιμάχονται,
Οἵτε πανημέριοι στυγερῷ κρίνονται ἄρηϊ
Ἄστεος ἐκ σφετέρου. ἅμα δ' ἠελίῳ καταδύντι
Πυρσοί τε φλεγέθουσιν ἐπήτριμοι, ὑψόσε δ' αὐγὴ
Γίγνεται ἀΐσσουσα, περικτιόνεσσιν ἰδέσθαι,
Αἴκεν πως σὺν νηυσὶν ἄρεως ἀλκτῆρες ἵκωνται·
Ὡς ἀπ' Ἀχιλλῆος κεφαλῆς σέλας αἰθέρ' ἵκανε.

Στῆ δ' ἐπὶ τάφρον ἰὼν ἀπὸ τείχεος· οὐδ' ἐς Ἀχαιοὺς
Μίσγετο· μητρὸς γὰρ πυκινὴν ὠπίζετ' ἐφετμήν.
Ἔνθα στὰς ἤϋσ'· ἀπάτερθε δὲ Παλλὰς Ἀθήνη
Φθέγξατ'· ἀτὰρ Τρώεσσιν ἐν ἄσπετον ὦρσε κυδοιμόν.
Ὡς δ' ὅτ' ἀριζήλη φωνὴ, ὅτε τ' ἴαχε σάλπιγξ
Ἄστυ περιπλομένων δηΐων ὑπὸ θυμοραϊστέων·
Ὡς τότ' ἀριζήλη φωνὴ γένετ' Αἰακίδαο.
Οἱ δ' ὡς οὖν ἄϊον ὄπα χάλκεον Αἰακίδαο,
Πᾶσιν ὀρίνθη θυμός· ἀτὰρ καλλίτριχες ἵπποι
Ἄψ ὄχεα τρόπεον· ὄσσοντο γὰρ ἄλγεα θυμῷ.
Ἡνίοχοι δ' ἔκπληγεν, ἐπεὶ ἴδον ἀκάματον πῦρ
Δεινὸν ὑπὲρ κεφαλῆς μεγαθύμου Πηλείωνος
Δαιόμενον· τὸ δ' ἔδαιε θεὰ γλαυκῶπις Ἀθήνη.
Τρὶς μὲν ὑπὲρ τάφρου μεγάλ' ἴαχε δῖος Ἀχιλλεύς·
Τρὶς δ' ἐκυκήθησαν Τρῶες κλειτοί τ' ἐπίκουροι.
Ἔνθὰ δὲ καὶ τότ' ὄλοντο δυώδεκα φῶτες ἄριστοι
Ἀμφὶ σφοῖς ὀχέεσσι καὶ ἔγχεσιν.

—*Iliad*, lib. xviii. vv. 203—231.

But up Achilles rose, the lov'd of heaven ;
And Pallas on his mighty shoulders cast

The shield of Jove ; and round about his head
She put the glory of a golden mist,
From which there burnt a fiery-flaming light.
And as, when smoke goes heaven-ward from a town,
In some far island which its foes besiege,
Who all day long with dreadful martialness
Have pour'd from their own town; soon as the sun
Has set, thick lifted fires are visible,
Which, rushing upward, make a light in the sky,
And let the neighbours know, who may perhaps
Bring help across the sea ; so from the head
Of great Achilles went up an effulgence.

Upon the trench he stood, without the wall,
But mix'd not with the Greeks, for he rever'd
His mother's word ; and so, thus standing there,
He shouted ; and Minerva, to his shout,
Added a dreadful cry ; and there arose
Among the Trojans an unspeakable tumult.
And as the clear voice of a trumpet, blown
Against a town by spirit-withering foes,
So sprang the clear voice of Æacides.
And when they heard the brazen cry, their hearts
All leap'd within them ; and the proud-maned horses
Ran with the chariots round, for they foresaw
Calamity ; and the charioteers were smitten,
When they beheld the ever-active fire
Upon the dreadful head of the great-minded one
Burning ; for bright-eyed Pallas made it burn.
Thrice o'er the trench divine Achilles shouted ;
And thrice the Trojans and their great allies
Roll'd back ; and twelve of all their noblest men
Then perish'd, crush'd by their own arms and chariots.

Of course there is no further question about the body of
Patroclus. It is drawn out of the press, and received by
the awful hero with tears.

The other passage is where Priam, kneeling before
Achilles, and imploring him to give up the dead body of

Hector, reminds him of his own father; who, whatever (says the poor old king) may be his troubles with his enemies, has the blessing of knowing that his son is still alive, and may daily hope to see him return. Achilles, in accordance with the strength and noble honesty of the passions in those times, weeps aloud himself at this appeal, feeling, says Homer, " desire " for his father in his very " limbs." He joins in grief with the venerable sufferer, and can no longer withstand the look of " his grey head and his grey *chin.*" Observe the exquisite introduction of this last word. It paints the touching fact of the chin's being imploringly thrown upward by the kneeling old man, and the very motion of his beard as he speaks.—

Ὣς ἄρα φωνήσας, ἀπέβη πρὸς μακρὸν Ὄλυμπον
Ἑρμείας· Πρίαμος δ' ἐξ ἵππων ἆλτο χαμᾶζε,
Ἰδαῖον δὲ κατ' αὖθι λίπεν· ὁ δὲ μίμνεν ἐρύκων
Ἵππους ἡμιόνους τε· γέρων δ' ἰθὺς κίεν οἴκου,
Τῇ ῥ' Ἀχιλεὺς ἵζεσκε, Διΐ φίλος· ἐν δέ μιν αὐτὸν
Εὗρ', ἕταροι δ' ἀπάνευθε καθείατο· τῷ δὲ δύ' οἴω
Ἥρως Αὐτομέδων τε, καὶ Ἄλκιμος ὄζος Ἄρηος,
Ποίπνυον παρεόντε· (νέον δ' ἀπέληγεν ἐδωδῆς,
Ἔσθων καὶ πίνων, ἔτι καὶ παρέκειτο τράπεζα·)
Τοὺς δ' ἔλαθ' εἰσελθὼν Πρίαμος μέγας, ἄγχι δ' ἄρα στὰς,
Χερσὶν Ἀχιλλῆος λάβε γούνατα, καὶ κύσε χεῖρας
Δεινὰς, ἀνδροφόνους, αἵ οἱ πολέας κτάνον υἷας.
Ὡς δ' ὅταν ἄνδρ' ἄτη πυκινὴ λάβῃ, ὅστ', ἐνὶ πάτρῃ
Φῶτα κατακτείνας, ἄλλον ἐξίκετο δῆμον,
Ἀνδρὸς ἐς ἀφνειοῦ, θάμβος δ' ἔχει εἰσορόωντας·
Ὡς Ἀχιλεὺς θάμβησεν, ἰδὼν Πρίαμον θεοειδέα·
Θάμβησαν δὲ καὶ ἄλλοι, ἐς ἀλλήλους δὲ ἴδοντο.
Τὸν καὶ λισσόμενος Πρίαμος πρὸς μῦθον ἔειπε·

Μνῆσαι πατρὸς σεῖο, θεοῖς ἐπιείκελ' Ἀχιλλεῦ,
Τηλίκου, ὥσπερ ἐγὼν, ὀλοῷ ἐπὶ γήραος οὐδῷ.
Καὶ μέν που κεῖνον περιναίεται ἀμφὶς ἐόντες
Τείρουσ', οὐδέ τις ἐστὶν, ἀρὴν καὶ λοιγὸν ἀμῦναι·

Ἀλλ' ἤτοι κεῖνός γε, σέθεν ζώοντος ἀκούων,
Χαίρει τ' ἐν θυμῷ, ἐπὶ τ' ἔλπεται ἤματα πάντα
Ὄψεσθαι φίλον υἱὸν, ἀπὸ Τροίηθεν ἰόντα·
Αὐτὰρ ἐγὼ πανάποτμος, ἐπεὶ τέκον υἷας ἀρίστους
Τροίῃ ἐν εὐρείῃ, τῶν δ' οὔτινα φημὶ λελεῖφθαι.
Πεντήκοντά μοι ἦσαν, ὅτ' ἤλυθον υἷες Ἀχαιῶν·
Ἐννεακαίδεκα μέν μοι ἰῆς ἐκ νηδύος ἦσαν,
Τοὺς δ' ἄλλους μοι ἔτικτον ἐνὶ μεγάροισι γυναῖκες.
Τῶν μὲν πολλῶν θοῦρος Ἄρης ὑπὸ γούνατ' ἔλυσεν·
Ὅς δέ μοι οἶος ἔην, εἴρυτο δὲ ἄστυ καὶ αὐτοὺς,
Τὸν σὺ πρώην κτεῖνας, ἀμυνόμενον περὶ πάτρης,
Ἕκτορα· τοῦ νῦν εἵνεχ' ἱκάνω νῆας Ἀχαιῶν,
Λυσόμενος παρὰ σεῖο, φέρω δ' ἀπερείσι' ἄποινα.
Ἀλλ' αἰδεῖο θεοὺς, Ἀχιλεῦ, αὐτόν τ' ἐλέησον,
Μνησάμενος σοῦ πατρός· ἐγὼ δ' ἐλεεινότερός περ,
Ἔτλην δ', οἷ' οὔπω τις ἐπιχθόνιος βροτὸς ἄλλος,
Ἀνδρὸς παιδοφόνοιο ποτὶ στόμα χεῖρ' ὀρέγεσθαι.
Ὣς φάτο· τῷ δ' ἄρα πατρὸς ὑφ' ἵμερον ὦρσε γόοιο,
Ἀψάμενος δ' ἄρα χειρὸς, ἀπώσατο ἦκα γέροντα.
Τὼ δὲ μνησαμένω, ὁ μὲν Ἕκτορος ἀνδροφόνοιο,
Κλαῖ' ἀδινὰ, προπάροιθε ποδῶν Ἀχιλῆος ἐλυσθείς·
Αὐτὰρ Ἀχιλλεὺς κλαῖεν ἑὸν πατέρ', ἄλλοτε δ' αὖτε
Πάτροκλον· τῶν δὲ στοναχὴ κατὰ δῶματ' ὀρώρει.
Αὐτὰρ, ἐπεὶ ῥα γόοιο τετάρπετο δῖος Ἀχιλλεύς,
Καί οἱ ἀπὸ πραπίδων ἦλθ' ἵμερος, ἠδ' ἀπὸ γυίων,
Αὐτίκ' ἀπὸ θρόνου ὦρτο, γέροντα δὲ χειρὸς ἀνίστη,
Οἰκτείρων πολιόν τε κάρη, πολιόν τε γένειον.

—*Iliad*, lib. xxiv. vv. 468—516.

So saying, Mercury vanished up to heaven ;
And Priam then alighted from his chariot,
Leaving Idæus with it, who remain'd
Holding the mules and horses ; and the old man
Went straight indoors, where the belov'd of Jove
Achilles sat, and found him. In the room
Were others, but apart ; and two alone,
The hero Automedon, and Alcimus,
A branch of Mars, stood by him. They had been
At meals, and had not yet remov'd the board.
Great Priam came, without their seeing him,
And kneeling down, he clasp'd Achilles' knees,

And kiss'd those terrible, homicidal hands,
Which had deprived him of so many sons.
And as a man who is press'd heavily
For having slain another, flies away
To foreign lands, and comes into the house
Of some great man, and is beheld with wonder,
So did Achilles wonder to see Priam;
And the rest wonder'd, looking at each other.
But Priam, praying to him, spoke these words :—
" God-like Achilles, think of thine own father !
To the same age have we both come, the same
Weak pass; and though the neighbouring chiefs may vex
Him also, and his borders find no help,
Yet when he hears that thou art still alive,
He gladdens inwardly, and daily hopes
To see his dear son coming back from Troy.
But I, bereav'd old Priam ! I had once
Brave sons in Troy, and now I cannot say
That one is left me. Fifty children had I,
When the Greeks came, nineteen were of one womb;
The rest my women bore me in my house.
The knees of many of these fierce Mars has loosen'd ;
And he who had no peer, Troy's prop and theirs,
Him hast thou kill'd now, fighting for his country,
Hector; and for his sake am I come here
To ransom him, bringing a countless ransom.
But thou, Achilles, fear the gods, and think
Of thine own father, and have mercy on me :
For I am much more wretched, and have borne
What never mortal bore, I think, on earth,
To lift unto my lips the hand of him
Who slew my boys."

       He ceased ; and there arose
Sharp longing in Achilles for his father;
And taking Priam by the hand, he gently
Put him away ; for both shed tears to think
Of other times ; the one, most bitter ones
For Hector, and with wilful wretchedness
Lay right before Achilles : and the other,

> For his own father now, and now his friend;
> And the whole house might hear them as they moan'd.
> But when divine Achilles had refresh'd
> His soul with tears, and sharp desire had left
> His heart and limbs, he got up from his throne,
> And rais'd the old man by the hand, and took
> Pity on his grey head and his grey chin.

O lovely and immortal privilege of genius! that can stretch its hand out of the wastes of time, thousands of years back, and touch our eyelids with tears. In these passages there is not a word which a man of the most matter-of-fact understanding might not have written, *if he had thought of it.* But in poetry, feeling and imagination are necessary to the perception and presentation even of matters of fact. They, and they only, see what is proper to be told, and what to be kept back; what is pertinent, affecting, and essential. Without feeling, there is a want of delicacy and distinction; without imagination there is no true embodiment. In poets, even good of their kind, but without a genius for narration, the action would have been encumbered or diverted with ingenious mistakes. The over-contemplative would have given us too many remarks; the over-lyrical, a style too much carried away; the over-fanciful, conceits and too many similes; the unimaginative, the facts without the feeling, and not even those. We should have been told nothing of the "grey chin," of the house hearing them as they moaned, or of Achilles gently putting the old man aside; much less of that yearning for his father, which made the hero tremble in every limb. Writers without the greatest passion and power do not feel in this way, nor are capable of expressing

the feeling ; though there is enough sensibility and imagi-
nation all over the world to enable mankind to be moved
by it, when the poet strikes his truth into their hearts.

The reverse of imagination is exhibited in pure absence
of ideas, in commonplaces, and, above all, in conventional
metaphor, or such images and their phraseology as have
become the common property of discourse and writing.
Addison's *Cato* is full of them :

> Passion unpitied and successless love
> *Plant daggers in my breast.*

> I've sounded my Numidians, man by man,
> And find them *ripe for a revolt.*

> The virtuous Marcia *towers above her sex.*

Of the same kind is his " courting the yoke "—" distract-
ing my very heart "—" calling up all " one's " father " in
one's soul—" working every nerve "—" copying a bright
example ; " in short, the whole play, relieved now and
then with a smart sentence or turn of words. The fol-
lowing is a pregnant example of plagiarism and weak
writing. It is from another tragedy of Addison's time,—
the *Mariamne* of Fenton :—

> Mariamne, *with superior charms,*
> *Triumphs o'er reason ;* in her look she *bears*
> A paradise of ever-blooming sweets ;
> Fair as the first idea beauty *prints*
> In the young lover's soul ; a winning grace
> Guides every gesture, and obsequious love
> *Attends* on all her steps.

" Triumphing o'er reason " is an old acquaintance of
everybody's. " Paradise in her look " is from the Italian

poets through Dryden. "Fair as the first idea," &c. is from Milton, spoilt;—" winning grace" and "steps" from Milton and Tibullus, both spoilt. Whenever beauties are stolen by such a writer, they are sure to be spoilt: just as when a great writer borrows, he improves.

To come now to Fancy,—she is a younger sister of Imagination, without the other's weight of thought and feeling. Imagination indeed, purely so called, is all feeling; the feeling of the subtlest and most affecting analogies; the perception of sympathies in the natures of things, or in their popular attributes. Fancy is a sporting with their resemblance, real or supposed, and with airy and fantastical creations.—

> —Rouse yourself; and the weak wanton Cupid
> Shall from your neck unloose his amorous fold,
> *And, like a dew-drop from the lion's mane,*
> *Be shook to air.*
> —*Troilus and Cressida*, Act iii. sc. 3.

That is imagination;—the strong mind sympathizing with the strong beast, and the weak love identified with the weak dew-drop.

> Oh!—and I forsooth
> In love! I that have been love's whip!
> *A very beadle to a humorous sigh;——*
> A domineering pedant o'er the boy;——
> This wimpled, whining, purblind, wayward boy;
> This senior-junior, giant-dwarf, Dan Cupid,
> *Regent of love-rhymes, lord of folded arms,*
> *The anointed sovereign of sighs and groans,* &c.
> —*Love's Labour's Lost*, Act iii. sc. 1.

That is fancy;—a combination of images not in their nature connected, or brought together by the feeling, but by the will and pleasure; and having just enough hold of analogy to betray it into the hands of its smiling subjector.

> Silent icicles
> *Quietly shining to the quiet moon.*
>
> —Coleridge's *Frost at Midnight.*

That, again, is imagination;—analogical sympathy; and exquisite of its kind it is.

> You are now sailed *into the north of my lady's opinion;* where you will hang *like an icicle on a Dutchman's beard,* unless you do redeem it by some laudable attempt.
>
> —*Twelfth Night,* Act iii. sc. 2.

And that is fancy;—one image capriciously suggested by another, and but half connected with the subject of discourse; nay, half opposed to it; for in the gaiety of the speaker's animal spirits, the "Dutchman's beard" is made to represent the lady !

Imagination belongs to Tragedy, or the serious muse; Fancy to the comic. *Macbeth, Lear, Paradise Lost,* the poem of Dante, are full of imagination : the *Midsummer Night's Dream* and the *Rape of the Lock,* of fancy : *Romeo and Juliet,* the *Tempest,* the *Fairy Queen,* and the *Orlando Furioso,* of both. The terms were formerly identical, or used as such; and neither is the best that might be found. The term Imagination is too confined : often too material. It presents too invariably the idea of a solid body ;—of "images" in the sense of the plastercast cry about the streets. Fancy, on the other hand, while it means nothing but a spiritual image or apparition (φάντασμα, appearance, *phantom*), has rarely that freedom

from visibility which is one of the highest privileges of
imagination. Viola, in *Twelfth Night*, speaking of some
beautiful music, says :—

> It gives a very echo to the seat,
> Where Love is throned.

In this charming thought, fancy and imagination are com-
bined ; yet the fancy, the assumption of Love's sitting on
a throne, is the image of a solid body; while the imagina-
tion, the sense of sympathy between the passion of love
and impassioned music, presents us no image at all. Some
new term is wanting to express the more spiritual sym-
pathies of what is called Imagination.

One of the teachers of Imagination is Melancholy ; and
like Melancholy, as Albert Durer has painted her, she
looks out among the stars, and is busied with spiritual
affinities and the mysteries of the universe. Fancy turns
her sister's wizard instruments into toys. She takes a
telescope in her hand, and puts a mimic star on her fore-
head, and sallies forth as an emblem of astronomy. Her
tendency is to the child-like and sportive. She chases
butterflies, while her sister takes flight with angels. She
is the genius of fairies, of gallantries, of fashions ; of
whatever is quaint and light, showy and capricious ; of the
poetical part of wit. She adds wings and feelings to the
images of wit ; and delights as much to people nature with
smiling ideal sympathies, as wit does to bring antipathies
together, and make them strike light on absurdity. Fancy,
however, is not incapable of sympathy with Imagination.
She is often found in her company ; always, in the case of
the greatest poets ; often in that of less, though with them

she is the greater favourite. Spenser has great imagination and fancy too, but more of the latter; Milton both also, the very greatest, but with imagination predominant; Chaucer, the strongest imagination of real life, beyond any writers but Homer, Dante, and Shakspeare, and in comic painting inferior to none; Pope has hardly any imagination, but he has a great deal of fancy; Coleridge little fancy, but imagination exquisite. Shakspeare alone, of all poets that ever lived, enjoyed the regard of both in equal perfection. A whole fairy poem of his writing will be found in the present volume. See also his famous description of Queen Mab and her equipage, in *Romeo and Juliet* :—

> Her waggon-spokes made of long-spinners' legs;
> The cover, of the wings of grasshoppers:
> The traces of the smallest spider's web;
> The collars of the moonshine's watery beams, &c.

That is Fancy, in its playful creativeness. As a small but pretty rival specimen, less known, take the description of a fairy palace from Drayton's *Nymphidia* :—

> This palace standeth in the air,
> By necromancy placèd there,
> That it no tempest needs to fear,
>   Which way soe'er it blow it:
> And somewhat southward tow'rd the noon,
> Whence lies a way up to the moon,
> And thence the Fairy can as soon
>   Pass to the earth below it.
> The walls of spiders' legs are made,
> Well mortisèd and finely laid;
> He was the master of his trade.
>   It curiously that builded :

> *The windows of the eyes of cats :*

(because they see best at night,)

> And for the roof instead of slats
> Is cover'd with the skins of bats
> *With moonshine that are gilded.*

Here also is a fairy bed, very delicate, from the same poet's
Muse's Elysium :

> Of leaves of roses, *white and red,*
> Shall be the covering of the bed ;
> The curtains, vallens, tester all
> Shall be the flower imperial ;
> And for the fringe it all along
> *With azure hare-bells shall be hung.*
> *Of lilies shall the pillows be*
> *With down stuft of the butterfly.*

Of fancy, so full of gusto as to border on imagination,
Sir John Suckling, in his *Ballad on a Wedding,* has given
some of the most playful and charming specimens in the
language.   They glance like twinkles of the eye, or cherries
bedewed :

> *Her feet beneath her petticoat*
> *Like little mice stole in and out,*
> *As if they fear'd the light :*
> But oh ! she dances such a way !
> *No sun upon an Easter day*
> Is half so fine a sight.

It is very daring, and has a sort of playful grandeur, to
compare a lady's dancing with the sun.   But as the sun
has it all to himself in the heavens, so she, in the blaze
of her beauty, on earth.   This is imagination fairly
displacing fancy.   The following has enchanted every-
body :—

> Her lips were red, *and one was thin*
> *Compared with that was next her chin,*
> *Some bee had stung it newly.*

Every reader has stolen a kiss at that lip, gay or grave.

With regard to the principle of Variety in Uniformity by which verse ought to be modulated, and one-ness of impression diversely produced, it has been contended by some, that Poetry need not be written in verse at all; that prose is as good a medium, provided poetry be conveyed through it; and that to think otherwise is to confound letter with spirit, or form with essence. But the opinion is a prosaical mistake. Fitness and unfitness for *song*, or metrical excitement, just make all the difference between a poetical and prosaical subject.; and the reason why verse is necessary to the form of poetry is, that the perfection of poetical spirit demands it;—that the circle of its enthusiasm, beauty, and power, is incomplete without it. I do not mean to say that a poet can never show himself a poet in prose; but that, being one, his desire and necessity will be to write in verse; and that, if he were unable to do so, he would not, and could not, deserve his title. Verse to the true poet is no clog. It is idly called a trammel and a ·difficulty. It is a help. It springs from the same enthusiasm as the rest of his impulses, and is necessary to their satisfaction and effect. Verse is no more a clog than the condition of rushing upward is a clog to fire, or than the roundness and order of the globe we live on is a clog to the freedom and variety that abound within its sphere. Verse is no dominator over the poet, except inasmuch as the bond is reciprocal, and the poet dominates over the verse. They are lovers, playfully challenging each other's rule, and delighted equally to rule and to obey. Verse is the final proof to the poet that his mastery over his art is complete. It is the shutting up of his powers in "*measureful* content;" the answer of form to his spirit; of strength and ease to his guidance. It is the willing action, the proud and fiery happiness, of the winged steed on whose back he has vaulted,

> To witch the world with wondrous horsemanship.

Verse, in short, is that finishing, and rounding, and "tuneful planetting" of the poet's creations, which is produced of necessity by the smooth tendencies of their energy or inward working, and the harmonious dance into which they are attracted round the orb of the beautiful. Poetry, in its complete sympathy with beauty, must, of necessity, leave no sense of the beautiful, and no power over its forms, unmanifested; and verse flows as inevitably from this condition of its integrity, as other laws of proportion do from any other kind of embodiment of beauty (say that of the human figure), however free and various the movements may be that play within their limits. What great poet ever wrote his poems in prose? or where is a good prose poem, of any length, to be found? The poetry of the *Bible* is understood to be in verse, in the original. Mr. Hazlitt has said a good word for those prose enlargements of some fine old song, which are known by the name of Ossian; and in passages they deserve what he said; but he judiciously abstained from saying anything about the form. Is Gesner's *Death of*

Abel a poem ? or Hervey's *Meditations ?* The *Pilgrim's Progress* has been called one; and, undoubtedly, Bunyan had a genius which tended to make him a poet, and one of no mean order : and yet it was of as ungenerous and low a sort as was compatible with so lofty an affinity; and this is the reason why it stopped where it did. He had a craving after the beautiful, but not enough of it in himself to echo to its music. On the other hand, the possession of the beautiful will not be sufficient without force to utter it. The author of *Telemachus* had a soul full of beauty and tenderness. He was not a man who, if he had had a wife and children, would have run away from them, as Bunyan's hero did, to get a place by himself in heaven. He was "a little lower than the angels," like our own Bishop Jewells and Berkeleys; and yet he was no poet. He was too delicately, not to say feebly, absorbed in his devotions to join in the energies of the seraphic choir.

Every poet, then, is a versifier; every fine poet an excellent one; and he is the best whose verse exhibits the greatest amount of strength, sweetness, straightforwardness, unsuperfluousness, *variety,* and *onc-ness ;*—one-ness, that is to say, consistency, in the general impression, metrical and moral; and variety, or every pertinent diversity of tone and rhythm, in the process. *Strength* is the muscle of verse, and shows itself in the number and force of the marked syllables ; as,

Sonòrous mètal blòwing màrtial sòunds.—*Paradise Lost.*

    Behèmoth, bìggest born of eàrth, ùphèav'd
    His vàstness.—*Id.*

> Blòw, wind, and cràck your chèeks ! ràge ! blòw !
> You càtărăcts, and hurricànoes, spòut
> Till you have drènch'd our stèeples, dròwn'd the còcks !
> You sùlphurous and thoùght-èxecuting fìres,
> Vaùnt-coùriers to òak-clèaving thùnderbòlts,
> Sìnge my whìte hèad ! And thòu, àll-shàking thùnder,
> Strìke flàt the thìck rotùndity o' the wòrld !—*Lear.*

Unexpected locations of the accent double this force, and render it characteristic of passion and abruptness. And here comes into play the reader's corresponding fineness of ear, and his retardations and accelerations in accordance with those of the poet :—

> Then in the keyhole turns
> The ìntrĭcăte wards, and every bolt and bar
> Unfastens.—On ă sŭddĕn òpen fly
> Wìth ĭmpètuous recoil and jarring sound
> The infernal doors, and on their hinges grate
> Harsh thunder.—*Par. Lost*, Book II.

> Abòmĭnăblĕ—unùttĕrăblĕ—and worse
> Than fables yet have feigned.—*Id.*

> Wàllŏwĭng ŭnwìèldў̆—ĕnòrmous in their gait.—*Id.*

Of unusual passionate accent, there is an exquisite specimen in the *Fairy Queen*, where Una is lamenting her desertion by the Red-Cross Knight :—

> But he, my lion, and my noble lord,
> How does he find in cruel heart to hate
> Her that him lov'd, and ever most ador'd
> *As the gòd of my lìfe ?* Why hath he me abhorr'd ?

See the whole stanza, with a note upon it, in the present volume.

The abuse of strength is harshness and heaviness ; the

reverse of it is weakness. There is a noble sentiment,—
it appears both in Daniel's and Sir John Beaumont's
works, but is most probably the latter's,—which is a perfect
outrage of strength in the sound of the words :—

> Only the firmest and the *constant'st* hearts
> God sets to act the *stout'st* and hardest parts.

Stout'st and *constant'st* for "stoutest" and "most con-
stant!" It is as bad as the intentional crabbedness of
the line in *Hudibras :*

> He that hangs or *beats out's* brains,
> The devil's in him if *he* feigns.

Beats out's brains, for "beats out his brains." Of heavi-
ness, Davenant's *Gondibert* is a formidable specimen,
almost throughout :—

> With silence (òrder's help, and màrk of càre)
> They chìde thàt nòise which hèedless yòuth affèct ;
> Still coùrse for ùse, for heàlth thèy clèanness wèar,
> And sàve in wèll-fìx'd àrms, all nìceness chèck'd.
> Thèy thoùght, thòse that, unàrm'd, expòs'd fràil life,
> But nàked nàture vàliantly betrày'd ;
> Whò wàs, though nàked, sàfe, till prìde màde strife,
> But màde defènce must ùse, nòw dànger's màde.

And so he goes digging and lumbering on, like a heavy
preacher thumping the pulpit in italics, and spoiling many
ingenious reflections.

Weakness in versification is want of accent and
emphasis. It generally accompanies prosaicalness, and
is the consequence of weak thoughts, and of the affectation
of a certain well-bred enthusiasm. The writings of the
late Mr. Hayley were remarkable for it; and it abounds

among the lyrical imitators of Cowley, and the whole of what is called our French school of poetry, when it aspired above its wit and " sense." It sometimes breaks down in a horrible, hopeless manner, as if giving way at the first step. The following ludicrous passage in Congreve, intended to be particularly fine, contains an instance :—

> And lo ! Silence himself is here ;
> Methinks I see the midnight god appear.
> In all his downy pomp array'd,
> Behold the reverend shade.
> *An ancient sigh he sits upon ! ! !*
> Whose memory of sound is long since gone,
> *And purposely annihilated for his throne ! ! !*
> —*Ode on the singing of Mrs. Arabella Hunt.*

See also the would-be enthusiasm of Addison about music :—

> For ever consecrate the *day*
> To music and *Cecilia;*
> Music, the greatest good that mortals know,
> And all of heaven we have below,
> Music can noble HINTS *impart ! ! !*

It is observable that the unpoetic masters of ridicule are apt to make the most ridiculous mistakes, when they come to affect a strain higher than the one they are accustomed to. But no wonder. Their habits neutralize the enthusiasm it requires.

Sweetness, though not identical with smoothness, any more than feeling is with sound, always includes it ; and smoothness is a thing so little to be regarded for its own sake, and indeed so worthless in poetry, but for some taste of sweetness, that I have not thought necessary to mention

it by itself; though such an all-in-all in versification was
it regarded not a hundred years back, that Thomas Warton,
himself an idolator of Spenser, ventured to wish the
following line in the *Fairy Queen*,

> And was admirèd much of fools, *wòmen*, and boys—

altered to

> And was admirèd much of women, fools, and boys—

thus destroying the fine scornful emphasis on the first
syllable of "women!" (an ungallant intimation, by the
way, against the fair sex, very startling in this no less
woman-loving than great poet). Any poetaster can be
smooth. Smoothness abounds in all small poets, as sweet-
ness does in the greater. Sweetness is the smoothness of
grace and delicacy,—of the sympathy with the pleasing
and lovely. Spenser is full of it,—Shakspeare—Beaumont
and Fletcher—Coleridge. Of Spenser's and Coleridge's
versification it is the prevailing characteristic. Its main
secrets are a smooth progression between variety and
sameness, and a voluptuous sense of the continuous,—
"linked sweetness long drawn out." Observe the first
and last lines of the stanza in the *Fairy Queen*, describing
a shepherd brushing away the gnats;—the open and the
close *e*'s in the one,

> As gèntle shèpherd in swēēt ēventide—

and· the repetition of the word *oft*, and the fall from the
vowel *a* into the two *u*'s in the other,—

> She brusheth *oft*, and *oft* doth màr their mūrmŭrings.

So in his description of two substances in the handling, both equally smooth ;—

Each smoother seems than each, and each than each seems smoother.

An abundance of examples from his poetry will be found in the volume before us. His beauty revolves on itself with conscious loveliness. And Coleridge is worthy to be named with him, as the reader will see also, and has seen already. Let him take a sample meanwhile from the poem called the *Day-Dream!* Observe both the variety and sameness of the vowels, and the repetition of the soft consonants :—

> My eyes make pictures when they're shut :—
> I see a fountain, large and fair,
> A willow and a ruin'd hut,
> And *thee* and *me* and Mary there.
> *O Mary! make thy gentle lap our pillow ;*
> *Bend o'er us, like a bower, my beautiful green willow.*

By *Straightforwardness* is meant the flow of words in their natural order, free alike from mere prose, and from those inversions to which bad poets recur in order to escape the charge of prose, but chiefly to accommodate their rhymes. In Shadwell's play of *Psyche*, Venus gives the sisters of the heroine an answer, of which the following is the *entire* substance, literally, in so many words. The author had nothing better for her to say :—

I receive your prayers with kindness, and will give success to your hopes. I have seen, with anger, mankind adore your sister's beauty and deplore her scorn : which they shall do no more. For I'll so resent their idolatry, as shall content your wishes to the full.

Now in default of all imagination, fancy, and expres-

sion, how was the writer to turn these words into poetry
or rhyme? Simply by diverting them from their natural
order, and twisting the halves of the sentences each before
the other.

> With kindness I your prayers receive,
> And to your hopes success will give.
> I have, with anger, seen mankind adore
> Your sister's beauty and her scorn deplore;
> Which they shall do no more.
> For their idolatry I'll so resent,
> As shall your wishes to the full content!!

This is just as if a man were to allow that there was
no poetry in the words, "How do you find yourself?"
"Very well, I thank you;" but to hold them inspired, if
altered into

> Yourself how do you find?
> Very well, you I thank.

It is true, the best writers in Shadwell's age were
addicted to these inversions, partly for their own reasons,
as far as rhyme was concerned, and partly because they
held it to be writing in the classical and Virgilian manner.
What has since been called Artificial Poetry was then
flourishing, in contradistinction to Natural; or Poetry
seen chiefly through art and books, and not in its
first sources. But when the artificial poet partook
of the natural, or, in other words, was a true poet
after his kind, his best was always written in his
most natural and straightforward manner. Hear Shad-
well's antagonist Dryden. Not a particle of inversion,
beyond what is used for the sake of emphasis in com-

mon discourse, and this only in one line (the last but
three), is to be found in his immortal character of the
Duke of Buckingham :—

> A man so various, that he seemed to be
> Not one, but all mankind's epitome:
> Stiff in opinions, *always in the wrong*,
> *Was everything by starts, and nothing long ;*
> But in the course of one revolving moon
> Was chemist, fiddler, statesman, and buffoon :
> Then all for women, rhyming, dancing, drinking,
> *Besides ten thousand freaks that died in thinking.*
> *Blest madman !* who could every hour employ
> *With something new to wish or to enjoy !*
> Railing and praising were his usual themes ,
> And both, to show his judgment, in extremes :
> So over-violent, or over-civil,
> *That every man with him was god or devil.*
> In squandering wealth was his peculiar art ;
> *Nothing went unrewarded, but desert.*
> Beggar'd by fools, whom still he found too late,
> *He had his jest, and they had his estate.*

Inversion itself was often turned into a grace in these
poets, and may be in others, by the power of being supe-
rior to it ; using it only with a classical air, and as a help
lying next to them, instead of a salvation which they are
obliged to seek.   In jesting passages also it sometimes
gave the rhyme a turn agreeably wilful, or an appearance
of choosing what lay in its way ; as if a man should pick
up a stone to throw at another's head, where a less con-
fident foot would have stumbled over it.   Such is Dryden's
use of the word *might*—the mere sign of a tense—in his
pretended ridicule of the monkish practice of rising to
sing psalms in the night.

And much they griev'd to see so nigh their hall
The bird that warn'd St. Peter of his fall ;
That he should raise his mitred crest on high,
And clap his wings and call his family
To sacred rites; and vex th' ethereal powers
With midnight matins at uncivil hours ;
Nay more, his quiet neighbours should molest
Just in the sweetness of their morning rest.

(What a line full of " another doze " is that !)

Beast of a bird ! supinely, when he *might*
Lie snug and sleep, to rise before the light !
What if his dull forefathers used that cry ?
Could he not let a bad example die ? *

I the more gladly quote instances like those of Dryden,
to illustrate the points in question, because they are
specimens of the very highest kind of writing in the heroic
couplet upon subjects not heroical. As to prosaicalness
in general, it is sometimes indulged in by young writers
on the plea of its being natural ; but this is a mere confu-
sion of triviality with propriety, and is usually the result
of indolence.

Unsuperfluousness is rather a matter of style in general,
than of the sound and order of words : and yet versification
is so much strengthened by it, and so much weakened by
its opposite, that it could not but come within the cate-
gory of its requisites. When superfluousness of words is
not occasioned by overflowing animal spirits, as in Beau-
mont and Fletcher, or by the very genius of luxury, as in
Spenser (in which cases it is enrichment as well as over-
flow), there is no worse sign for a poet altogether, except
pure barrenness. Every word that could be taken away
from a poem, unreferable to either of the above reasons for

it, is a damage; and many such are death; for there is nothing that posterity seems so determined to resent as this want of respect for its time and trouble. The world is too rich in books to endure it. Even true poets have died of this Writer's Evil. Trifling ones have survived, with scarcely any pretensions but the terseness of their trifles. What hope can remain for wordy mediocrity? Let the discerning reader take up any poem, pen in hand, for the purpose of discovering how many words he can strike out of it that give him no requisite ideas, no relevant ones that he cares for, and no reasons for the rhyme beyond its necessity, and he will see what blot and havoc he will make in many an admired production of its day, —what marks of its inevitable fate. Bulky authors in particular, however safe they may think themselves, would do well to consider what parts of their cargo they might dispense with in their proposed voyage down the gulfs of time; for many a gallant vessel, thought indestructible in its age, has perished:—many a load of words, expected to be in eternal demand, gone to join the wrecks of self-love, or rotted in the warehouses of change and vicissitude. I have said the more on this point, because in an age when the true inspiration has undoubtedly been re-awakened by Coleridge and his fellows, and we have so many new poets coming forward, it may be as well to give a general warning against that tendency to an accumulation and ostentation of *thoughts*, which is meant to be a refutation in full of the pretensions of all poetry less cogitabund, whatever may be the requirements of its class. Young writers should bear in mind, that even some of

the very best materials for poetry are not poetry built; and
that the smallest marble shrine, of exquisite workmanship,
outvalues all that architect ever chipped away. Whatever·
can be so dispensed with is rubbish.

Variety in versification consists in whatsoever can be
done for the prevention of monotony, by diversity of·
stops and cadences, distribution of emphasis, and retarda-·
tion and acceleration of time; for the whole real secret.
of versification is a musical secret, and is not attainable·
to any vital effect save by the ear of genius. All the mere·
knowledge of feet and numbers, of accent and quantity,
will no more impart it, than a knowledge of the *Guide to
Music* will make a Beethoven or a Paisiello. It is a·
matter of sensibility and imagination; of the beautiful in
poetical passion, accompanied by musical; of the impera-·
tive necessity for a pause here, and a cadence there, and a·
quicker or slower utterance in this or that place, created
by analogies of sound with sense, by the fluctuations of·
feeling, by the demands of the gods and graces that·
visit the poet's harp, as the winds visit that of Æolus.
The same time and quantity which are occasioned by the·
spiritual part of this secret, thus become its formal ones,
—not feet and syllables, long and short, iambics or·
trochees; which are the reduction of it to its *less* than dry
bones. You might get, for instance, not only ten and.
eleven, but thirteen or fourteen syllables into a rhyming,
as well as blank, heroical verse, if time and the feeling·
permitted; and in irregular measure this is often done;
just as musicians put twenty notes in a bar instead of two,
quavers instead of minims, according as the feeling they·

are expressing impels them to fill up the time with short
and hurried notes, or with long; or as the choristers in a
cathedral retard or precipitate the words of the chaunt,
according as the quantity of its notes, and the colon which
divides the verse of the psalm, conspire to demand it.
Had the moderns borne this principle in mind when they
settled the prevailing systems of verse, instead of learning
them, as they appear to have done, from the first drawling
and one-syllabled notation of the church hymns, we should
have retained all the advantages of the more numerous
versification of the ancients, without being compelled to
fancy that there was no alternative for us between our
syllabical uniformity and the hexameters or other special
forms unsuited to our tongues. But to leave this ques-
tion alone, we will present the reader with a few sufficing
specimens of the difference between monotony and variety
in versification, first from Pope, Dryden, and Milton, and
next from Gay and Coleridge. The following is the
boasted melody of the nevertheless exquisite poet of the
Rape of the Lock,—exquisite in his wit and fancy, though
not in his numbers. The reader will observe that it is
literally *see-saw,* like the rising and falling of a plank,
with a light person at one end who is jerked up in the
briefer time, and a heavier one who is set down more
leisurely at the other. It is in the otherwise charming
description of the heroine of that poem :—

> On her white breast—a sparkling cross she wore,
> Which Jews might kiss—and infidels adore;
> Her lively looks—a sprightly mind disclose,
> Quick as her eyes—and as unfix'd as those

Favours to none—to all she smiles extends,
Oft she rejects—but never once offends ;
Bright as the sun—her eyes the gazers strike,
And like the sun—they shine on all alike ;
Yet graceful ease—and sweetness void of pride,
Might hide her faults—if belles had faults to hide ;
If to her share—some female errors fall,
Look on her face—and you'll forget them all.

Compare with this the description of Iphigenia in one of Dryden's stories from Boccaccio : —

It happen'd—on a summer's holiday,
That to the greenwood shade—he took his way,
For Cymon shunn'd the church—and used not much to pray :
His quarter-staff—which he could ne'er forsake,
Hung half before—and half behind his back :
He trudg'd along—not knowing what he sought,
And whistled as he went—for want of thought.

By chance conducted—or by thirst constrain'd,
The deep recesses of a grove he gain'd :—
Where—in a plain defended by a wood,
Crept through the matted grass—a crystal flood,
By which—an alabaster fountain stood ;
And on the margent of the fount was laid—
Attended by her slaves—a sleeping maid ;
Like Dian and her nymphs—when, tir'd with sport,
To rest by cool Eurotas they resort.—
The dame herself—the goddess well express'd,
Not more distinguished by her purple vest—
Than by the charming features of the face—
And e'en in slumber—a superior grace :
Her comely limbs—compos'd with decent care,
Her body shaded—by a light cymarr,
Her bosom to the view—was only bare ;
Where two beginning paps were scarcely spied—
For yet their places were but signified.—
The fanning wind upon her bosom blows—
To meet the fanning wind—the bosom rose ,
The fanning wind—and purling stream—continue her repose.

For a further variety take, from the same author's *Theodore and Honoria*, a passage in which the couplets are run one into the other, and all of it modulated, like the former, according to the feeling demanded by the occasion :—

> Whilst listening to the murmuring leaves he stood—
> More than a mile immers'd within the wood—
> At once the wind was laid.I—The whispering sound
> Was dumb.I—A rising earthquake rock'd the ground.
> With deeper brown the grove was overspread—⎫
> A sudden horror seiz'd his giddy head— ⎬
> And his ears tinkled—and his colour fled. ⎭
>
> Nature was in alarm.—Some danger nigh
> Seem'd threaten'd—though unseen to mortal eye.
> Unus'd to fear—he summon'd all his soul,
> And stood collected in himself—and whole:
> Not long.—

But for a crowning specimen of variety of pause and accent, apart from emotion, nothing can surpass the account, in *Paradise Lost*, of the Devil's search for an accomplice :—

>   There was a plàce,
> Nòw nòt—though Sìn—not Tìme—first wroùght the chànge,
> Where Tìgris—at the foot of Pàradise,
> Into a gùlf—shòt under ground—till pàrt
> Ròse up a foùntain by the Trèe of Lìfe.
> *In* with the river sunk—and *with it ròse*
> Sàtan—invòlv'd in rìsing mìst—then soùght
> Whère to lie hìd.—Sèa he had search'd—and lànd
> From Eden over Pòntus—and the pòol
> Mæòtis—*ùp* beyond the river *Ob ;*
> Dòwnward as fàr antàrctic ;—and in lèngth
> West from Oròntes—to the òcean bàrr'd
> At Dàriën—thènce to the lànd whère flòws
> Gànges, and Indus.—Thùs the òrb he ròam'd

With nàrrow sèarch;—and with inspèction deep
Consìder'd èvery crèature—which of àll
Mòst opportùne mìght sèrve his wìles—and foùnd
The sèrpent—sùbtlest bèast of all the fièld.

If the reader cast his eye again over this passage, he
will not find a verse in it which is not varied and har-
monized in the most remarkable manner. Let him notice
in particular that curious balancing of the lines in the
sixth and tenth verses:—

In with the river sunk, &c.

and

Up beyond the river *Ob.*

It might, indeed, be objected to the versification of
Milton, that it exhibits too constant a perfection of this
kind. It sometimes forces upon us too great a sense of
consciousness on the part of the composer. We miss the
first sprightly runnings of verse,—the ease and sweetness
of spontaneity. Milton, I think, also too often condenses
weight into heaviness.

Thus much concerning the chief of our two most
popular measures. The other, called octosyllabic, or the
measure of eight syllables, offered such facilities for *namby-
pamby*, that it had become a jest as early as the time of
Shakspeare, who makes Touchstone call it the "butter-
woman's rate to market," and the "very false gallop of
verses." It has been advocated, in opposition to the
heroic measure, upon the ground that ten syllables lead
a man into epithets and other superfluities, while eight
syllables compress him into a sensible and pithy gentle-
man. But the heroic measure laughs at it. So far from

compressing, it converts one line into two, and sacrifices
everything to the quick and importunate return of the
rhyme.   With Dryden compare Gay, even in the strength
of Gay,—

> The wind was high, the window shakes;
> With sudden start the miser wakes;
> Along the silent room he stalks,

(A miser never "stalks;" but a rhyme was desired for
"walks")

> Looks back, and trembles as he walks:
> Each lock and every bolt he tries,
> In every creek and corner pries;
> Then opes the chest with treasure stor'd,
> And stands in rapture o'er his hoard;

("Hoard" and "treasure stor'd" are just made for one
another,)

> But now, with sudden qualms possess'd,
> He wrings his hands, he beats his breast;
> By conscience stung, he wildly stares,
> And thus his guilty soul declares.

And so he denounces his gold, as miser never denounced
it; and sighs because

> Virtue resides on earth no more!

Coleridge saw the mistake which had been made with
regard to this measure, and restored it to the beautiful
freedom of which it was capable, by calling to mind the
liberties allowed its old musical professors the minstrels,
and dividing it by *time* instead of *syllables*;—by the *beat
of four*, into which you might get as many syllables as you
could, instead of allotting eight syllables to the poor time,
whatever it might have to say.   He varied it further with

alternate rhymes and stanzas, with rests and omissions precisely analogous to those in music, and rendered it altogether worthy to utter the manifold thoughts and feelings of himself and his lady Christabel. He even ventures, with an exquisite sense of solemn strangeness and licence (for there is witchcraft going forward), to introduce a couplet of blank verse, itself as mystically and beautifully modulated as anything in the music of Gluck or Weber.—

'Tis the middle of night by the castle clock,
And the owls have awaken'd the crowing cock
Tu-whit!—Tu-whoo!
And hark, again! the crowing cock,
How drowsily he crew.
Sir Leoline, the baron rich,
Hath a toothless mastiff bitch;
From her kennel beneath the rock
She maketh answer to the clock,
Fòur fŏr thĕ quàrtĕrs ănd twelve fŏr thĕ hoùr,
Ever and aye, by shine and shower,
Sixteen short howls, not over loud:
Some say, she sees my lady's shroud.

Is the night chilly and dark?
The night is chilly, but not dark.
The thin grey cloud is spread on high,
It covers, but not hides, the sky.
The moon is behind, and at the full,
And yet she looks both small and dull.
The night is chilly, the cloud is grey;

(These are not superfluities, but mysterious returns of importunate feeling)

'Tis a month before the month of May,
And the spring comes slowly up this way.
The lovely lady, Christabel,
Whom her father loves so well,

4

What makes her in the wood so late,
A furlong from the castle-gate ?
She had dreams all yesternight .
Of her own betrothèd knight ;
And shè ĭn thĕ midnight wood will **pray**
For the wèal ŏf hĕr lover that's far **away**.

She stole along, she nothing spoke,
The sighs she heav'd were soft and low,
*A*nd nought was green upon the oak,
But moss and rarest mistletoe ;
She kneels beneath the huge oak tree,
*A*nd in silence prayeth she.

The lady sprang up suddenly,
The lovely lady, Christabel !
It moan'd as near as near can be,
But what it is, she cannot tell.
On the other side it seems to be
Of thĕ hùge, broàd breàsted, òld oàk trĕe.

The night is chill, the forest bare ;
Is it the wind that moaneth bleak ?

(This " bleak moaning " is a witch's)

There is not wind enough in the air
To move away the ringlet curl
From the lovely lady's cheek—
There is not wind enough to twirl
The òne rèd lèaf, the làst ŏf ĭts clan,
That dáncĕs ăs òftĕn ăs dànce it càn,
Hángĭng sŏ light and hàngĭng sŏ high,
On thĕ tòpmost twig thăt lŏoks ùp ăt thĕ **sky**.

Hush, beating heart of Christabel !
Jesu Maria, shield her well !
She folded her arms beneath her cloak,
And stole to the other side of the oak.
What sees she there ?

There she sees a damsel bright,
Drest in a robe of silken white,
That shadowy in the moonlight shone :
The neck that made that white robe wan,
Her stately neck and arms were bare :
Her blue-vein'd feet unsandall'd were ;
And wildly glitter'd, here and there,
The gems entangled in her hair.
I guess 'twas *frightful* there to see
A lady so richly clad as she—
Beautiful exceedingly.

The principle of Variety in Uniformity is here worked
out in a style "beyond the reach of art." Everything is
diversified according to the demand of the moment, of the
sounds, the sights, the emotions ; the very uniformity of
the outline is gently varied ; and yet we feel that *the whole
is one and of the same character,* the single and sweet uncon-
sciousness of the heroine making all the rest seem more
conscious, and ghastly, and expectant. It is thus that
versification itself becomes part of the sentiment of a poem,
and vindicates the pains that have been taken to show its
importance. I know of no very fine versification unac-
companied with fine poetry ; no poetry of a mean order
accompanied with verse of the highest.

As to Rhyme, which might be thought too insignificant
to mention, it is not at all so. The universal consent of
modern Europe, and of the East in all ages, has made it
one of the musical beauties of verse for all poetry but epic
and dramatic, and even for the former with Southern
Europe,—a sustainment for the enthusiasm, and a demand
to enjoy. The mastery of it consists in never writing it
for its own sake, or at least never appearing to do so ; in

knowing how to vary it, to give it novelty, to render it
more or less strong, to divide it (when not in couplets) at
the proper intervals, to repeat it many times where luxury
or animal spirits demand it (see an instance in Titania's
speech to the Fairies), to impress an affecting or startling
remark with it, and to make it, in comic poetry, a new and
surprising addition to the jest.

> Large was his bounty and his soul sincere,
> Heav'n did a recompence as largely send;
> He gave to misery all he had, *a tear ;*
> He gain'd from heav'n ('twas all he wish'd) *a friend.*
> > —-Gray's *Elegy.*

> The fops are proud of scandal ; for they cry
> At every lewd, low character, " That's *I.*"
> > —Dryden's *Prologue to the Pilgrim.*

> What makes all doctrines plain and clear ?
> *About two hundred pounds a year.*
> And that which was proved true before,
> Prove false again ? *Two hundred more.*—*Hudibras*

> Compound for sins they are *inclin'd to,*
> By damning those they have *no mind to.*—*Id.*

> ———Stor'd with deletery *med'cines,*
> Which whosoever took is *dead since.*—*Id.*

Sometimes it is a grace in a master like Butler to force
his rhyme, thus showing a laughing wilful power over the
most stubborn materials :—

> > Win
> The women, and make them draw in
> The men, as Indians with a *female*
> Tame elephant inveigle *the* male.—*Id.*

> He made an instrument to know
> If the moon shines at full or no ;
> That would, as soon as e'er she *shone, straight*
> Whether 'twere day or night *demonstrate ;*
> Tell what her diameter to an *inch is,*
> And prove that she's not made of *green cheese.*
>
> —*Hudibras.*

Pronounce it, by all means, *grinches,* to make the joke more wilful. The happiest triple rhyme, perhaps, that ever was written, is in *Don Juan :—*

> But oh ! ye lords of ladies *intellectual,*
> Inform us truly,—haven't they *hen-peck'd you all ?*

The sweepingness of the assumption completes the flowing breadth of effect.

Dryden confessed that a rhyme often gave him a thought. Probably the happy word " sprung " in the following passage from Ben Jonson was suggested by it ; but then the poet must have had the feeling in him :

> —Let our trumpets sound,
> And cleave both air and ground
>   With beating of our drums.
> Let every lyre be strung,
> Harp, lute, theorbo, *sprung*
>   *With touch of dainty thumbs.*

Boileau's trick for appearing to rhyme naturally was to compose the second line of his couplet first ! which gives one the crowning idea of the " artificial school of poetry." Perhaps the most perfect master of rhyme, the easiest and most abundant, was the greatest writer of comedy that the world has seen,—Molière.

If a young reader should ask, after all, What is the quickest way of knowing bad poets from good, the best poets from the next best, and so on? the answer is, the only and twofold way : first, the perusal of the best poets with the greatest attention; and, second, the cultivation of that love of truth and beauty which made them what they are. Every true reader of poetry partakes a more than ordinary portion of the poetic nature; and no one can be completely such, who does not love, or take an interest in, everything that interests the poet, from the firmament to the daisy,—from the highest heart of man to the most pitiable of the low. It is a good practice to read with pen in hand, marking what is liked or doubted. It rivets the attention, realizes the greatest amount of enjoyment, and facilitates reference. It enables the reader also, from time to time, to see what progress he makes with his own mind, and how it grows up towards the stature of its exalter.

If the same person should ask, What class of poetry is the highest ? I should say, undoubtedly, the Epic ; for it includes the drama, with narration besides ; or the speaking and action of the characters, with the speaking of the poet himself, whose utmost address is taxed to relate all well for so long a time, particularly in the passages least sustained by enthusiasm. Whether this class has included the greatest poet, is another question still under trial; for Shakspeare perplexes all such verdicts, even when the claimant is Homer ; though, if a judgment may be drawn from his early narratives (*Venus and Adonis*, and the *Rape of Lucrece*), it is to be doubted whether even Shakspeare could have told a story like Homer, owing to that incessant activity and superfœtation of thought, a

little less of which might be occasionally desired even in
his plays;—if it were possible, once possessing anything
of his, to wish it away. Next to Homer and Shakspeare
come such narrators as the less universal, but still intenser
Dante ; Milton, with his dignified imagination ; the uni-
versal, profoundly simple Chaucer ; and luxuriant, remote
Spenser—immortal child in poetry's most poetic solitudes :
then the great second-rate dramatists ; unless those who
are better acquainted with Greek tragedy than I am,
demand a place for them before Chaucer : then the airy
yet robust universality of Ariosto ; the hearty, out-of-door
nature of Theocritus, also a universalist ; the finest lyrical
poets (who only take short flights, compared with the
narrators) ; the purely contemplative poets who have more
thought than feeling ; the descriptive, satirical, didactic,
epigrammatic. It is to be borne in mind, however, that
the first poet of an inferior class may be superior to fol-
lowers in the train of a higher one, though the superiority
is by no means to be taken for granted ; otherwise Pope
would be superior to Fletcher, and Butler to Pope. Imagi-
nation, teeming with action and character, makes the
greatest poets ; feeling and thought the next; fancy (by
itself) the next ; wit the last. Thought by itself makes
no poet at all; for the mere conclusions of the under-
standing can at best be only so many intellectual matters
of fact. Feeling, even destitute of conscious thought,
stands a far better poetical chance ; feeling being a sort of
thought without the process of thinking,—a grasper of the
truth without seeing it. And what is very remarkable,
feeling seldom makes the blunders that thought does. An

idle distinction has been made between taste and judg-
ment. Taste is the very maker of judgment. Put an
artificial fruit in your mouth, or only handle it, and you
will soon perceive the difference between judging from
taste or tact, and judging from the abstract figment called
judgment. The latter does but throw you into guesses
and doubts. Hence the conceits that astonish us in the
gravest, and even subtlest thinkers, whose taste is not pro-
portionate to their mental perceptions : men like Donne,
for instance ; who, apart from accidental personal impres-
sions, seem to look at nothing as it really is, but only as
to what may be thought of it. Hence, on the other hand,
the delightfulness of those poets who never violate truth
of feeling, whether in things real or imaginary ; who are
always consistent with their object and its requirements ;
and who run the great round of nature, not to perplex and
be perplexed, but to make themselves and us happy. And
luckily, delightfulness is not incompatible with greatness,
willing soever as men may be in their present imperfect
state to set the power to subjugate above the power to
please. Truth, of any great kind whatsoever, makes great
writing. This is the reason why such poets as Ariosto,
though not writing with a constant detail of thought and
feeling like Dante, are justly considered great as well as
delightful. Their greatness proves itself by the same
truth of nature, and sustained power, though in a different
way. Their action is not so crowded and weighty ; their
sphere has more territories less fertile ; but it has enchant-
ments of its own, which excess of thought would spoil, —
luxuries, laughing graces, animal spirits ; and not to

recognize the beauty and greatness of those, treated as
they treat them, is simply to be defective in sympathy.
Every planet is not Mars or Saturn. There is also Venus
and Mercury. There is one genius of the south, and
another of the north, and others uniting both. The reader
who is too thoughtless or too sensitive to like intensity of
any sort, and he who is too thoughtful or too dull to like
anything but the greatest possible stimulus of reflection or
passion, are equally wanting in complexional fitness for a
thorough enjoyment of books. Ariosto occasionally says
as fine things as Dante, and Spenser as Shakspeare ; but
the business of both is to enjoy ; and in order to partake
their enjoyment to its full extent, you must feel what
poetry is in the general as well as the particular, must be
aware that there are different songs of the spheres, some
fuller of notes, and others of a sustained delight; and as
the former keep you perpetually alive to thought or
passion, so from the latter you receive a constant har-
monious sense of truth and beauty, more agreeable per-
haps on the whole, though less exciting. Ariosto, for
instance, does not *tell a story* with the brevity and concen-
trated passion of Dante ; every sentence is not so full of
matter, nor the style so removed from the indifference of
prose ; yet you are charmed with a truth of another sort,
equally characteristic of the writer, equally drawn from
nature and substituting a healthy sense of enjoyment for
intenser emotion. Exclusiveness of liking for this or that
mode of truth, only shows, either that a reader's percep-
tions are limited, or that he would sacrifice truth itself to
his favourite form of it. Sir Walter Raleigh, who was as

trenchant with his pen as his sword, hailed the *Faerie Queene* of his friend Spenser in verses in which he said that Petrarch was thenceforward to be no more heard of; and that in all English poetry there was nothing he counted "of any price" but the effusions of the new author. Yet Petrarch is still living; Chaucer was not abolished by Sir Walter; and Shakspeare is thought somewhat valuable. A botanist might as well have said, that myrtles and oaks were to disappear, because acacias had come up. It is with the poet's creations, as with Nature's, great or small. Wherever truth and beauty, whatever their amount, can be worthily shaped into verse, and answer to some demand for it in our hearts, there poetry is to be found; whether in productions grand and beautiful as some great event, or some mighty, leafy solitude, or no bigger and more pretending than a sweet face or a bunch of violets; whether in Homer's epic or Gray's *Elegy*, in the enchanted gardens of Ariosto and Spenser, or the very pot-herbs of the *Schoolmistress* of Shenstone, the balms of the simplicity of a cottage. Not to know and feel this, is to be deficient in the universality of Nature herself, who is a poetess on the smallest as well as the largest scale, and who calls upon us to admire all her productions; not indeed with the same degree of admiration, but with no refusal of it, except to defect.

I cannot draw this essay towards its conclusion better than with three memorable words of Milton; who has said, that poetry, in comparison with science, is "simple, sensuous, and passionate." By simple, he means unperplexed and self-evident; by sensuous, genial and full of imagery;

by passionate, excited and enthusiastic. I am aware that
different constructions have been put on some of these
words; but the context seems to me to necessitate those
before us. I quote, however, not from the original, but
from an extract in the *Remarks on Paradise Lost* by
Richardson.

What the poet has to cultivate above all things is love
and truth ;—what he has to avoid, like poison, is the
fleeting and the false. He will get no good by proposing
to be " in earnest at the moment." His earnestness must
be innate and habitual; born with him, and felt to be
his most precious inheritance. " I expect neither profit
nor general fame by my writings," says Coleridge, in the
Preface to his Poems; " and I consider myself as having
been amply repaid without either. Poetry has been to me
its ' *own exceeding great reward ;* ' it has soothed my
afflictions; it has multiplied and refined my enjoyments ;
it has endeared solitude; and it has given me the habit
of wishing to discover the good and the beautiful in all
that meets and surrounds me."—*Pickering's edition,* p. 10.

" Poetry," says Shelley, " lifts the veil from the hidden
beauty of the world, *and makes familiar objects be as if they
were not familiar.* It reproduces all that it represents ;
and the impersonations clothed in its Elysian light stand
thenceforward in the minds of those who have once con-
templated them, as memorials of that gentle and exalted
content which extends itself over all thoughts and actions
with which it co-exists. The great secret of morals is
love, or a going out of our own nature, and an identifica-
tion of ourselves with the beautiful which exists in thought,

action, or person, not our own. A man, to be greatly good, must imagine intensely and comprehensively; he must put himself in the place of another, and of many others: the pains and pleasures of his species must become his own. The great instrument of moral good is imagination; and poetry administers to the effect by acting upon the cause."—*Essays and Letters*, vol. i. p. 16.

I would not willingly say anything after perorations like these; but as treatises on poetry may chance to have auditors who think themselves called upon to vindicate the superiority of what is termed useful knowledge, it may be as well to add, that if the poet may be allowed to pique himself on any one thing more than another, compared with those who undervalue him, it is on that power of undervaluing nobody, and no attainments different from his own, which is given him by the very faculty of imagination they despise. The greater includes the less. They do not see that their inability to comprehend him argues the smaller capacity. No man recognizes the worth of utility more than the poet: he only desires that the meaning of the term may not come short of its greatness, and exclude the noblest necessities of his fellow-creatures. He is quite as much pleased, for instance, with the facilities for rapid conveyance afforded him by the railroad, as the dullest confiner of its advantages to that single idea, or as the greatest two-idea'd man who varies that single idea with hugging himself on his "buttons" or his good dinner. But he sees also the beauty of the country through which he passes, of the towns, of the heavens, of the steam-engine itself, thundering and fuming along like a magic horse, of the affections that are carrying, perhaps, half the passengers on their journey, nay, of those of the great two-idea'd man ; and, beyond all this, he discerns the incalculable amount of good, and knowledge, and refinement, and mutual consideration, which this wonderful invention is fitted to circulate over the globe, perhaps to the displacement of war itself, and certainly to the diffusion of millions of enjoyments.

"And a button-maker, after all, invented it !" cries our friend.

Pardon me—it was a nobleman. A button-maker may be a very excellent, and a very poetical man too, and yet not have been the first man visited by a sense of the gigantic powers of the combination of water and fire. It was a nobleman who first thought of this most poetical bit of science. It was a nobleman who first thought of it,— a captain who first tried it,—and a button-maker who perfected it. And he who put the nobleman on such thoughts, was the great philosopher, Bacon, who said that poetry had "something divine in it," and was necessary to the satisfaction of the human mind.

SPENSER.

BORN, PROBABLY ABOUT THE YEAR 1553- -
DIED, 1598.

THREE things must be conceded to the objectors against this divine poet: first, that he wrote a good deal of allegory; second, that he has a great many superfluous words; third, that he was very fond of alliteration. He is accused also (by little boys) of obsolete words and spelling; and it must be added, that he often forces his rhymes; nay, spells them in an arbitrary manner on purpose to make them fit. In short, he has a variety of faults, real or supposed, that would be intolerable in writers in general. This is true. The answer is, that his genius not only makes amends for all, but overlays them, and makes them beautiful, with "riches fineless." When acquaintance with him is once begun, he repels none but the anti-poetical. Others may not be able to read him continuously; but more or less, and as an enchanted stream "to dip into," they will read him always.

In Spenser's time, orthography was unsettled. Pronunciation is always so. The great poet, therefore, sometimes spells his words, whether rhymed or otherwise, in a manner apparently arbitrary, for the purpose of inducing the reader to give them the sound fittest for the sense. Alliteration, which, as a ground of melody, had been a principle in Anglo-Saxon verse, continued such a favourite with old English poets whom Spenser loved, that, as late as the reign of Edward III., it stood in the place of rhyme itself. Our author turns it to beautiful account. Superfluousness, though eschewed with a fine instinct by Chaucer in some of his latest works, where the narrative was fullest of action and character, abounded in his others; and, in spite of the classics, it had not been recognized as a fault in Spenser's time, when books were still rare, and a writer thought himself bound to pour out all he felt and knew. It accorded also with his genius; and in him is not an excess of weakness, but of will and luxury. And as to allegory, it was not only the taste of the day, originating in gorgeous pageants of church and state, but in Spenser's hands it became such an embodiment of poetry itself, that its objectors really deserve no better answer than has been given them by Mr. Hazlitt, who asks, if they thought the allegory would "bite them." The passage will be found a little further on.

Spenser's great characteristic is poetic luxury. If you go to him for a story, you will be disappointed; if for a style, classical or concise, the point against him is conceded; if for pathos, you must weep for personages half-real and too beautiful; if for mirth, you must laugh out of good breeding, and because it pleaseth the great, sequestered man to be facetious. But if you love

poetry well enough to enjoy it for its own sake, let no evil
reports of his " allegory " deter you from his acquaintance,
for great will be your loss.   His allegory itself is but one
part allegory, and nine parts beauty and enjoyment ; some-
times an excess of flesh and blood.   His forced rhymes,
and his sentences written to fill up, which in a less poet
would be intolerable, are accompanied with such endless
grace and dreaming pleasure, fit to

> Make heaven drowsy with the harmony,

. that although it is to be no more expected of anybody to
read him through at once, than to wander days and nights
in a forest, thinking of nothing else, yet any true lover of
poetry, when he comes to know him, would as soon quarrel
with repose on the summer grass.   You may get up and
go away, but will return next day at noon to listen to his
waterfalls, and to see, " with half-shut eye," his visions of
knights and nymphs, his gods and goddesses, whom he
brought down again to earth in immortal beauty.

Spenser, in some respects, is more southern than the
south itself.   Dante, but for the covered heat which occa-
sionally concentrates the utmost sweetness as well as
venom, would be quite northern compared with him.   He
is more luxurious than Ariosto or Tasso, more haunted
with the presence of beauty.   His wholesale poetical belief,
mixing up all creeds and mythologies, but with less
violence, resembles that of Dante and Boccaccio ; and it
gives the compound the better warrant in the more agree-
able impression.   Then his versification is almost perpetual
honey.

Spenser is the farthest removed from the ordinary
cares and haunts of the world of all the poets that ever
wrote, except perhaps Ovid ; and this, which is the reason
why mere men of business and the world do not like him,
constitutes his most bewitching charm with the poetical.
He is not so great a poet as Shakspeare or Dante ;—he
has less imagination, though more fancy, than Milton.
He does not see things so purely in their elements as
Dante ; neither can he combine their elements like Shak-
speare, nor bring such frequent intensities of words, or of
wholesale imaginative sympathy, to bear upon his subject
as any one of them ; though he has given noble diffuser
instances of the latter in his Una, and his Mammon, and
his accounts of Jealousy and Despair.

But when you are " over-informed " with thought and
passion in Shakspeare, when Milton's mighty grandeurs
oppress you, or are found mixed with painful absurdities,
or when the world is vexatious and tiresome, and you have
had enough of your own vanities or struggles in it, or
when " house and land " themselves are " gone and
spent," and your riches must lie in the regions of the
" unknown," then Spenser is " most excellent." His
remoteness from everyday life is the reason perhaps why
Somers and Chatham admired him ; and his possession of
every kind of imaginary wealth completes his charm with
his brother poets. Take him in short for what he is,
whether greater or less than his fellows, the poetical
faculty is so abundantly and beautifully predominant in
him above every ·other, though he had passion, and
thought, and plenty of ethics, and was as learned a man

as Ben Jonson, perhaps as Milton himself, that he has
always been felt by his countrymen to be what Charles
Lamb called him, the " Poet's Poet." He has had more
idolatry and imitation from his brethren than all the rest
put together. The old undramatic poets, Drayton, Browne,
Drummond, Giles and Phineas Fletcher, were as full of
him as the dramatic were of Shakspeare. Milton studied
and used him, calling him the " sage and serious
Spenser;" and adding, that he " dared be known to think
him a better teacher than Scotus or Aquinas." Cowley said
that he became a poet by reading him. Dryden claimed
him for a master. Pope said he read him with as much
pleasure when he was old, as young. Collins and Gray loved
him; Thomson, Shenstone, and a host of inferior writers,
expressly imitated him; Burns, Byron, Shelley, and Keats
made use of his stanza; Coleridge eulogized him; and he
is as dear to the best living poets as he was to their prede-
cessors. Spenser has stood all the changes in critical
opinion; all the logical and formal conclusions of the
understanding, as opposed to imagination and lasting sym-
pathy. Hobbes in vain attempted to depose him in favour
of Davenant's *Gondibert*. Locke and his friend Molyneux
to no purpose preferred Blackmore! Hume, acute and
encroaching philosopher as he was, but not so universal in
his philosophy as great poets, hurt Spenser's reputation
with none but the French (who did not know him); and,
by way of involuntary amends for the endeavour, he set up
for poets such men as Wilkie and Blacklock! In vain, in
vain. " In spite of philosophy and fashion," says a better
critic of that day (Bishop Hurd), " Faerie Spenser still

ranks highest amongst the poets; I mean with all those
who are either of that house, or have any kindness for it.
Earth-born critics may blaspheme;

> But all the *gods* are ravish'd with delight
> Of his celestial song and musick's wondrous might."
> —*Remarks on the Plan and Conduct of the Faerie Queene* (*in Todd's
> edition of Spenser*, vol. ii. p. 183).

"In reading Spenser," says Warton, "if the critic is
not satisfied, yet the reader is transported."—(*Id*. p. 65.)

"Spenser," observes Coleridge, "has the wit of the
southern, with the deeper inwardness of the northern
genius. Take especial note of the marvellous independ-
ence and true imaginative absence of all particular space
or time in the *Faerie Queene*. It is in the domains
neither of history nor geography: it is ignorant of all
artificial boundary, all material obstacles; it is truly in
land of Faerie, that is, of mental space. The poet has
placed you in a dream, a charmed sleep: and you neither
wish nor have the power to inquire, where you are, or how
you got there."—*Literary Remains*, vol. i. p. 94.

"In reading the *Faerie Queene*," says Hazlitt, "you
see a little withered old man by a wood-side opening a
wicket, a giant, and a dwarf lagging far behind, a damsel
in a boat upon an enchanted lake, wood-nymphs and
satyrs; and all of a sudden you are transported into a
lofty palace, with tapers burning, amidst knights and
ladies, with dance and revelry, and song, ' and mask and
antique pageantry.'—But some people will say that all this
may be very fine, but they cannot understand it on account
of the allegory. They are afraid of the allegory, as if they

thought it would bite them; they look at it as a child looks at a painted dragon, and think that it will strangle them in its shining folds. This is very idle. If they do not meddle with the allegory, the allegory will not meddle with them. Without minding it at all, the whole is as plain as a pike-staff. It might as well be pretended, that we cannot see Poussin's pictures for the allegory, as that the allegory prevents us from understanding Spenser."— *Lectures on the English Poets* (Templeman's edition, 12mo p. 67).

ARCHIMAGO'S HERMITAGE,

AND

THE HOUSE OF MORPHEUS.

Archimago, a hypocritical magician, lures Una and the Red-cross Knight into his abode; and while they are asleep, sends to Morpheus, the god of sleep, for a false dream to produce discord between them.

> *A little lowly hermitage it was,*
> *Down in a dale, hard by a forest's side,*
> *Far from resort of people* that did pass
> In travel to and fro : a little wide
> There was a holy chapel edifyde,
> Wherein the hermit duly wont to say
> His holy things each morn and eventide :
> Thereby a crystal stream did gently play,
> Which from a sacred fountain *welld forth alway.* (¹)

> Arrivèd there, the little house they fill, (²)
> Nor look for entertainment where none was; (³)
> Rest is their feast, and all things at their will :
> *The noblest mind the best contentment has.* (⁴)

With fair discourse the evening so they pass.
For that old man of pleasing words had store,
And well could file his tongue as smooth as glass :
He told of saints and popes, *and evermore*
He strow'd an Ave-Mary after and before.

The drooping night thus creepeth on them fast ;
And the sad humour, *loading their eye-lids,*
As messenger of Morpheus, on them cast
Sweet slumbering dew ; the which to sleep them bids.
Unto their lodgings then his guests he rids ;
Where, when all drown'd in deadly sleep he finds,
He to his study goes ; and there amids
His magic books, and arts of sundry kinds,
He seeks out mighty charms to trouble sleepy minds.

Then choosing out few words most horrible ·
(*Let none them read!*) (⁵) thereof did verses frame ;
With which, and other spells like terrible,
He bade awake black Pluto's grisly dame ;
And cursèd Heaven ; and spake reproachful shame
Of highest God, the Lord of life and light:
A bold bad man ! that dar'd to call by name
Great Gorgon, (⁶) prince of darkness and dead night ;
At which Cocytus quakes, and Styx is put to flight.

And forth he call'd out of deep darkness dread
Legions of sprites, the which, like little flies, (⁷)
Fluttering about his ever-damnèd head,
Await whereto their service he applies ;
To aid his friends, or fray his enemies ;
Of those he chose out two, the falsest two,
And fittest for to forge true-seeming lies ;
The one of them he gave a message to,
The other by himself stay'd other work to do.

He, making speedy way through spersèd air,
And through the world of waters wide and deep, (⁸)
To Morpheus' house doth hastily repair. (⁹)
Amid the bowels of the earth full steep

And low, where dawning day doth never peep,
His dwelling is ; *there Tethys his wet bed
Doth ever wash*, and Cynthia still doth steep
In silver dew his ever-drooping head,
While sad Night over him her mantle black doth spread.

Whose double gates he findeth lockèd fast ;
The one fair fram'd of burnish'd ivory,
The other all with silver overcast ;
And wakeful dogs before them *far do lie*,
Watching to banish Care their enemy,
Who oft is wont to trouble gentle Sleep.
By them the sprite doth pass in quietly,
And unto Morpheus comes, whom drownèd deep
In drowsy fit he finds : of nothing he takes keep.

*And more to lull him in his slumber soft,
A trickling stream from high rock tumbling down
And ever-drizzling rain upon the loft,
Mix'd with a murmuring wind, much like the soun'
Of swarming bees, did cast him in a swoun :
No other noise, nor people's troublous cries,
As still are wont to annoy the wallèd town,
Might there be heard ; but careless Quiet lies
Wrapt in eternal silence, far from enemies.* ([10])

The messenger approaching to him spake ;
But his waste words return'd to him in vain :
So sound he slept, that nought might him awake.
Then rudely he him thrust, and push'd with pain,
Whereat he gan to stretch : but he again
Shook him so hard, that forcèd him to speak.
As one then in a dream, whose drier brain
Is tost with troubled sights and fancies weak,
He mumbled soft, but would not all his silence break.

The sprite then gan more boldly him to wake,
And threaten'd unto him the dreaded name
Of Hecaté : whereat he gan to quake,
And lifting up his lumpish head, with blame

Half angry askèd him, for what he came.
" Hither," quoth he, " me Archimago sent ;
He that the stubborn sprites can wisely tame ;
He bids thee to him send for his intent
A fit false dream, that can delude the sleeper's sent." (¹¹)

The god obey'd ; and calling forth straightway
A diverse Dream (¹²) out of his prison dark,
Deliver'd it to him, and down did lay
His heavy head, devoid of careful cark ;
Whose senses all were straight benumb'd and stark.
He, back returning by the ivory door,
Remounted up as light as cheerful lark ;
And on his little wings the Dream he bore
In haste unto his lord, where he him left afore.

(¹) *Wellèd forth alway.*

The modulation of this charming stanza is exquisite.
Let us divide it into its pauses, and see what we have been
hearing :—

A little lowly hermitage it was, |
Down in a dale, | hard by a forest's side, |
Far from resort of people | that did pass
In travel to and fro : | a little wide |
There was a holy chapel edifyde, |
Wherein the hermit duly wont to say
His holy things | each morn and eventide : |
Thereby a crystal stream did gently play, |
Which from a sacred fountain wellèd forth alway.

Mark the variety of the pauses, of the accentuation of
the syllables, and of the intonation of the vowels ; all
closing in that exquisite last line, as soft and continuous
as the water it describes. The repetition of the words
little and *holy* add to the sacred snugness of the abode.

We are to fancy the little tenement on the skirts of a forest, that is to say, within, but not deeply within, the trees; the chapel is near it, but not close to it, more embowered; and the rivulet may be supposed to circuit both chapel and hermitage, running partly under the trees between mossy and flowery banks, for hermits were great cullers of simples; and though Archimago was a false hermit, we are to suppose him living in a true hermitage. It is one of those pictures which remain for ever in the memory; and the succeeding stanza is worthy of it.

(²) *Arrivèd there, the little house they fill.*

Not literally the *house,* but the apartment as a specimen of the house; for we see by what follows that the hermitage must have contained at least four rooms: one in which the knight and the lady were introduced, two more for their bed-chambers, and a fourth for the magician's study.

(³) *Nor look for entertainment where none was.*

" Entertainment " is here used in the restricted sense of treatment as regards food and accommodation; according to the old inscription over inn-doors—" Entertainment for man and horse."

(⁴) *The noblest mind the best contentment has.*

This is one of Spenser's many noble sentiments expressed in as noble single lines, as if made to be recorded in the copy-books of full-grown memories. As, for example, one which he is fond of repeating:—

No service loathsome to a gentle mind.
Entire affection scorneth nicer hands.
True love loathes disdainful nicety.

And that fine Alexandrine,—

Weak body well is chang'd for mind's redoubled force.

And another, which Milton has imitated in *Comus*—

Virtue gives herself light in darkness for to wade,

([5]) (*Let none them read!*)

As if we could! And yet while we smile at the impossibility, we delight in this solemn injunction of the Poet's, so child-like, and full of the imaginative sense of the truth of what he is saying.

([6]) *A bold bad man! that dar'd to call by name*
Great Gorgon.

This is the ineffable personage whom Milton, with a propriety equally classical and poetical, designates as

. . . . The dreaded name
Of Demogorgon.—*Par. Lost*, book ii. v. 965.

Ancient believers apprehended such dreadful consequences from the mention of him, that his worst and most potent invokers are represented as fearful of it; nor am I aware that any poet, Greek or Latin, has done it, though learned commentators on Spenser imply otherwise. In the passages they allude to, in *Lucan* and *Statius*, there is no name uttered. The adjuration is always made by a periphrasis. This circumstance is noticed by Boccaccio, who has given by far the best, and indeed, I believe, the only account of this very rare god, except what is abridged from his pages in a modern Italian mythology, and furnished by his own authorities, Lactantius and Theodantus, the latter an author now lost. Ben Jonson calls him "Boccaccio's Demogorgon." The passage is in the first book of his *Genealogie Deorum*, a work of prodigious erudition for that age, and full of the gusto of a man of genius. According to Boccaccio, Demogorgon (*Spirit Earthworker*) was the great deity of the rustical Arcadians, and the creator of all things out of brute matter. He describes him as a pale and sordid-looking wretch, inhabiting the centre of the earth, all over moss and dirt, squalidly wet, and emitting an earthy smell; and he laughs at the credulity of the ancients in thinking to make a god of such a fellow. He is very glad, however, to talk about him; and doubtless had a lurking respect for him, inasmuch as mud and dirt are among the elements of things material, and therefore partake of a certain mystery and divineness.

(⁷) *Legions of sprites, the which, like little flies.*

Flies are old embodiments of evil spirits;—Anacreon forbids us to call them incarnations, in reminding us that insects are fleshless and bloodless, ἀναιμόσαρκα. Beelzebub signifies the Lord of Flies.

(⁸) *The world of waters wide and deep.*

How complete a sense of the ocean under one of its aspects! Spenser had often been at sea, and his pictures of it, or in connexion with it, are frequent and fine accordingly, superior perhaps to those of any other English poet, Milton certainly, except in that one famous imaginative passage in which he describes a fleet at a distance as seeming to " hang in the clouds." And Shakspeare throws himself wonderfully into a storm at sea, as if he had been in the thick of it; though it is not known that he ever quitted the land. But nobody talks so much about the sea, or its inhabitants, or its voyagers, as Spenser. He was well acquainted with the Irish Channel. Coleridge observes (*ut sup.*), that " one of Spenser's arts is that of alliteration, which he uses with great effect in doubling the impression of an image." The verse above noticed is a beautiful example.

(⁹) *To Morpheus' house doth hastily repair,* &c.

Spenser's earth is not the Homeric earth, a circular flat, or disc, studded with mountains, and encompassed with the " ocean stream." Neither is it in all cases a globe. We must take his cosmography as we find it, and as he wants it; that is to say, poetically, and according to the feeling required by the matter in hand. In the present instance, we are to suppose a precipitous country striking gloomily and far downwards to a cavernous sea-shore, in which the bed of Morpheus is placed, the ends of its curtains dipping and fluctuating in the water, which reaches it from underground. The door is towards a flat on the land-side, with dogs lying " far before it ; " and the moonbeams reach it, though the sun never does. The passage is imitated from Ovid (lib. ii. ver. 592), but with wonderful concentration, and superior *home* appeal to the imagination. Ovid will have no dogs, nor any sound at all but that of Lethe rippling over its pebbles. Spenser has dogs, but afar off, and a lulling sound overhead of wind and rain. These are the sounds that men delight to hear in the intervals of their own sleep.

(¹⁰) *Wrapt in eternal silence, far from enemies.*

The modulation of this most beautiful stanza (perfect, except for the word *tumbling*) is equal to that of the one describing the hermitage, and not the less so for being less varied both in pauses and in vowels, the subject demanding a greater monotony. A poetical reader need hardly be told, that he should humour such verses with a corresponding tone in the recital. Indeed it is difficult to read them without lowering or deepening the voice, as though we were going to bed ourselves, or thinking of the rainy night that has lulled us. A long rest at the happy pause in the last line, and then a strong accent on the word *far*, put us in possession of all the remoteness of the scene ;—and it is improved, if we make a similar pause at *heard* :—

> No other noise, or people's troublous cries,
> As still are wont to annoy the wallèd town,
> Might there be heard ;—but careless Quiet lies
> Wrapt in eternal silence,—*far* from enemies.

Upton, one of Spenser's commentators, in reference to the *trickling stream*, has quoted in his note on this passage some fine lines from Chaucer, in which, describing the " dark valley " of Sleep, the poet says there was nothing whatsoever in the place, save that

> .... A few wells
> Came running fro the clyffes adowne,
> That made a deadly sleeping sowne.

Sowne (in the old spelling) is also Spenser's word. In the text of the present volume it is written *soun'*, to show that it is the same as the word *sound* without the *d* ;—like the French and Itálian, *son, suono.*

" 'Tis hardly possible," says Upton, " for a more picturesque description to come from a poet or a painter than this whole magical scene."—See Todd's *Variorum Spenser*, vol. ii. p. 38.

Meantime, the magician has been moulding a shape of air to represent the virtuous mistress of the knight; and when the Dream arrives, he sends them both to deceive him, the one sitting by his head and abusing "the organs of his fancy " (as Milton says of the devil with Eve), and the other behaving in a manner very unlike her prototype. The delusion succeeds for a time.

(11) *A fit false dream, that can delude the sleeper's sent.*

Scent, sensation, perception. Skinner says that *sent,* which we falsely write *scent,* is derived *à sentiendo.* The word is thus frequently spelt by Spenser.—TODD.

(12) *A diverse Dream.*

" A dream," says Upton, " that would occasion diversity or distraction ; or a frightful, hideous dream, from the Italian, *sogno diverso.*"—Dante, *Inferno*, canto vi.

> Cerbero, fiera crudele e *diversa.*
> (Cerberus, the fierce beast, cruel and diverse.)

Berni, *Orlando Innamorato*, lib. i. canto 4, stanza 66.

> Un grido orribile e *diverso.*
> (There rose a cry, horrible and diverse), &c.
> —*See Todd's Edition, as above*, p. 42.

The obvious sense, however, as in the case of Dante's
Cerberus, I take to be *monstrously varied*,—inconsistent
with itself. The dream is to make the knight's mistress
contradict her natural character.

THE CAVE OF MAMMON

AND

GARDEN OF PROSERPINE.

Sir Guyon, crossing a desert, finds Mammon sitting amidst his gold
in a gloomy valley. Mammon, taking him down into his cave,
tempts him with the treasures there, and also with those in the
Garden of Proserpine.

"Spenser's strength," says Hazlitt, "is not strength
of will or action, of bone and muscle, nor is it coarse and
palpable; but it assumes a character of vastness and
sublimity seen through the same visionary medium" (he
has just been alluding to one), "and blended with the
appalling associations of preternatural agency. We need
only turn in proof of this to the Cave of Despair, or the
Cave of Mammon, or to the account of the change of
Malbecco into Jealousy."—*Lectures*, p. 77.

> That house's form within was rude and strong, ([13])
> Like a huge cave hewn out of rocky clift,
> *From whose rough vault the ragged breaches hung*
> *Emboss'd with massy gold of glorious gift,*
> *And with rich metal loaded every rift,*
> *That heavy ruin they did seem to threat;*
> And over them Arachne high did lift
> Her cunning web, and spread her subtle net,
> Enwrappèd in foul smoke and clouds more black than jet.

Both roof, and floor, and walls, were all of gold,
But overgrown with dust and old decay,
And hid in darkness, that none could behold
The hue thereof; for view of cheerful day
Did never in that house itself display;
But a faint shadow of uncertain light,
Such as a lamp whose life does fade away ;
Or as the moon, clothèd with cloudy night,
Does show to him that walks in fear and sad affright.

In all that room was nothing to be seen
But huge great iron chests, and coffers strong,
All barr'd with double bends, that none could ween
Them to enforce by violence or wrong;
On every side they placèd were along.
But all the ground with skulls was scatterèd,
And dead men's bones, which round about were flung;
Whose lives, it seemèd, whilome there were shed,
And their vile carcases now left unburièd.

They forward pass, nor Guyon yet spake word,
Till that they came unto an iron door,
Which to them opened of its own accord,
And show'd of riches such exceeding store
As eye of man did never see before,
Nor ever could within one place be found,
Though all the wealth which is, or was of yore,
Could gathered be through all the world around,
And that above were added to that under ground.

The charge thereof unto a covetous sprite
Commanded was, who thereby did attend,
And warily awaited, day and night,
From other covetous fiends it to defend,
Who it to rob and ransack did intend.
Then Mammon, turning to that warrior, said:
" Lo here the worldè's bliss ! lo here the end,
To which all men do aim, rich to be madè !
Such grace now to be happy is before thee laid."

" Certes," said he, " I n'ill thine offered grace, ([14])
Nor to be made so happy do intend.
Another bliss before mine eyes I place,
Another happiness, another end :
To them that list, these base regards I lend ;
But I in arms, and in achievements brave,
Do rather choose my fitting hours to spend,
And to be lord of those that riches have,
Than them to have myself, and be their servile slave."

*   *   *   *

The Knight is led further on, and shown more trea-
sures, and afterwards taken into the palace of Ambition ;
but all in vain.

Mammon emmovèd was with inward wrath ;
Yet forcing it to fain, him forth thence led,
Through griesly shadows, by a beaten path,
Into a garden goodly garnishèd
With herbs and fruits, whose kinds must not be read ·
Not such as earth out of her fruitful womb ([15])
Throws forth to men, sweet and well savourèd,
But direful deadly black, both leaf and bloom,
Fit to adorn the dead and deck the dreary tomb.

There mournful cypress grew in greatest store ; ([16])
And trees of bitter gall ; and heben sad ;
Dead sleeping poppy ; and black hellebore ;
Cold coloquintida ; and tetra *mad ;*
Mortal samnitis ; and cicuta bad,
With which the unjust Athenians made to die
Wise Socrates, who thereof quaffing glad,
Pour'd out his life and *last philosophy*
To the fair Critias, his dearest belamy !

The garden of Prosèrpina this hight ; ([17])
And in the midst thereof a silver seat,
With a thick arbour goodly over-dight,
In which she often us'd from open heat

Herself to shroud, and pleasures to entreat :
Next thereunto did grow a goodly tree,
With branches broad dispread and body great,
Clothed with leaves, that none the wood might see,
And loaded all with fruit as thick as it might be.

Their fruit were golden apples glistering bright,
That goodly was their glory to behold ;
On earth liké never grew, nor living wight
Like ever saw, but they from hence were sold ; ([18])
For those, which Hercules with conquest bold
Got from great Atlas' daughters, hence began,
And planted there did bring forth fruit of gold ;
And those, with which th' Eubœan young man wan
Swift Atalanta, when through craft he her outran.

Here also sprung that goodly golden fruit,
With which Acontius got his lover true,
Whom he had long time sought with fruitless suit ;
Here eke that famous golden apple grew,
The which amongst the gods false Até threw ;
For which *the Idæan ladies* disagreed, ([19])
Till partial Paris deem'd it Venus' due,
And had of her fair Helen for his meed,
That many noble Greeks and Trojans made to bleed.

The warlike Elf much wonder'd at this tree,
So fair and great, that shadow'd all the ground,
And his broad branches, laden with rich fee,
Did stretch themselves without the utmost bound
Of this great garden, compass'd with a mound :
Which overhanging, they themselves did steep ([20])
In a black flood, which flow'd about it round ;
That is the river of Cocytus deep,
In which full many souls do endless wail and weep.

Which to behold, he climb'd up to the bank ;
And, looking down, saw many damnèd wights ([21])
In those sad waves, which direful deadly stank,
Plungèd continually of cruel sprites,

6

That with their piteous cries and yelling shrights,
They made the further shore resounden wide :
Amongst the rest of those same rueful sights,
One cursèd creature he by chance espied,
That drenchèd lay full deep under the garden side.

Deep was he drenchèd to the utmost chin,
Yet gapèd still as coveting to drink
Of the cold liquor which he waded in :
And, stretching forth his hand, did often think
To reach the fruit which grew upon the brink;
But both *the fruit from hand,* and *flood from mouth,*
Did fly aback, and made him vainly swinck;
The whiles he starv'd with hunger, and with drouth
He daily died, yet never throughly dyën couth. ([22])

The knight, him seeing labour so in vain,
Ask'd who he was, and what he meant thereby ?
Who, groaning deep, thus answered him again :
" Most cursed of all creatures under sky,
Lo, Tantalus I here tormented lie !
Of whom high Jove wont whilome feasted be ;
Lo, here I now for want of food do die !
But, if that thou be such as I thee see,
Of grace I pray thee give to eat and drink to me ! "

" Nay, nay, *thou greedy Tantalus,*" quoth he ;
" Abide the fortune of thy present fate ;
And unto all that live in high degree,
Example be of mind intemperate,
To teach them how to use their present state."
Then gan the cursed wretch aloud to cry,
Accusing highest Jove and gods ingrate :
And eke blaspheming Heaven bitterly,
As author of injustice, there to let him die.

He look'd a little further, and espied
Another wretch, whose carcase deep was drent
Within the river which the same did hide :
But both his hands, most filthy feculent,

Above the water were on high extent,
And fain'd to wash themselves incessantly,
Yet nothing cleaner were for such intent,
But rather fouler seemèd to the eye;
So lost his labour vain, and idle industry.

The knight him calling, askèd who he was?
Who, lifting up his head, him answered thus;
" I Pilate am, ([23]) the falsest judge, alas!
And most unjust; that, by unrightëous
And wicked doom, to Jews despiteous
Delivered up the Lord of Life to die,
And did acquit a murderer felonous;
The whilst my hands I wash'd in purity,
The whilst my soul was soil'd with foul iniquity."

Infinite more tormented in like pain
He there beheld, too long here to be told:
Nor Mammon would there let him long remain,
For terror of the tortures manifold,
In which the damnèd souls he did behold,
But roughly him bespake: " Thou fearful fool,
Why takest not of that same fruit of gold?
Nor sittest down on that same silver stool,
To rest thy weary person in the shadow cool?"

All which he did to do him deadly fall
In frail intemperance through sinful bait;
To which if he inclinèd had at all,
That dreadful fiend, which did behind him wait,
Would him have rent in thousand pieces straight:
But he was wary wise in all his way,
And well perceivèd his deceitful sleight,
Nor sufferèd lust his safety to betray:
So goodly did beguile the guiler of his prey.

And now he has so long remainèd there,
That vital power gan wax both weak and wan
For want of food and sleep, which two upbear,
Like mighty pillars, this frail life of man,

That none without the same enduren can ;
For now three days of men were full outwrought,
Since he this hardy enterprise began :
Therefore great Mammon fairly he besought
Into the world to guide him back, as he him brought.

The god, though loth, yet was constrain'd t' obey ;
For longer time than that no living wight
Below the earth might suffered be to stay ;
So back again him brought to living light.
But all as soon as his enfeebled sprite
Gan suck this vital air into his breast,
As overcome with too exceeding might,
The life did flit away out of her nest,
And all his senses were in deadly fit opprest.

(¹³) *That house's form within was rude and strong,* &c.

Hazlitt, with his fine poetical taste, speaking of the
two stanzas here following, and the previous one beginning,
And over all, &c., says, that they are unrivalled for the
" portentous massiveness of the forms, the splendid chiaro-
scuro and shadowy horror."—*Lectures on the English
Poets,* third edition, p. 77. It is extraordinary that in the
new " *Elegant Extracts* " published under his name, seven
lines of the first stanza, beginning at the words, " From
whose rough vault," are left out. Their exceeding weight,
the contrast of the dirt and squalor with the gold, and the
spider's webs dusking over all, compose chief part of the
grandeur of the description (as indeed he has just said).
Hogarth, by the way, has hit upon the same thought of a
spider's web for his poor's-box, in the wedding-scene in
Mary-le-bone church. So do tragedy and comedy meet.

(¹⁴) N'ill, *ne-will,* will not.

(¹⁵) *Not such as earth,* &c.

Upton thinks it not unlikely that Spenser imagined the direful deadly and black fruits which this infernal. garden bears, from a like garden which Dante describes, *Inferno,* canto 13, v. 4 :—

> Non frondi verdi, ma di color fosco,
> Non rami schietti, ma nodosi e'nvolti,
> Non pomi v' eran, ma stecchi con tosco.

> (No leaves of green were theirs, but dusky sad,
> No fair straight boughs, but gnarl'd and tangled all;
> No rounded fruits, but poison-bearing thorns.)

Dante's garden, however, has no flowers. It is a *human grove ;* that is to say, made of trees that were once human beings,—an aggravation (according to his customary improvement upon horrors) of a like solitary instance in *Virgil,* which Spenser has also imitated in his story of *Fradubio,* book i, canto 2, st. 30.

(¹⁶) *There mournful cypress grew in greatest store,* &c.

Among the trees and flowers here mentioned, *heben* is ebony; *coloquintida,* the bitter gourd or apple ; tetra, the *tetrum solanum,* or deadly nightshade ; *samnitis,* Upton takes to be the Sabine, or savine-tree ; and *cicuta* is the hemlock, which Socrates drank when he poured out to his friends his " last philosophy." How beautifully said is that ! But the commentators have shown that it was a slip of memory in the poet to make Critias their representative on the occasion,—that apostate from his philosophy not having been present. *Belamy* is *bel ami,* fair friend,

—a phrase answering to *good friend* in the old French writers.

. ([17]) *The garden of Proserpina this hight.*

The idea of a garden and a golden tree for Proserpina is in Claudian, *De Raptu Proserpinæ*, lib. 2, v. 290. But Spenser has made the flowers funereal, and added the "silver seat,"—a strong yet still delicate contrast to the black flowers, and in cold sympathy with them. It has also a certain fair and lady-like fitness to the possessor of the arbour. May I venture, with all reverence to Spenser, to express a wish that he had made a compromise with the flowers of Claudian, and retained them by the side of the others? Proserpine was an unwilling bride, though she became a reconciled wife. She deserved to enjoy her Sicilian flowers; and besides, in possessing a nature superior to her position, she would not be without innocent and cheerful thoughts. Perhaps, however, our "sage and serious Spenser" would have answered, that she could see into what was good in these evil flowers, and so get a contentment from objects which appeared only melancholy to others. It is certainly a high instance of modern imagination, this venturing to make a pleasure-garden out of the flowers of pain.

([18]) *But they from hence were sold.*

Upton proposes that, "with a little variation," this word *sold* should be read *stold;* "that is," says he, "procured by stealth:"—he does not like to say stolen. "The wise *convey* it call." Spenser certainly would have no objection to spell the word in any way most convenient;

and I confess I wish, with Upton, that he had exercised
his licence in this instance; though he might have argued
that the infernal powers are not in the habit of letting
people have their goods for nothing. In how few of the
instances that follow did the possession of the golden
apples turn out well! Are we sure that it prospered in
any? For Acontius succeeded with *his* apple by a trick;
and after all, as the same commentator observes, it was
not with a golden apple, but common mortal-looking fruit,
though gathered in the garden of Venus. He wrote a
promise upon it to marry him, and so his mistress read,
and betrothed herself. The story is in Ovid : *Heroides,
Epist.* xx. xxi.

(¹⁹) *For which the Idæan ladies disagreed.*

"He calls the three goddesses that contended for
the prize of beauty, boldly but elegantly enough, Idæan
Ladies."—JORTIN. "He calls the Muses and the Graces,
likewise, *Ladies*."—CHURCH. "The ladies may be fur-
ther gratified by Milton's adaptation of their title to the
celebrated daughters of Hesperus, whom he calls *Ladies* of
the Hesperides."—TODD. The ladies of the present
day, in which so much good poetry and reading have
revived, will smile at the vindication of a word again
become common, and so frequent in the old poets and
romancers.

(²⁰) *Which overhanying, they themselves did steep
In a black flood, which flow'd about it round, &c.*

The tree, observe, grew in the middle of "this great
garden," and yet overhung its utmost bounds, and steeped

itself in the black river by which it was encircled. We
are to imagine the branches with their fruit stretching
over the garden like one enormous arbour or trellice, and
mixing a certain lustrous light with the gloom and the
funereal flowers. You walk in the shadow of a golden
death. What an excessive and gorgeous luxury beside
the blackness of hell !

> ([21]) *And, looking down, saw many damnèd wights*
> *In those sad waves, which direful deadly stank.*
> *Plungèd continually of cruel sprites,*
> *That with their piteous cries, &c.*

Virgil appears to have been the first who ventured to
find sublimity in a loathsome odour. I say " appears,"
because many Greek writers have perished whom he
copied, and it is probable the invention was theirs. A
greater genius, Dante, followed him in this as in other
respects ; and, probably, would have set the example had it
not been given him. Sackvile followed both ; and the
very excess of Spenser's sense of the beautiful and attrac-
tive would render him fully aware of the capabilities of
this intensity of the repulsive. Burke notices the subject
in his treatise *On the Sublime and Beautiful.* The fol-
lowing is the conclusion of his remarks :—" It is one of
the tests by which the sublimity of an image is to be tried,
not whether it becomes mean when associated with mean
ideas, but whether, when united with images of an allowed
grandeur, the whole composition is supported with dignity.
Things which are terrible are always great ; but when
things possess disagreeable qualities, or such as have
indeed some degree of danger, but of a danger easily over-

come, they are merely odious, as toads and spiders."—
Part the Second, Section the Twenty-first. Both points
are easily illustrated. Passing by a foul ditch, you are
simply disgusted, and turn aside : but imagine yourself
crossing a mountain, and coming upon a hot and slimy
valley in which a pestilential vapour ascends from a city,
the inhabitants of which have died of the plague and been
left unburied ; or fancy the great basin of the Caspian Sea
deprived of its waters, and the horror which their refuse
would send up over the neigbouring regions.

(²⁸) *He daily died, yet never throughly dyën couth.*

Die could; he never could thoroughly die. Truly
horrible ; and, as Swift says of his hanging footman,
"very satisfactory to the beholders." Yet Spenser's
Tantalus, and his Pontius Pilate, and indeed the whole of
this *latter* part of his hell, strike us with but a poor sort
of cruelty compared with any like number of pages out of
the tremendous volume of Dante. But the far greater
part of our extract, the sooty golden cave of Mammon,
and the mortal beauty of the garden of Proserpine, with
its golden fruit hanging in the twilight ; all, in short, in
which Spenser combines his usual luxury with grandeur,
are as fine as anything of the kind which Dante or any
one else ever conceived.

(²⁹) *"I Pilate am,"* &c.

Let it not be supposed that I intend the slightest
glance of levity towards the divine name which has become
identified with charity. But charity itself will allow us

to imagine the astonishment of this Roman Governor of Jerusalem, could he have foreseen the destinies of *his* name. He doubtless thought, that if another age spoke of him at all, it would treat him as a good-natured man who had to rule over a barbarous people, and make a compromise between his better judgment and their laws and prejudices. No name, except Judas's, has received more execration from posterity. Our good-natured poet has here put him in the " loathly lakes " of Tartarus.

ı

A GALLERY OF PICTURES FROM SPENSER.

SPENSER CONSIDERED AS THE POET OF THE PAINTERS.

IT has been a whim of late years with some transcen-
dental critics, in the excess of the reaction of what may
be called spiritual poetry against material, to deny utterly
the old family relationship between poetry and painting.
They seem to think that, because Darwin absurdly pro-
nounced nothing to be poetry which could not be painted,
they had only to avail themselves of the spiritual supe-
riority of the art of the poet, and assert the contrary
extreme. Now, it is granted that the subtlest creations of
poetry are neither effected by a painter-like process, nor
limited to his powers of suggestion. The finest idea the
poet gives you of anything is by what may be called sleight
of mind, striking it without particular description on the
mind of the reader, feeling and all, moral as well as
physical, as a face is struck on a mirror. But to say,
nevertheless, that the poet does not include the painter in
his more visible creations, is to deprive him of half his
privileges, nay, of half of his very poems. Thousands of
images start out of the *canvas* of his pages to laugh at
the assertion. Where did the great Italian painters get
half of the most bodily details of their subjects but out of

the poets ? and what becomes of a thousand landscapes,
portraits, colours, lights and shades, groupings, effects,
intentional and artistical pictures, in the writings of all
the poets inclusive, the greatest especially ?

I have taken opportunity of this manifest truth to
introduce under one head a variety of the most beautiful
passages in Spenser, many of which might otherwise have
seemed too small for separate exhibition ; and I am sure
that the more poetical the reader, the more will he be
delighted to see these manifestations of the pictorial side
of poetry. He will not find them destitute of that subtler
spirit of the art, which picture cannot express.

"After reading," said Pope, " a canto of Spenser two
or three days ago to an old lady, between seventy and
eighty years of age, she said that I had been showing her
a gallery of pictures. I don't know how it is, but she said
very right. There is something in Spenser that pleases
one as strongly in old age as it did in one's youth.
I read the *Faerie Queene* when I was about twelve,
with infinite delight ; and I think it gave me as much,
when I read it over about a year or two ago."—*Spence's
Anecdotes.*

The canto that Pope here speaks of was probably one
of the most allegorical sort, very likely that containing the
Mask of Cupid. In the one preceding it, there is a pro-
fessed gallery of pictures, supposed to be painted on
tapestry. But Spenser's allegorical pictures are only his
most obvious ones : he has a profusion of others, many of
them still more exquisitely painted. I think that if he
had not been a great poet, he would have been a great

painter; and in that case there is ground for believing
that England would have possessed, and in the person of
one man, her Claude, her Annibal Caracci, her Correggio,
her Titian, her Rembrandt, perhaps even her Raphael. I
suspect that if Spenser's history were better known, we
should find that he was a passionate student of pictures, a
haunter of the collections of his friends Essex and Lei-
cester. The tapestry just alluded to he criticises with all
the gusto of a connoisseur, perhaps with an eye to pictures
in those very collections. In speaking of a Leda, he says,
bursting into an admiration of the imaginary painter,—

> O wondrous skill and *sweet wit of the man,*
> *That her in daffodillies sleeping made,*
> *From scorching heat her dainty limbs to shade!*

And then he proceeds with a description full of life and
beauty, but more proper to be read with the context than
brought forward separately. The colouring implied in
these lines is in the very core of the secret of that branch
of the art; and the unpainted part of the tapestry is
described with hardly less beauty :

> For, round about, the walls yclothèd were
> With goodly arras of great majesty,
> Woven with gold and silk so close and near,
> That the rich metal *lurkèd privily,*
> As feigning to be hid from envious eye ;
> Yet here, and there, and everywhere, unwares
> It show'd itself, and *shone unwillingly ;*
> *Like to a discolour'd snake, whose hidden snares*
> *Through the green grass his long bright burnish'd back declares.*

Spenser should have a new set of commentators,—the
painters themselves. They might do for him in their own

art, what Wharton did in his,—trace him among his
brethren. Certainly no works would "illustrate" better
than Spenser's with engravings from the old masters (I
should like no better amusement than to hunt him through
the print-shops!), and from none might a better gallery
be painted by new ones. I once wrote an article on the
subject in a magazine; and the late Mr. Hilton (I do not
know whether he saw it) projected such a gallery, among
his other meritorious endeavours. It did not answer to
the originals, either in strength or sweetness; but a very
creditable and pleasing specimen may be seen in the
National Gallery,—*Serena rescued from the Savages by
Sir Calepine.*

In corroboration of the delight which Spenser took in
this more visible kind of poetry, it is observable that he
is never more free from his superfluousness than when
painting a picture. When he gets into a moral, or intel-
lectual, or narrative vein, we might often spare him a good
deal of the flow of it; but on occasions of sheer poetry
and painting, he is too happy to wander so much from
his point. If he is tempted to expatiate, every word is to
the purpose. Poetry and painting indeed would in Spenser
be identical, if they could be so; and they are more so,
too, than it has latterly been the fashion to allow; for
painting does not deal in the purely visible. It deals
also in the suggestive and the allusive, therefore in
thoughts beyond the visible proof of the canvas; in inti-
mations of sound; in references to past and future. Still
the medium is a visible one, and is at the mercy of the
spectator's amount of comprehension. The great privilege

of the poet is, that, using the medium of speech, he can make his readers poets; can make them aware and *possesssed* of what he intends, enlarging their comprehension by his details, or enlightening it by a word. A painter might have the same feeling as Shakspeare respecting the moonlight "sleeping" on a bank; but how is he to evince it? He may go through a train of the profoundest thoughts in his own mind; but into what voluminous fairy circle is he to compress them? Poetry can paint whole galleries in a page, while her sister art requires heaps of canvas to render a few of her poems visible.

This, however, is what everybody knows. Not so, that Spenser emulated the Raphaels and Titians in a profusion of pictures, many of which are here *taken from their walls*. They give the Poet's Poet a claim to a new title,—that of Poet of the Painters. The reader has seen what Mr. Hazlitt says of him in connection with Rubens; but the passage adds, what I have delayed quoting till now, that "none but Rubens could have painted the fancy of Spenser;" adding further, that Rubens "could not have painted the sentiment, the airy dream that hovers over it." I venture to think that this fine critic on the two sister arts wrote the first of these sentences hastily; and that the truth of the second would have shown him, on reflection, with what painters, greater than Rubens, the poet ought to have been compared. The great Fleming was a man of a genius as fine and liberal as his nature; yet who that looks for a moment at the pictures which ensue, shall say that he would have been justified in

putting his name to them ? Sentiments and airy dreams
hover over them all,—say rather, abide and brood over
many,—with such thoughtfulness as the Italian aspect
only can match. More surprising is Mr. Coleridge's
assertion, that Spenser's descriptions are "not, in the
true sense of the word, picturesque ; but composed of a
wondrous series of images, as in dreams."—*Lectures* (*ut
sup.*) vol. i. p. 93. If, by true sense of the word, he
means the acquired sense of piquancy of contrast, or a
certain departure from the smoothness of beauty in order
to enhance it, Spenser certainly is not in the habit of
putting many thorns in his roses. His bowers of bliss, he
thought, did not demand it. The gentle beast that Una
rode would not have cut a very piquant figure in the
forest scenery of Mr. Gilpin. But if Coleridge means
picturesque in the sense of fitness for picture, and very
striking fitness, then the recollections of the masks, or the
particular comparison of Prince Arthur's crest with the
almond-tree (which is the proof he adduces) made him
forget the innumerable instances in which the pictorial
power is exhibited. Nor was Spenser unaware, nay, he
was deeply sensible of the other feeling of the picturesque,
as may be seen by his sea-gods' beards (when Proteus
kisses Amoret), his "rank grassy fens," his "weeds of
glorious feature," his oaks "half dead," his satyrs, gloomy
lights, beautiful but unlucky grounds, &c. &c. &c. (for in
this sense of the word, there are feelings of the invisible
corresponding with the stronger forms of the picturesque).
He has himself noticed the theory in his *Bower of Bliss*,
and thus anticipated the modern taste in landscape garden-

ing, the idea of which is supposed to have originated with
Milton :—

> One would have thought (*so cunningly the rude*
> *And scornèd parts were mingled with the fine*)
> That Nature had for wantonness ensued
> Art, and that Art at Nature did repine.
> So, striving each the other to undermine,
> Each did the other's work more beautify.

But the reader will judge for himself.

I have attached to each of the pictures in this Spenser
Gallery the name of the painter of whose genius it
reminded me ; and I think the connoisseur will allow
that the assignment was easy, and that the painter-poet's
range of art is equally wide and wonderful.

CHARISSA; OR, CHARITY.

Character : Spiritual Love.   Painter for it, Raphael.

> She was a woman in her freshest age,
> Of wondrous beauty and of bounty rare,
> With goodly grace and comely personage,
> That was on earth not easy to compare ;
> *Full of great love ;* but Cupid's wanton snare
> As hell she hated, chaste in work and will ;
> Her neck and breasts were ever open bare,
> That ay thereof her babes might suck their fill ;
> The rest was all in yellow robes arrayèd still.

> A multitude of babes about her hung
> Playing their sports, that joy'd her to behold,
> Whom still she fed, whilst they were weak and young,
> But thrust them forth still as they waxèd old ;

7

And on her head she wore a tire of gold
Adorn'd with gems and owches wondrous **fair**,*
Whose passing price uneath † was to be told;
And by her side there *sate a gentle pair* (²⁴)
Of turtle doves, she *sitting in an ivory chair*.

—————

(²⁴) *And by her side*, &c.

This last couplet brings at once before us all the dispassionate graces and unsuperfluous treatment of Raphael's allegorical females.

———————

HOPE.

Character: Sweetness without Devotedness.   Painter, Correggio.

With him went Hope in rank, a handsome maid,
Of cheerful look, and lovely to behold:
In silken samite she was light array'd,
And her fair locks were woven up in gold. (²⁵)
She alway smil'd;—and in her hand did hold
An holy-water sprinkle dipp'd in dew,
With which she sprinkled favours manifold
On whom she list, and did great **liking shew**;
Great liking unto many, but true love to few.

—————

(²⁵) *And her fair locks*, &c.

What a lovely line is that! and with a beauty how simple and sweet is the sentiment portrayed in the next

———————

* *Owches wondrous fair:* Owches are *carcanets*, or ranges of jewels.

† *Uneath :* Scarcely, with difficulty.

three words,—" She alway smil'd ! " But almost every line of the stanza is lovely, including the felicitous Catholic image of the

Holy-water sprinkle dipp'd in dew.

Correggio is in every colour and expression of the picture.

CUPID USURPING THE THRONE OF JUPITER.
Character : Potency in Weakness. Painter, Raphael.

In Satyr's shape Antiope he snatch'd ;
And like a fire, when he Ægine essay'd ;
A shepherd, when Mnemosyne he catch'd ;
And like a serpent to the Thracian maid.
While thus on earth great Jove these pageants play'd,
The wingèd boy did thrust into his throne ;
And scoffing, thus unto his mother said:
" Lo ! now the heavens obey to me alone,
And take me for their Jove, whilst Jove to earth is gone."

MARRIAGE PROCESSION OF THE THAMES AND MEDWAY.
Character : Genial Strength, Grace, and Luxury. Painter, Raphael.

First came great Neptune with his three-forked mace,
That rules the seas and makes them rise or fall ,
His dewy locks did drop with brine apace,
Under his diadem imperial ;
And by his side his queen, with coronal,
Fair Amphitrite, most divinely fair,
Whose ivory shoulders weren covered all,
As with a robe, with her own silver hair,
And deck'd with pearls which the Indian seas for her prepare.

These marchèd far afore the other crew,
And all the way before them as they went
Triton his trumpet shrill before him blew,
For goodly triumph and great jolliment,
That made the rocks to roar as they were rent.

Or take another part of the procession, with dolphins and sea-nymphs listening as they went, to

ARION.

Then was there heard a most celestial sound
Of dainty music, which did next ensue
Before the spouse. *That was Arion, crown'd,*
Who playing on his harp, unto him drew
The ears and hearts of all that goodly crew ;
That even yet the dolphin which him bore
Through the Ægean seas from pirates' view
Stood still by him, astonish'd at his lore,
And all the raging seas for joy forgot to roar.

So went he playing on the watery plain. ([26])

([26]) *So went he,* &c.

This sweet, placid, and gently progressing line is one of Spenser's happy samples of alliteration. And how emphatic is the information—

That was Arion, crown'd.

SIR GUYON BINDING FUROR.

Character : Superhuman Energy and Rage. Painter, Michael Angelo.

In his strong arms he stiffly him embrac'd,
Who, him gain-striving, nought at all prevail'd ;
Then him to ground he cast and rudely haled,
And both his hands fast bound behind his back,
And both his feet in fetters to an iron rack.

With hundred iron chains he did him bind,
And hundred knots that him did sore constrain ;
Yet his *great iron teeth* he still did grind
And grimly gnash, threat'ning revenge in vain.
His burning eyes, whom bloody streaks did stain,
Starèd full wide, and threw forth sparks of fire ;
And more for rank despite, than for great pain,
Shak'd his long lócks, colour'd like copper wire, ([27])
And bit his tawny beard, to show his raging ire.

([27]) *Colour'd like copper wire.*

A felicity suggested perhaps by the rhyme. It has all
the look, however, of a copy from some painting ; perhaps
one of Julio Romano's.

UNA (OR FAITH IN DISTRESS).

Character: Loving and Sorrowful Purity glorified.

(May I say, that I think it would take Raphael and
Correggio united to paint this, on account of the exquisite
chiaro-scuro ? Or might not the painter of the Magdalen
have it all to himself?)

Yet she, most faithful lady, all this while, ([28])
Forsaken, woeful, solitary maid,
Far from all people's press, as in exile,
In wilderness and wasteful deserts stray'd
To seek her knight, who subtily betray'd
Through that late vision which the enchanter wrought,
Had her abandon'd. She, of nought afraid,
Through *woods and wasteness wide* him daily sought.
Yet wishèd tidings none of him unto her brought.

One day nigh weary of the irksome way,
From her unhasty beast she did alight,
And on the grass her dainty limbs did lay
In secret shadow far from all men's sight:
From her fair head her fillet she undight
And laid her stole aside : *her angel's face
As the great eye of heaven shinèd bright,
And made a sunshine in the shady place;*
Did never mortal eye behold such heavenly grace.

It fortunèd, out of the thickest wood
A ramping lion rushèd suddenly,
Hunting full greedy after savage blood :
Soon as the royal virgin he did spy,
With gaping mouth at her ran greedily,
To have at once devour'd her tender corse ;
But to the prey whenas he drew more nigh,
His bloody rage assuagèd with remorse,
And with the sight amaz'd, forgot his furious force.

Instead thereof he kiss'd her weary feet,
And lick'd her lily hand with fawning tongue,
As he her wrongèd innocence did weet.
O how can beauty master the most strong,
And simple truth subdue avenging wrong !
Whose yielded pride and proud submissiön,
Still dreading death when she had markèd long,
Her heart gan melt in great compassiön :
And drizzling tears did shed for pure affection.

" *The lion, lord of every beast in field,*"
Quoth she, " his princely puissance doth abate,
And mighty proud to humble weak does yield,
Forgetful of the hungry rage, which late
Him prick'd with pity of my sad estate :—
But he my lion, and my noble lord,
How does he find in cruel heart to hate
Her, that him lov'd, and ever most ador'd
As the gòd of my life ? Why hath he me abhorr'd ? " (◈

(²⁸) *Yet she,* &c.

Coleridge quotes this stanza as "a good instance of what he means" in the following remarks in his *Lectures :* —"As characteristic of Spenser, I would call your particular attention in the first place to the indescribable sweetness and fluent projections of his verse, very clearly distinguishable from the deeper and more inwoven harmonies of Shakspeare and Milton." Good, however, as the stanza is, and beautiful the second line, it does not appear to me so happy an instance of what Coleridge speaks of as many which he might have selected.

The verses marked in the second stanza are one of the most favourite quotations from the *Fairy Queen.*

(²⁹) *As the god of my life ?* &c.

Pray let not the reader consent to read this first half of the line in any manner less marked and peremptory. It is a striking instance of the beauty of that "acceleration and retardation of true verse" which Coleridge speaks of. There is to be a hurry on the words *as the,* and a passionate emphasis and passing stop on the word *god ;* and so of the next three words.

JUPITER AND MAIA.

Character: Young and Innocent but Conscious and Sensuous Beauty.
Painter, Correggio.

Behold how goodly my fair love does lie
                In proud humility !
Like unto Maia, whenas Jove her took
In Tempè, *lying on the flowery grass,*
'Twixt sleep and wake, after she weary was
With bathing in the Acidalian brook.

NIGHT AND THE WITCH DUESSA,

TAKING SANSJOY IN THEIR CHARIOT TO ÆSCULAPIUS TO BE
RESTORED TO LIFE.

Character: Dreariness of Scene ; Horridness of Aspect and Wicked
Beauty, side by side. Painter, Julio Romano.

Then to her iron waggon she betakes
And with her bears the *foul well-favoured witch* .
Through mirksome air her ready way she makes,
Her twofold team (of which two black as pitch
And two were brown, yet each to each unlich*)
Did softly swim away, nor ever stamp
Unless she chanc'd their stubborn mouths to twitch ;
Then, *foaming tar,* their bridles they would champ,
And trampling the fine element would fiercely ramp.

So well they sped, that they be come at length
Unto the place whereas the Paynim lay
Devoid of outward sense and native strength,
Cover'd with charmed cloud from view of day

---

* *Each to each unlich :* **Unlike.**

And sight of men, since his late luckless fray.
His cruel wounds, with cruddy blood congeal'd,
They binden up so wisely as they may,
And handle softly, till they can be heal'd,
So lay him in her chariot, close in night conceal'd.

And all the while she stood upon the ground,
The wakeful dogs did never cease to bay ;
As giving warning of the unwonted sound,
With which her iron wheels did them affray,
And her dark griesly look them much dismay.
The messenger of death, the ghastly owl,
With dreary shrieks did also her bewray ;
And hungry wolves continually did howl
At her abhorrèd face, so filthy and so foul. ([30])

Then turning back in silence soft they stole,
And brought the heavy corse with easy pace
To yawning gulf of deep Avernus hole.
By that same hole, an entrance, dark and base,
With smoke and sulphur hiding all the place,
Descends to hell : there creature never pass'd
That back returnèd without heavenly grace ;
But dreadful furies which their chains have brast,
And damnèd sprites sent forth, to make ill men aghast.

By that same way the direful dames do drive
Their *mournful* chariot, *fill'd with rusty blood.* ([31])
And down to Pluto's house are come belive :
Which passing through, on every side them stood
The trembling ghosts with *sad amazèd mood,*
Chattering their iron teeth, and staring wide
With stony eyes ; and all the hellish brood
Of fiends infernal flock'd on every side,
To gaze on earthly wight, that with the night durst ride.

([30]) *So filthy and so foul.*

Why he should say this of Night, except perhaps in
connection with the witch, I cannot say. It seems to me

to hurt the "abhorrèd face." Night, it is true, may be reviled, or made grand or lovely, as a poet pleases. There is both classical and poetical warrant for all. But the goddess with whom the witch *dared* to ride (as the poet finely says at the close) should have been exhibited, it would seem, in a more awful, however frightful guise.

(31) *Their mournful chariot, fill'd with rusty blood.*

There is something wonderfully dreary, strange, and terrible in this picture. By "rusty blood" (which is very horrid) he must mean the blood half congealing; altered in patches, like rusty iron. Be this as it may, the word "rusty," as Warton observes, "seems to have conveyed the idea of somewhat very loathsome and horrible to our author."

VENUS, IN SEARCH OF CUPID, COMING TO DIANA.

Character: Contrast of Impassioned and Unimpassioned Beauty—Cold and Warm colours mixed. Painter, Titian.

(Yet I know not whether Annibal Caracci would not better suit the demand for personal expression in this instance. But the recollection of Titian's famous Bath of Diana is forced upon us.)

> Shortly unto the wasteful woods she came,
> Whereas she found the goddess with her crew,
> After late chace of their embrewèd game,
> Sitting beside a fountain in a rew ;

Some of them washing with the liquid dew
From off their dainty limbs the dusty sweat
And soil, which did defile their lively hue ;
Others lay shaded from the scorching heat ;
The rest upon her person gave *attendance great.*

She having hung upon a bough on high
Her bow and painted quiver, had unlac'd
Her silver buskins from her nimble thigh,
And her *lank* loins ungirt and breasts unbrac'd,
After her heat the breathing cold to taste ;
Her golden locks, that late in tresses bright
Embraided were for hindering of her haste,
Now loose about her shoulders lay undight,
And were with sweet ambrosia all besprinkled light.

Soon as she Venus saw behind her back,
She was asham'd to be so loose surpris'd,
And wak'd half wrath against her damsels slack,
That had not her thereof before aviz'd,
But suffer'd her so carelessly disguiz'd
Be overtaken : *soon her garments loose* ([32])
Upgathering in her bosom she compriz'd,
Well as she might, and to the goddess rose,
Whiles all her nymphs did like a garland her inclose.

([32]) *Soon her garments loose, &c.*

This picture is from Ovid ; but the lovely and beauti-
fully coloured comparison of the garland is Spenser's own.

MAY.

Character : Budding Beauty in male and female ; Animal Passion,
Luminous Vernal colouring. Painter, Titian.

Then came *fair May, the fairest maid* on ground, ([33])
Deck'd all with dainties of her season's pride,
And throwing flowers out of her lap around :
Upon two brethren's shoulders she did ride,
The Twins of Leda; which, on either side,
Supported her *like to their sovereign queen :*
Lord ! how all creatures laugh'd when her they spied,
And leap'd and danc'd as they had ravish'd been :
And Cupid's self about her fluttĕrĕd all in green.

([33]) *Then came, &c.*

Raphael would have delighted (but Titian's colours
would be required) in the lovely and liberal uniformity of
this picture,—the young goddess May supported aloft;
the two brethren on each side ; animals and flowers below ;
birds in the air, and Cupid streaming overhead in his
green mantle. Imagine the little fellow, with a body of
Titian's carnation, tumbling in the air, and playfully
holding the mantle, which is flying amply behind, rather
than concealing him.

This charming stanza beats the elegant but more
formal invocation to May by Milton, who evidently had it
in his recollection. Indeed the latter is almost a com-
pilation from various poets. It is, however, too beautiful
to be omitted here.

Now the bright morning-star, day's harbinger,
Comes dancing from the east, and leads with her
The flowery May, who from her green lap throws
The yellow cowslip and the pale primrose.

Hail bounteous May, that dost inspire
Mirth, and youth, and warm desire!
Woods and groves are of thy dressing,
Hill and dale doth boast thy blessing.
Thus we salute thee with our early song,
And welcome thee, and wish thee long.

Spenser's "Lord! how all creatures laugh'd," is an instance of joyous and impulsive expression not common with English poets, out of the pale of comedy. They have geniality in abundance, but not animal spirits.

AN ANGEL, WITH A PILGRIM AND A FAINTING KNIGHT.

Character: Active Superhuman Beauty, with the finest colouring and contrast. Painter, Titian.

During the while that Guyon did abide
In Mammon's house, the palmer, whom whilere
That wanton maid of passage had denied,
By further search had passage found elsewhere;
And being on his way, approachèd near
While Guyon lay in trance: when suddenly
He heard a voice that callèd loud and clear,
" Come hither, hither, O come hastily! "
That all the fields resounded with the rueful cry.

The palmer leant his ear unto the noise,
To weet who call'd so importunèdly;
Again he heard a more enforcèd voice,
That bade him come in haste. He by-and-bye

His feeble feet directed to the cry;
Which to that shady delve him brought at last,
Where Mammon earst did sun his treasury :
There the good Guyon he found slumbering fast
In senseless dream ; which sight at first him sore aghast.

Beside his head there sat a fair young man, ([34])
Of wondrous beauty and of freshest years,
Whose tender bud to blossom new began,
And flourish fair above his equal peers ;
His snowy front, curlèd with golden hairs,
Like Phœbus' face adorn'd with sunny rays,
Divinely shone; *and two sharp wingèd shears,*
Deckèd with diverse plumes, like painted jays,
Were fixèd at his back *to cut his airy ways.*

([34]) *Beside his head,* &c.

The superhuman beauty of this angel should be
Raphael's, yet the picture, as a whole, demands Titian;
and the painter of Bacchus was not incapable of the most
imaginative exaltation of countenance. As to the angel's
body, no one could have painted it like him,—nor the
beautiful jay's wings; not to mention the contrast between
the pilgrim's weeds and the knight's armour. See a
picture of Venus blinding Cupid, beautifully engraved
by Sir Robert Strange, in which the Cupid has variegated
wings.

AURORA AND TITHONUS.

Character: Young and Genial Beauty, contrasted with Age,—the accessories full of the mixed warmth and chillness of morning. Painter, Guido.

The joyous day gan early to appear,
And fair Aurora from the dewy bed
Of aged Tithon gan herself to rear
With rosy cheeks, for shame as blushing red.
*Her golden locks, for haste, were loosely shed
About her ears,* when Una did her mark
Climb to her chariot, all with flowers spread,
From heaven high to chace the cheerless dark:
With merry note her loud salutes the mounting lark.

THE BRIDE AT THE ALTAR.

Character: Flushed yet Lady-like Beauty, with ecstatic Angels regarding her. Painter, the same.

Behold, while she before the altar stands,
Hearing the holy priest that to her speaks,
And blesses her with his two happy hands,
How the red roses flush up in her cheeks!
And the pure snow, with goodly vermeil stain,
    Like crimson dyed in grain!
That ev'n the angels, which continually
About the sacred altar do remain,
Forget their service and about her fly,
Oft peeping in her face, that seems more fair (³⁵)
    The more they on it stare;
But her sad eyes, still fastened on the ground,
Are governèd with goodly modesty,
That suffers not one look to glance awry,
Which may let in a little thought unsound.

(³⁵) *Oft peeping in her face, &c.*

I cannot think the words *peeping* and *stare* the best
which the poet could have used ; but he is aggravating
the beauties of his bride in a long epithalamium, and
sacrificing everything to her superiority.   The third line
is felicitous.

A NYMPH BATHING.

Character · Ecstasy of Conscious and Luxurious Beauty.   Painter,
the same.

—Her fair locks, which formerly were bound
Up in one knot, she low adown did loose,
Which flowing long and thick, her cloth'd around,
And the ivory in golden mantle gown'd ;
So that fair spectacle was from him reft,
Yet that which reft it, no less fair was found :
So hid in locks and waves from looker's theft,
Nought but her lovely face she for his looking left

Withal she laughèd, and she blush'd withal, (³⁶)
That blushing to her laughter gave more grace,
And laughter to her blushing.

(³⁶) *Withal she laughèd, &c.*

Perhaps this is the loveliest thing of the kind, mixing
the sensual with the graceful, that ever was painted.   The
couplet, *So hid in locks and waves,* &c. would be an exces-
sive instance of the sweets of alliteration, could we bear to
miss a particle of it.

THE CAVE OF DESPAIR.

Character : Savage and Forlorn Scenery, occupied by Squalid Misery.
Painter, Salvator Rosa.

Ere long they come where that same wicked wight
His dwelling has, low in a hollow cave,
Far underneath a craggy cliff ypight,
Dark, doleful, dreary, like a greedy grave,
That still for carrion carcasses doth crave;
On top whereof ay dwelt the ghastly owl,
Shrieking his baleful note, which ever drave
Far from that haunt all other cheerful fowl,
And all about it wand'ring ghosts did wail and howl:

And all about *old stocks and stubs of trees,*
Whereon nor fruit nor leaf was ever seen,
Did hang upon the *ragged rocky knees,*
On which had many wretches hangèd been,
Whose carcasses were scattered on the green,
And thrown about the cliffs.   Arrivèd there,
That bare-head knight, for dread and doleful teen,*
Would fain have fled, nor durst approachen near,
But th' other forc'd him stay and comforted in fear.

That darksome cave they enter, where they find
That cursed man low sitting on the ground,
Musing full sadly in his sullen mind ;
His griesly locks, long growen and unbound,
Disordered hung about his shoulders round,
And hid his face through which the hollow eyne
Look'd deadly dull, and starèd as astoun'd ;
His raw-bone cheeks, through penury and pine,
Were shrunk into his jaws, as he did never dine.

---

* *Teen.* Anxiety.

> His garment nought but many ragged clouts,
> With thorns together pinn'd and patchèd was,
> The which his naked sides he wrapp'd abouts;
> And him beside there lay upon the grass
> A dreary corse, whose life away did pass,
> All wallow'd in his own yet lukewarm blood,
> That from his wound yet wellèd fresh alas!
> In which a rusty knife fast fixèd stood,
> And made an open passage for the gushing flood.

Still finer than this description are the morbid sophistry
and the fascinations of terror that follow it in the original;
but as they are less poetical or pictorial then argumen-
tative, the extract is limited accordingly. There is a
tradition that when Sir Philip Sidney read this part of
the *Fairy Queen*, he fell into transports of admiration.

A KNIGHT IN BRIGHT ARMOUR LOOKING INTO A CAVE.

Character : A deep effect of Chiaro-scuro, making deformity visible.
Painter, Rembrandt.

> But full of fire and greedy hardiment,
> The youthful knight would not for aught be stay'd,
> But forth unto the darksome hole he went,
> And lookèd in. *His glistering armour made*
> *A little glooming light, much like a shade ;* [37]
> *By which he saw the ugly monster plain,*
> Half like a serpent horribly display'd,
> But th' other half did woman's shape retain,
> Most loathsome, filthy foul, and full of vile disdain.

---

[37] *A little glooming light, much like a shade.*

Spenser is very fond of this effect, and has repeatedly
painted it. I am not aware that anybody noticed it

before him. It is evidently the original of the passage in
Milton :—

> Where glowing embers through the room
> Teach light to counterfeit a gloom.

Observe the pause at the words *lookèd in.*

MALBECCO SEES HELLENORE DANCING WITH THE SATYRS.

Character : Luxurious Abandonment to Mirth. Painter, Nicholas Poussin.

—Afterwards, close creeping as he might,   ·
He in a bush did hide his fearful head :
The jolly satyrs, full of fresh delight,
Came dancing forth, and with them nimbly led
Fair Hellenore, with garlands all bespread,
Whom their May-lady they had newly made :
She, proud of that new honour which they redd,*
And of their lovely fellowship full glad,
Danc'd lively ; *and her face did with a laurel shade.*

The silly man then in a thicket lay,
Saw all this goodly sport, and grievèd sore,
Yet durst he not against it do or say,
But did his heart with bitter thoughts *engore*
To see the unkindness of his Hellenore.
All day they dancèd with great lustyhead,
And with their hornèd feet *the green grass wore,*
The whiles their goats upon the browses
Till drooping Phœbus gan to hide his golden head.

---

* *That new honour which they redd :* Areaded, awarded.

LANDSCAPE,

WITH DAMSELS CONVEYING A WOUNDED SQUIRE ON HIS HORSE.

Character: Select Southern Elegance, with an intimation of fine Architecture. Painter, Claude. (Yet " mighty " woods hardly belong to him.)

> Into that forest far they thence him led,
> Where was their dwelling, in a pleasant glade
> With mountains round about environèd;
> And mighty woods which did the valley shade
> And like a stately theatre it made,
> Spreading itself into a spacious plain;
> And in the midst a little river play'd
> Amongst the pumy stones, which seem'd to plain
> With gentle murmur, that his course they did restrain.

> Beside the same a dainty place there lay,
> Planted with myrtle trees and laurels green,
> In which the birds sung many a lovely lay
> Of God's high praise and of their sweet love's teen,
> As it an earthly paradise had been;
> In whose enclosèd shadows there was pight
> A fair pavilion, scarcely to be seen.

THE NYMPHS AND GRACES DANCING TO A SHEPHERD'S PIPE; OR,

APOTHEOSIS OF A POET'S MISTRESS.

Character: Nakedness without Impudency; Multitudinous and Innocent Delight; Exaltation of the principal Person from Circumstances rather than her own Ideality. Painter, Albano.

> Unto this place whenas the elfin knight
> Approach'd, him seemèd that the merry sound
> Of a shrill pipe he playing heard on height,
> And many feet fast thumping the hollow ground:

That through the woods their echo did rebound;
He nigher drew, to weet what might it be ;
There he a troop of ladies dancing found
Full merrily, and making gladful glee,
And in the midst a shepherd piping he did see.

He durst not enter into the open green,
For dread of them unwares to be descry'd,
For breaking off their dance, if he were seen ;
But in the covert of the wood did bide,
Beholding all, yet of them unespied ;
There he did see (that pleased much his sight
That even he himself his eyes envìed)
A hundred naked maidens lily white,
All rangèd in a ring, and dancing in delight.

All they without were rangèd in a ring
And dancèd round, but in the midst of them
Three other ladies did both dance and sing,
The whilst the rest them round about did hem,
And like a garland did in compass stem ;
And in the midst of those same three was placed
Another damsel, as a precious gem
Amidst a ring most richly well enchaced,
That with her goodly presence all the rest much graced.

* * * *

Those were the Graces, daughters of delight,
Handmaids of Venus, which are wont to haunt
Upon this hill, and dance there day and night ;
Those three to men all gifts of grace do graunt,
And all that Venus in herself doth vaunt
Is borrowèd of them ; but that fair one
That in the midst was placed paravaunt,
Was she to whom that shepherd pip'd alone,
That made him pipe so merrily as never none.

She was, to weet, that jolly shepherd's lass
Which pipèd there unto that merry rout ;
That jolly shepherd which there piped, was
Poor Colin Clout (who knows not Colin Clout ?) ;

> He pip'd apace, whilst they him danc'd about.
> *Pipe, jolly shepherd! pipe thou now apace*
> *Unto thy love, that made thee low to lout;*
> *Thy love is present there with thee in place,*
> *Thy love is there advanc'd to be another Grace.* ([38])

([38]) *Thy love is there advanc'd,* &c.

And there she remains, dancing in the midst of the Graces for ever, herself a Grace, made one by the ordinance of the poor but great poet who here addresses himself under his pastoral title, and justly prides himself on the power of conferring immortality on his love. The apostrophe is as affecting as it is elevating, and the whole scene conceived in the highest possible spirit of mixed wildness and delicacy.

A PLUME OF FEATHERS AND AN ALMOND-TREE.

In this instance, which is the one he adduces in proof of his remark on the picturesque, the reader must agree with Coleridge, that the description (I mean of the almond-tree), however charming, is not fit for a picture: it wants accessories; to say nothing of the reference to the image illustrated, and the feeling of too much minuteness and closeness in the very distance. Who is to paint the tender locks " every one," and the whisper of " every little breath ? "

> Upon the top of all his lofty crest
> A bunch of hairs discolour'd diversly,
> With sprinkled pearl and gold full richly dress'd,
> Did shake and seem to dance for jollity.

Like to an almond tree, ymounted high,
On top of green Selinis all alone,
With blossoms brave bedeckèd daintily,
Whose tender locks do tremble every one,
At every'little breath that under heaven is blown.

What an exquisite last line! but the whole stanza is perfection. The word jollity seems to show the *plumpness* of the plume; what the fop in Molière calls its *embonpoint:*

Mascarille.—Holà, porteurs, holà! Là, là, là, là, là, là. Je pense que ces marauds-là ont dessein de me briser à force de heurter contre les murailles et les pavés.

1 *Porteur.*—Dame! c'est que la porte est étroite. Vous avez voulu aussi que nous soyons entrés jusqu'ici.

Mascarille.—Je le crois bien. Voudriez-vous, faquins, que j'exposasse l'embonpoint de mes plumes aux inclémences de la saison pluvieuse, et que j'allasse imprimer mes souliers en boue?—*Les Précieuses Ridicules,* sc. 7.

[*Mascarille* (to the sedan chairmen).—Stop, stop! What the devil is all this? Am I to be beaten to pieces against the walls and pavement?

Chairman.—Why, you see the passage is narrow. You told us to bring you right in.

Mascarille.—Unquestionably. Would you have me expose the *embonpoint* of my feathers to the inclemency of the rainy season, and leave the impression of my pumps in the mud?]

Our gallery shall close with a piece of
ENCHANTED MUSIC.

Eftsoons they heard a most melodious sound
Of all that might delight a dainty ear,
Such as, at once, might not on living ground,
Save in this paradise, be heard elsewhere:

Right hard it was for wight which did it hear
To weet what manner music that might be,
For all that pleasing is to living ear
Was there consorted in one harmony ;
Birds, voices, instruments, winds, waters, all agree.

The joyous birds, shrouded in cheerful shade,
Their notes unto the voice attemp'red sweet :
Th' angelical, soft, trembling voices made
To th' instruments divine respondence meet ;
The silver sounding instruments did meet
With the base murmur of the water's fall ;
The water's fall, with difference discreet,
Now soft, now loud, unto the wind did call ;
The gentle warbling wind low answerèd to all. ([39])

([39]) *The gentle warbling wind, &c.*

This exquisite stanza is a specimen of perfect modulation, upon the principles noticed in the description of *Archimago's Hermitage.* The reader may, perhaps, try it upon them. " Compare it," says Upton, " with Tasso's *Gierusalemme Liberata,* canto 16, st. 12." Readers who understand Italian will gladly compare it, and see how far their countryman has surpassed the sweet poet of the south.

MARLOWE.

BORN, ACCORDING TO MALONE, ABOUT 1565,—
DIED, 1593.

If ever there was a born poet, Marlowe was one. He perceived things in their spiritual as well as material relations, and impressed them with a corresponding felicity. Rather, he struck them as with something sweet and glowing that rushes by ;—perfumes from a censer,— glances of love and beauty. And he could accumulate images into as deliberate and lofty a grandeur. Chapman said of him, that he stood

> Up to the chin in the Pierian flood.

Drayton describes him as if inspired by the recollection :—

> Next Marlowe, bathèd in the Thespian springs,
> Had in him *those brave translunary things,*
> *That the first poets had ; his raptures were*
> *All air and fire*, which made his verses clear:
> *For that fine madness still he did retain,*
> *Which rightly should possess a poet's brain.*

But this happy genius appears to have had as unhappy a will, which obscured his judgment. It made him con-

descend to write fustian for the town, in order to rule over
it ; subjected him to the charge of impiety, probably for
nothing but too scornfully treating irreverent notions of
the Deity ; and brought him, in the prime of his life, to a
violent end in a tavern. His plays abound in wilful and
self-worshipping speeches, and every one of them turns
upon some kind of ascendancy at the expense of other
people. He was the head of a set of young men from the
university, the Peeles, Greens, and others, all more or less
possessed of a true poetical vein, who, bringing scholar-
ship to the theatre, were intoxicated with the new graces
they threw on the old bombast, carried to their height the
vices as well as wit of the town, and were destined to see,
with indignation and astonishment, their work taken out
of their hands, and done better, by the uneducated inter-
loper from Stratford-upon-Avon.

Marlowe enjoys the singular and (so far) unaccountable
honour of being the only English writer to whom Shak-
speare seems to have alluded with approbation. ' In *As
You Like It*, Phœbe says,

> Dead Shepherd ! now I know thy saw of might,—
> " Who ever lov'd that lov'd not at first sight ? "

The " saw " is in Marlowe's *Hero and Leander*, a poem
not comparable with his plays.

The ranting part of Marlowe's reputation has been
chiefly owing to the tragedy of *Tamburlaine*, a passage in
which is laughed at in *Henry the Fourth*, and has become
famous. Tamburlaine cries out to the captive monarchs
whom he has yoked to his car,—

> Holla, ye pampered jades of Asia,
> What! can ye draw but twenty miles a day,
> And have so proud a chariot at your heels,
> And such a coachman as great Tamburlaine?

Then follows a picture drawn with real poetry :—

> The horse that *guide the golden eye of Heaven,*
> *And blow the morning from their nostrils* (read *nosterils*),
> Making their fiery gait above the clouds,
> Are not so honour'd in their governor,   .
> As you, ye slaves, in mighty Tamburlaine.

It has latterly been thought that a genius like Marlowe could have had no hand in a play so bombastic as this huffing tragedy. But besides the weighty and dignified, though monotonous tone of his versification in many places (what Ben Jonson, very exactly as well as finely, calls "Marlowe's mighty *line*"), there are passages in it of force and feeling, of which I doubt whether any of his contemporaries were capable in so sustained a degree, though Green and Peele had felicitous single lines, and occasionally a refined sweetness. Take, for instance, the noble verses to be found in the description of Tamburlaine himself, which probably suggested to Milton his "Atlantean shoulders "—" fit to bear mightiest monarchies "— and to Beaumont a fine image, which the reader will see in his *Melancholy* :—

> Of stature tall and straightly fashionèd,
> *Like his desire lift upward and divine,*
> So large of limbs, his joints so strongly knit,
> Such breadth of shoulders as might mainly bear
> Old Atlas' burthen :—
> *Pale of complexion, wrought in him with passion,* &c.

By "passion" we are to understand, not anger, but deep emotions. Peele or Green might possibly have written the beautiful verse that closes these four lines :

> Kings of Argier, Moroccus, and of Fesse,
> You that have marched with happy Tamburlaine
> As far as from the frozen place of heaven
> *Unto the watery morning's ruddy bower :—*

but the following is surely Marlowe's own :—

> *As princely lions when they rouse themselves,*
> *Stretching their paws and threatening herds of beasts,*
> *So in his armour looketh Tamburlaine :*

and in the following is not only a hint of the scornful part of his style, such as commences the extract from the *Jew of Malta*, but the germ of those lofty and harmonious nomenclatures, which have been thought peculiar to Milton :

> So from the east unto the farthest west
> Shall Tamburlaine extend his puissant arm
> The gallies and *those pilling brigandines*
> That yearly sail to the Venetian gulf,
> And hover in the Straits for Christian wreck,
> *Shall lie at anchor in the isle Arant,*
> *Until the Persian fleet and men of wars,*
> *Sailing along the Oriental sea,*
> *Have fetch'd about the Indian continent,*
> *Even from Persepolis to Mexico,*
> *And thence unto the Straits of Jubaltàr.*

Milton never surpassed the elevation of that close. Who also but Marlowe is likely to have written the fine passage extracted into this volume, under the title of *Beauty beyond Expression*, in which the thought argues as much expression as the style a confident dignity ? *Tamburlaine* was most likely a joint-stock piece, got up from the manager's chest by Marlowe, Nash, and perhaps half-a-dozen others ; for there are two consecutive plays on the subject, and the theatres of our own time are not unacquainted with this species of manufacture.

But I am forgetting the plan of my book. Marlowe, like Spenser, is to be looked upon as a poet who had no native precursors. As Spenser is to be criticised with an eye to his poetic ancestors, who had nothing like the *Fairy Queen,* so is Marlowe with reference to the authors of *Gorboduc.* He got nothing from them ; he prepared the way for the versification, the dignity, and the pathos of his successors, who have nothing finer of the kind to show than the death of Edward the Second—not Shakspeare himself ; — and his imagination, like Spenser's, haunted those purely poetic regions of ancient fabling and modern rapture, of beautiful forms and passionate expressions, which they were the first to render the common property of inspiration, and whence their language drew "empyreal air." Marlowe and Spenser are the first of our poets who perceived the beauty of words ; not as apart from their significance, nor upon occasion only, as Chaucer did (more marvellous in that than themselves, or than the originals from whom he drew), but as a habit of the poetic mood, and as receiving and reflecting beauty through the feeling of the ideas.

THE JEW OF MALTA'S IDEA OF WEALTH.

So that of thus much that return was made,
And of the third part of the Persian ships,
There was the venture summ'd and satisfied.
As for those Samnites, and the men of Uz,
That bought my Spanish oils and wines of Greece, (¹)
Here have I purs'd their paltry silverlings.
Fie ; what a trouble 't is to count this trash !
Well fare the Arabians, who so richly pay
The things they traffic for with wedge of gold,
Whereof a man may easily in a day
Tell that which may maintain him all his life.
The needy groom, that never finger'd groat,
Would make a miracle of thus much coin ;
But he whose steel-barr'd coffers are cramm'd full,
And all his life-time hath been tired (read *ti-er-ed*),
Wearying his fingers' ends with telling it,
Would in his age be loth to labour so,
And for a pound to sweat himself to death.
Give *me* the merchants of the Indian mines,
That trade in metal of the purest mould ;
The Wealthy Moor, that in the eastern rocks
Without control can pick his riches up,
And in his house heap pearl like pebble-stones ,
Receive them free, and sell them by the weight ;
Bags of fiery opals, sapphires, amethysts,
Jacinths, hard topaz, grass-green emeralds,
Beauteous rubies, sparkling diamonds,
And seld-seen costly stones of so great price,
As one of them indifferently rated,
And of a carat of this quantity,
May serve, in peril of calamity,
To ransom great kings from captivity :
This is the ware wherein consists my wealth ;
And thus, methinks, should men of judgment frame
Their means of traffic from the vulgar trade,

And as their wealth increaseth, so inclose
Infinite riches in a little room.
But now how stands the wind?
Iuto what corner peers my halcyon's bill? *
Ha! to the east? yes; see how stand the vanes?
East and by south.   Why then, I hope my ships
I sent for Egypt and the bordering isles
Are gotten up by Nilus' winding banks;
Mine argosies from Alexandria, (²)
Loaden with spice and silks, now under sail,
Are smoothly gliding down by Candy shore
To Malta, through our Mediterranean Sea.

(¹) " *Samnites* " and " *men of Uz*," and " *Spanish oils !* "

That is to say, countrymen and contemporaries of old
Rome, of Arabian Job, and the modern Spanish merchants!
Marlowe, though he was a scholar, cared no more for geo-
graphy and consistent history than Shakspeare.   He took
the world as he found it at the theatre, where it was a
mixture of golden-age innocence, tragical enormity, and a
knowledge superior to all petty and transitory facts.

(²) *Mine argosies from Alexandria,* &c.

Note the wonderful sweetness of these four lines,
particularly the last.   The variety of the vowels, the
delicate alliteration, and the lapse of the two concluding
verses, are equal, as a study, to anything in Spenser.

---

* *My halcyon's bill :* The halcyon is the figure on the vane.

A VISION OF HELEN.

She passes between two Cupids, having been summoned from the
next world by desire of Faustus.

Faust. Was this *the face that launch'd a thousand ships,*
And burnt the topmost towers of Ilium?
Sweet Helen, make me immortal with a kiss.—
Her lips suck forth my soul! *see where it flies.*
Come, Helen, come, give me my soul again.
Here will I dwell, for heav'n is in these lips,
And all is dross that is not Helena.
I will be Paris; and for love of thee,
Instead of Troy, shall Wittenberg be sack'd;
And I will combat with weak Menelaus,
And wear my colours on my plumèd crest:
Yea, I will wound Achilles in the heel,
And then return to Helen for a kiss.
Oh, thou art fairer than the evening air,
Clad in the beauty of a thousand stars;
Brighter art thou than flaming Jupiter, ([3])
When he appear'd to hapless Semele;
More lovely than the monarch of the sea,
In wanton Arethusa's azure arms;
.And none but thou shalt be my paramour!

([3]) *Brighter art thou,* &c.

Much cannot be said of the five lines here ensuing;
but their retention was necessary to the entire feeling or
classical association of the speech, if not to a certain
lingering modulation.

MYTHOLOGY AND COURT AMUSEMENTS.

Gaveston meditates how to govern Edward the Second.

I must have wanton poets, pleasant wits,
Musicians, that *with touching of a string*
May draw the pliant king which way I please.
Music and poetry are his delight:
Therefore I'll have Italian masks by night;
Sweet speeches, comedies, and pleasing shows;
And in the day when he shall walk abroad,
Like sylvan nymphs my pages shall be clad:
My men, like satyrs grazing on the lawns,
Shall with their goat-feet dance the antic hay.
Sometimes a lovely boy in Dian's shape,
With hair that gilds the water as it glides,
Shall bathe him in a spring; and there, hard by,
One, like Actæon, peeping through the grove,
Shall by the angry goddess be transform'd;
And running in the likeness of a hart,
By yelping hounds pull'd down, shall seem to die—
Such things as these best please his Majesty.

BEAUTY BEYOND EXPRESSION.

If all the pens that ever poets held
Had fed the feeling of their masters' thoughts.
And ev'ry sweetness that inspired their hearts,
And minds, and muses on admirèd themes;
If all the heavenly quintessence they 'stil
From their immortal flowers of poesy,
Wherein, as in a mirror, we perceive
The highest reaches of a human wit;
If these had made one poem's period,
And all combin'd in beauty's worthiness,
Yet should there hover in their restless heads
One thought, one grace, one wonder, at the best,
Which into words no virtue can digest.

9

THE PASSIONATE SHEPHERD TO HIS LOVE.

Come live with me and be my love,
And we will all the pleasures prove,
That hill and valley, grove and field,
And all the craggy mountains yield.
There will we sit upon the rocks,
And see the shepherds feed their flocks
By shallow rivers, to whose falls
Melodious birds sing madrigals.
There will I make thee beds of roses,   .
With a thousand fragrant posies;
A cap of flowers and a kirtle
Embroider'd all with leaves of myrtle;
A gown made of the finest wool,
Which from our pretty lambs we pull;
Slippers lin'd choicely for the cold,
With buckles of the purest gold;
A belt of straw, and ivy buds,
With coral clasps, and amber studs.

The shepherd swains shall dance and sing
For thy delight each May morning;
And if these pleasures may thee move,
Then live with me, and be my love.

This song is introduced, not so much for its poetical excellence (though it is quite what a poet would write on the occasion), as because it is one of those happy embodiments of a thought which all the world thinks at some time or other; and which therefore *takes* wonderfully with them when somebody utters it. The "golden buckles" and "amber studs" are not to be considered as a contradiction to the rest of the imagery; for we are to suppose it a gentlewoman to whom the invitation is addressed, and with whom her bridegroom proposes to go and play at shepherd and shepherdess, at once realizing the sweets of lowliness and the advantages of wealth. A charming fancy! and realized too sometimes; though Sir Walter Raleigh could not let it alone, but must needs refute it in some excellent verses, too good for the occasion. Sir Walter, a great but wilful man (in some respects like Marlowe himself, and a true poet too—I wish he had written more poetry), could pass and ultimately lose his life in search of El Dorados,—whole countries made of gold, — but doubted whether an innocent young lady and gentleman, or so, should aim at establishing a bit of Arcadia.

There are so many copies of this once-popular production, all different, and none quite consistent, owing, no doubt, to oral repetitions and the licence of musical setting (for no copy of it is to be found coëval with its production), that, after studious comparison of several, I have exercised a certain discretion in the one here printed, and omitted also an ill-managed repetition of the burden : —not, of course, with the addition of a syllable. Such readers, therefore, as it may concern, are warned not to take the present copy for granted, at the expense of the others ; but to compare them all, and make his choice.

SHAKSPEARE.

BORN, 1564—DIED, 1616.

SHAKSPEARE is here in his purely poetical creations, apart (as much as it is possible for such a thinker and humanist to be) from thought and humanity. There is nothing wanting either to the imagination or fancy of Shakspeare. The one is lofty, rich, affecting, palpable, subtle; the other full of grace, playfulness, and variety. He is equal to the greatest poets in grandeur of imagination; to all in diversity of it; to all in fancy; to all in everything else, except in a certain primæval intensity, such as Dante's and Chaucer's; and in narrative poetry, which (to judge from *Venus and Adonis,* and the *Rape of Lucrece*) he certainly does not appear to have had a call to write. He over-informed it with reflection. It has been supposed that when Milton spoke of Shakspeare as

> *Fancy's child*
> Warbling his native wood-notes wild,

the genealogy did him injustice. But the critical distinction between Fancy and Imagination was hardly determined till of late. Collins himself, in his *Ode on the Poetical Character,* uses the word Fancy to imply both, even when speaking of Milton ; and so did Milton, I conceive, when speaking of Shakspeare. The propriety of the words, "native wood-notes wild," is not so clear. I take them to have been hastily said by a learned man of an unlearned. But Shakspeare, though he had not a college education, was as learned as any man, in the highest sense of the word, by a scholarly intuition. He had the spirit of learning. He was aware of the education he wanted, and by some means or other supplied it. He could anticipate Milton's own Greek and Latin :

Tortive and errant from his course of growth—

The multitudinous seas incarnadine—

A pudency so rosy, &c.

In fact, if Shakspeare's poetry has any fault, it is that of being too learned ; too over-informed with thought and allusion. His wood-notes wild surpass Haydn and Bach. His wild roses were all twenty times double. He thinks twenty times to another man's once, and makes all his serious characters talk as well as he could himself,—with a superabundance of wit and intelligence. He knew, however, that fairies must have a language of their own ; and hence, perhaps, his poetry never runs in a more purely poetical vein than when he is speaking in their persons ;—I mean it is less mixed up with those heaps of comments and reflections which, however the wilful or metaphysical critic may think them suitable on all occasions, or succeed in persuading us not to wish them absent, by reason of their stimulancy to one's mental activity, are assuredly neither always proper to dramatic,

still less to narrative poetry; nor yet so opposed to all
idiosyncrasy on the writer's part as Mr. Coleridge would
have us believe. It is pretty manifest, on the contrary,
that the over-informing intellect which Shakspeare thus
carried into all his writings, must have been a personal
as well as literary peculiarity; and as the events he speaks
of are sometimes more interesting in their nature than
even a superabundance of his comments can make them,
readers may be pardoned in sometimes wishing that he
had let them speak a little more briefly for themselves.
Most people would prefer Ariosto's and Chaucer's narra-
tive poetry to his; the *Griselda*, for instance, and the
story of *Isabel*,—to the *Rape of Lucrece*. The intense
passion is enough. The misery is enough. We do not
want even the divinest talk about what Nature herself
tends to petrify into silence. *Curæ ingentes stupent.*
Our divine poet had not quite outlived the times
when it was thought proper for a writer to say every-·
thing that came into his head. He was a student of
Chaucer; he beheld the living fame of Spenser; and his
fellow-dramatists did not help to restrain him. The
players told Ben Jonson that Shakspeare never blotted
a line; and Ben says he was thought invidious for ob-
serving that he wished he had blotted a thousand. He
sometimes, he says, required stopping. (*Aliquando suffla-
minandus erat.*) Was this meant to apply to his con-
versation as well as writing? Did he manifest a like
exuberance in company? Perhaps he would have done so,
but for modesty and self-knowledge. To keep his elo-
quence altogether within bounds was hardly possible; and

who could have wished it had been? Would that he had had a Boswell a hundred times as voluminous as Dr. Johnson's to take all down! Bacon's *Essays* would have seemed like a drop out of his ocean. He would have swallowed dozens of Hobbeses by anticipation, like larks for his supper.

. If Shakspeare, instead of proving himself the greatest poet in the world, had written nothing but the fanciful scenes in this volume, he would still have obtained a high and singular reputation,—that of Poet of the Fairies. For he may be said to have invented the Fairies; that is to say, he was the first that turned them to poetical account; that bore them from clownish neighbourhoods to the richest soils of fancy and imagination.

WHOLE STORY OF THE TEMPEST

ENCHANTMENT, MONSTROSITY, AND LOVE.

The whole story of the *Tempest* is really contained in this scene :—

> *Mira.* I pray you, sir,
> (For still 'tis beating in my mind,) your reason
> For raising this sea-storm?
> *Pro.* Know thus far forth :—
> By accident most strange, bountiful fortune,
> Now my dear lady, hath mine enemies
> Brought to this shore: and by my prescience
> I find my zenith doth depend upon
> A most auspicious star; whose influence

If now I court not, but omit, my fortunes
Will ever after droop.   Here cease more questions;
Thou art inclin'd to sleep; 'tis a good dulness,
And give it way;—I know thou canst not choose.—

                                [Miranda sleeps.

Come away, servant, come; I am ready now;
Approach, my Ariel; come.

                         Enter ARIEL.

   Ari. All hail, great master! grave sir, hail! I come
To answer thy best pleasure, be 't to fly,
To swim, to dive into the fire, to ride
On the curl'd clouds: to thy strong bidding task
Ariel, and all his quality.
   Pro.   Hast thou, spirit,
Perform'd to point the tempest that I bade thee?
   Ari. To every article.
I boarded the king's ship; now on the beak,
Now in the waist, the deck, in every cabin,
I flam'd amazement.   Sometimes I 'd *divide,*
And burn in many places; on the top-mast,
The yards, and bowsprit, would I flame distinctly,
Then meet and join: Jove's lightnings, *the precursors*
O' the dreadful thunder-claps, more momentary
And *sight-outrunning* were not: the fire, and cracks
Of sulphurous roaring, the most mighty Neptune
Seem'd to besiege, and make his bold waves tremble;
Yea, his dread trident shake.
   Pro.   My brave spirit!
Who was so firm, so constant, that this coil
Would not infect his reason?
   Ari.   Not a soul
But felt a fever of the mad, and play'd
Some tricks of desperation: all, but mariners,
Plung'd in the foaming brine, and quit the vessel,
Then all a-fire with me: the king's son, Ferdinand,
With hair up-staring (then like reeds, not hair),
Was the first man that leap'd; cried, " *Hell is empty,*
And all the devils are here."

Pro.   Why, that's my spirit!
But was not this nigh shore?
Ari.   Close by, my master.
Pro. But are they, Ariel, safe?
Ari.   Not a hair perish'd;
On their sustaining garments not a blemish,
But fresher than before; and as thou bad'st me,
In troops I have dispers'd them 'bout the isle:
The king's son have I landed by himself;
Whom I left cooling of the air with sighs,
In an odd angle of the isle, and sitting,
His arms in *this sad knot.*
Pro.   Of the king's ship,
The mariners, say how thou hast dispos'd,
And all the rest o' the fleet?
Ari.   Safely in harbour
Is the king's ship; in the deep nook, where once
Thou call'dst me up at midnight to fetch dew
From the still-vexed Bermoothes, there she's hid;
The mariners all under hatches stow'd;
Whom, with a charm join'd to their suffer'd labour,
I have left asleep; and for the rest o' the fleet,
Which I dispers'd, they all have met again;
And are upon the Mediterranean flote,
Bound sadly home for Naples;
Supposing that they saw the king's ship wreck'd,
And his great person perish.
Pro.   Ariel, thy charge
Exactly is perform'd; but there's more work:
What is the time o' the day?
Ari.   Past the mid season.
Pro. At least two glasses. The time 'twixt six and now
Must by us both be spent most preciously.
Ari. Is there more toil? Since thou dost give me pains,
Let me remember thee what thou hast promis'd,
Which is not yet perform'd me.
Pro.   How now? moody?
What is 't thou canst demand?
Ari.   My liberty.
Pro. Before the time be out? no more.

Ari.　　　　　　　　　I pray thee
Remember, I have done thee worthy service ;
Told thee no lies, made no mistakings, serv'd
Without or grudge or grumblings : thou didst promise
To bate me a full year.
　　Pro.　　　　　　　　Dost thou forget
From what a torment I did free thee?
　　Ari.　　　　　　　　No.
　　Pro. Thou dost ; and think'st
It much to *tread* the *ooze* of the salt deep ;
To run upon the sharp wind of the north ;
To do me business in the veins of the earth,
When it is bak'd with frost.
　　Ari.　　　　　　　　I do not, sir.
　　Pro. Thou liest, malignant thing ! Hast thou forgot'
The foul witch Sycorax, who, with age and envy,
Was grown into a hoop ? Hast thou forget her ?
　　Ari. No, sir.
　　Pro.　　　. Thou hast : where was she born ? speak ; tell me.
　　Ari. Sir, in Argier.
　　Pro.　　　　　　O, was she so ? I must,
Once in a month, recount what thou hast been,
Which thou forget'st. This damn'd witch, Sycorax,
For mischiefs manifold, and sorceries *terrible*
To enter human hearing, from Argier,
Thou know'st, was banish'd ; for one thing she did,
They would not take her life. Is not this true ?
　　Ari.　　　　　　　　Ay, sir.
　　Pro. This blue-eyed hag was hither brought with child,
And here was left by the sailors. Thou, my slave,
As thou report'st thyself, was then her servant :
And, for thou wast a spirit too delicate
To act her *earthy and abhorr'd commands*,
Refusing her grand hests, she did confine thee
By help of her more potent ministers,
And in her most unmitigable rage,
Into a cloven pine : within which rift
Imprison'd, thou didst painfully remain
A dozen years ; within which space she died,
And left thee there ; where thou didst vent thy groans,

As fast as mill-wheels strike : Then was this island
(Save for the son that she did *litter* here,
A freckled whelp, hag-born) not honoured with
A human shape.
    Ari.   Yes ; Caliban her son.
    Pro. Dull thing, I say so ; he, that Caliban,
Whom now I keep in service. Thou best know'st
What torment I did find thee in ; *thy groans*
Did make wolves howl, and penetrate the breasts
Of ever angry bears : it was a torment
To lay upon the damn'd, which Sycorax
Could not again undo ; it was mine art,
When I arriv'd, and heard thee, that made gape
The pine and let thee out.
    Ari.   I thank thee, master.
    Pro. If thou more murmur'st, I will rend an oak,
And peg thee in his knotty entrails, till
Thou hast howl'd away twelve winters.
    Ari.   Pardon, master :
I will be correspondent to command,
And do my spiriting gently.
    Pro.   Do so ; and after two days
I will discharge thee.
    Ari.   That's my noble master !
What shall I do ? say what : what shall I do ?
    Pro. Go make thyself like to a nymph o' the sea ;
Be subject to no sight but mine ; invisible
To every eyeball else. Go, take this shape,
And hither come in't : hence, with diligence.   [*Exit Ariel.*
Awake, dear heart, awake ! thou hast slept well :
Awake !
    Mira. The strangeness of your story put
Heaviness in me.
    Pro.   Shake it off : come on ;
We'll visit Caliban, my slave, who never
Yields us kind answer.
    Mira.   'Tis a villain, sir,
I do not love to look on.
    Pro.   But as 'tis,
We cannot miss him ; he does make our fire,

Fetch in our wood, and serves in offices
That profit us.   What ho! slave! Caliban!
Thou earth thou! speak.
    Cali. (*within.*) There's wood enough within.
    Pro. Come forth, I say: there's other business for thee
Come forth, thou tortoise! when?

Re-enter Ariel, *like a water-nymph.*

Fine apparition! my quaint Ariel!
Hark in thine ear.
    Ari. My lord, it shall be done.
                                                              [*Exit.*
    Pro. Thou poisonous slave, got by the devil himself
Upon thy wicked dam, come forth!

Enter Caliban.

    Cali. As wicked dew as e'er my mother brush'd
With raven's feather from unwholesome fen
Drop on you both! a south-west blow on ye,
And blister you all o'er!
    Pro. For this, be sure, to-night thou shalt have cramps,
Side-stitches that shall pen thy breath up; urchins
Shall, for that vast of night that they may work,
All exercise on thee: thou shalt be pinch'd
As thick as honey-combs, each pinch more stinging
Than bees that made them.
    Cali.   I must eat my dinner!
This island's mine, by Sycorax, my mother,
Which thou tak'st from me.   When thou camest first,
Thou strokedst me, and madest much of me; wouldst give me
Water with berries in't; and teach me how
To name the bigger light, and how the less,
That burn by day and night: and then I lov'd thee,
And show'd thee all the qualities o' the isle,
The fresh springs, brine-pits, barren place, and fertile;
Cursèd be I that did so!   All the charms
Of Sycorax, toads, beetles, bats, light on you!

For I am all the subjects that you have,
Which first was mine own king; and here you sty me
In this hard rock, whiles you do keep from me
The rest of the island.
 Pro.   - Thou most lying slave,
Whom stripes may move, not kindness,—I have us'd thee,
Filth as thou art, with human care: and lodg'd thee
In mine own cell, till thou didst seek to violate
The honour of my child.
 Cali. O ho, O ho! would it had been done!
Thou didst prevent me; I had peopled else
This isle with Calibans.
 Pro.   Abhorrèd slave,
Which any print of goodness will not take,
Being capable of all ill! I pitied thee,
Took pains to make thee speak, taught thee each hour
One thing or other; when thou didst not, savage,
Know thine own meaning, but wouldst gabble, like
A thing most brutish, I endow'd thy purposes
With words that made them known: but thy vile race,
Though thou didst learn, had that in't which good natures
Could not abide to be with; therefore wast thou
Deservedly confin'd into this rock,
Who hadst deserved more than a prison.
 Cali. You taught me language; and my profit on't
Is, *I know how to curse:* the red plague rid you,
For learning me your language!
 Pro.   Hag-seed, hence!
Fetch us in fuel; and be quick, thou wert best,
To answer other business. Shrug'st thou, malice?
If thou neglect'st, or dost unwillingly
What I command, I'll rack thee with old cramps;
Fill all thy bones with achès; make thee roar,
That beasts shall tremble at thy din.
 Cali.   No, 'pray thee!
I must obey: his art is of such power, [*Aside.*
It would control my dam's god, Setebos,
And make a vassal of him.
 Pro.   So, slave; hence!
            [*Exit Caliban.*

Re-enter ARIEL *invisible, playing and singing ;* FERDINAND
following him.

ARIEL'S SONG.

Come unto these yellow sands,
    And then take hands;
Court'sied when you have, and kiss'd
    (The wild waves whist),
Foot it featly here and there ;
And, sweet sprites, the burden bear.
        Hark, hark !
    [*Burden.* Bowgh, wowgh.   (*Dispersedly*)]
        The watch-dogs bark:
    [*Bur.* Bowgh, wowgh.   (*Dispersedly*)]
        Hark, hark ! I hear
The strain of *strutting* chanticlere
Cry, Cock-a-doodle-doo !

Fer. Where should this music be ? i' the air, or the earth ?
It sounds no more ;—and sure it waits upon
Some god of the island.   Sitting on a bank,
Weeping again the king my father's wreck,
This music *crept* by me *upon the waters ;*
Allaying both their fury and my passion
With its sweet air; thence I have follow'd it,
Or it hath drawn me rather—But 'tis gone—
No, it begins again.

ARIEL *sings.*
Full fathom five thy father lies ;
    Of his bones are coral made ;
Those are pearls that were his eyes ;
    Nothing of him that doth fade,
But doth suffer a sea-change
Into something rich and strange.
Sea-nymphs hourly ring his knell ;
Hark ! now I hear them,—ding, dong, bell.
                        [*Burden.* Ding-dong.

Fer. The ditty does remember my drowned father.
This is no mortal business, nor no sound
That the earth owes.—I hear it now above me.

Pro. The fringèd curtains of thine eye advance, (¹)
And say what thou seest yond!
    Mira.   What is 't? a spirit?
Lord, how it looks about! Believe me, sir,
It carries a brave form :—but 't is a spirit.
    Pro. No, wench; it eats and sleeps, and hath such senses
As we have,—such. This gallant, which thou seest,
Was in the wreck; and but he's something stain'd
With grief, that's beauty's canker, thou might'st call him
A goodly person: he hath lost his fellows,
And strays about to find them.
    Mira.   I might call him
A thing divine; for nothing natural
I ever saw so noble.
    Pro.   It goes on,   [*Aside.*.
As my soul prompts it:—Spirit, fine.spirit! I'll free thee
Within two days for this.
    Fer.   Most sure, the goddess
On whom these airs attend!—Vouchsafe, my prayer
May know if you remain upon this island;
And that you will some good instruction give,
How I may bear me here. My prime request,
Which I do last pronounce, is, *O, you wonder!*
If you be maid, or no?
    Mira.   No wonder, sir;
But certainly a maid.
    Fer.   My language! heavens!
I am the best of them that speak this speech,
Were I but where 't is spoken.
    Pro.   How! the best?
What wert thou, if the King of Naples heard thee?
    Fer. A single thing, as I am now, that wonders
To hear thee speak of Naples. He does hear me;
And, that he does, I weep: *myself am Naples;* (²)
Who with mine eyes, ne'er since at ebb, beheld
The king my father wreck'd.
    Mira.   Alack for mercy!
    Fer. Yes, faith, and all his lords; the Duke of Milan,
And his brave son, being twain.

> *Pro.*   The Duke of **Milan**,
> And his more braver daughter, could control thee,
> If now 'twere fit to do 't.—At the first sight   [*Aside.*
> *They have chang'd eyes!*—Delicate Ariel,
> I'll set thee free for this!

(¹) *The fringèd curtains of thine eye advance.*

Why Shakspeare should have condescended to the elaborate nothingness, not to say nonsense of this metaphor (for what is meant by advancing " curtains ?"), I cannot conceive ; that is to say, if he did condescend ; for it looks very like the interpolation of some pompous, declamatory player. Pope has put it into his treatise on the Bathos.

(²) *Myself am Naples.*

This is a very summary and kingly style. Shakspeare is fond of it. " How now, France ? " says King John to King Philip. " I'm dying, Egypt ? " says Antony to Cleopatra.

MACBETH AND THE WITCHES.

This scene fortunately comprises a summary of the whole subsequent history of Macbeth.

A dark Cave.   In the middle, a Cauldron boiling.   Thunder.
Enter three Witches.

1st *Wi.* Thrice the brinded cat hath mew'd.
2nd *Wi.* Thrice ; and once the hedge-pig whin'd.
8rd. *Wi.* Harper cries :—'Tis time, 'tis time.

1st *Wi.* Round about the cauldron go ;
   In the poison'd entrails throw
   Toad, that under a cold stone
   Days and nights hast thirty-one
   Swelter'd venom sleeping got,
   Boil thou first i' the charmèd pot !
All. Double, double, toil and trouble ;
   Fire, burn ; and, cauldron, bubble.
2nd *Wi.* Fillet of a fenny snake,
   In the cauldron boil and bake :
   Eye of newt, and toe of frog,
   Wool of bat, and tongue of dog,
   Adder's fork, and blind-worm's sting.
   Lizard's leg, and owlet's wing,
   For a charm of powerful trouble,
   Like a hell-broth boil and bubble.
All. Double, double, toil and trouble ;
   Fire, burn ; and, cauldron, bubble,
3r l *Wi.* Scale of dragon, tooth of wolf;
   Witches' mummy ; maw, and gulf,
   Of the ravin'd salt-sea shark ;
   Root of hemlock, digg'd i' the dark;
   Liver of blaspheming Jew ;
   Gall of goat, and slips of yew,
   Sliver'd in the moon's eclipse ;
   Nose of Turk, and Tartar's lips ;
   Finger of birth-strangled babe,
   Ditch-deliver'd by a drab,
   Make the gruel thick and slab ;
   Add thereto a tiger's chawdron,
   For the ingredients of our cauldron.
All. Double, double, toil and trouble,
   Fire burn ; and, cauldron, bubble.
2nd *Wi.* Cool it with a baboon's blood,
   Then the charm is firm and good.

Enter Hecate *and the other three* Witches.

Hec. O, well done ! I commend your pains ;
And every one shall share i' the gains.

10

And now about the cauldron sing,
Like elves and fairies in a ring,
Enchanting all that you put in.

(Music and a Song, " Black spirits," &c.)

2nd Wi. By the pricking of my thumbs,
Something wicked this way comes.
Open, locks, whoever knocks.

Enter MACBETH.

Mac. How now, you secret, black, and midnight hags.
What is't you do?
All.　　　　*A deed without a name.*
Mac. I conjure you, by that which you profess
(Howe'er you come to know it), answer me :
Though you untie the winds, and let them *fight*
Against the churches : though the yeasty waves
Confound and swallow navigation up ;
Though bladed corn be lodg'd, and trees blown down ;
Though castles topple on their warders' heads ;
Though palaces and pyramids do slope
Their heads to their foundations ; though the treasure
Of nature's germins tumble all together,
Even till destruction sicken, answer me
To what I ask you.
　　1st Wi.　　　Speak.
　　2nd Wi.　　　　Demand.
　　3rd Wi.　　　　　We'll answer.
　　1st Wi. Say, if thou'dst rather hear it from our mouths,
Or from our masters' ?
　　Mac.　　　Call them, let me see them.
　　1st Wi. Pour in *sow's blood, that hath eaten*
Her nine farrow ; grease that's sweaten
From the murderer's gibbet, throw
Into the flame.
　　All.　　　Come, high or low ;
Thyself, and office, deftly show.

　　Thunder. An Apparition of an armed Head rises
　　Mac. Tell me, thou unknown power,—

1st Wi.   *He knows thy thought ,*
Hear his speech, but say thou nought.
App. Macbeth! Macbeth! Macbeth! beware Macduff;
Beware the Thane of Fife.—*Dismiss me ;*—Enough.
                                            [*Descends.*
Mac. Whate'er thou art, for thy good caution thanks;
Thou hast harp'd my fear aright:—But one word more ;—
1st Wi. He will not be commanded : Here's another,
More potent than the first.

Thunder. An Apparition of a bloody Child rises. (³)

App. Macbeth! Macbeth! Macbeth!—
Mac.   Had I three ears, I'd hear thee.
App. Be bloody, bold, and resolute ; laugh to scorn
The power of man, for none of woman born
Shall harm Macbeth.   [*Descends.*
Mac. Then live, Macduff: what need I fear of thee?
But yet I'll make assurance doubly sure,
And take a bond of fate: thou shalt not live ;
That I may tell pale-hearted fear it lies,
And sleep in spite of thunder.—What is this?

*Thunder.   An Apparition of a Child crowned, with a tree in his
                - hand, rises.*

That rises like the issue of a king;
And wears upon his baby-brow the round
And top of sovereignty?
All.   Listen, but speak not to 't.
App. Be lion-mettled, proud; and take no care
Who chafes, who frets, or where conspirers are ;
Macbeth shall never vanquish'd be, until
Great Birnam wood to high Dunsinane hill
Shall come against him.
                                            [*Descends.*
Mac.   That will never be ;
Who can impress the forest; bid the tree
Unfix his earth-bound root? Sweet bodements! good!
Rebellious head, rise never, till the wood
Of Birnam rise, and our high-plac'd Macbeth
Shall live the lease of nature, pay his breath

To time and mortal custom.—Yet my heart
Throbs to know one thing : Tell me (if your art
Can tell so much), shall Banquo's issue ever
Reign in the kingdom ?
    All.   Seek to know no more.
  Mac. I will be satisfied : deny me this,
And an eternal curse fall on you ! Let me know—
Why sinks that cauldron ? and what noise is this?
                              [*Hautboys.*

  1st Wi. Show !
  2nd Wi.   Show !
  3rd Wi.   Show !
  All. Show his eyes and grieve his heart,
     Come like shadows, so depart.

*Eight Kings appear, and pass over the stage in order ; the last with a
         glass in his hand ; Banquo following.*

  Mac. Thou art too like the spirit of Banquo ; down !
Thy crown does sear mine eyeballs :—And thy hair,
Thou other gold-bound brow, is like the first ;—
A third is like the former.—Filthy hags !
Why do you show me this ? a fourth ? Start, eyes !
What ! will the line stretch out to the crack of doom ?
Another yet ?—A seventh ? I'll see no more :
And yet the eighth appears, who bears a glass
Which shows me many more ; and some I see,
That twofold balls and treble sceptres carry :
Horrible sight !—Ay, now, I see, 'tis true ;
For the *blood-bolter'd Banquo smiles upon me,
And points at them for his.*—What, is this so ?
  1st Wi. Ay, sir, all this is so :—But why
     Stands Macbeth thus amazèdly ?
     Come, sisters, cheer we up his sprites,
     And show the best of our delights :
     I'll charm the air to give a sound,
     While you perform your antique round ;
     That this great king may kindly say,
     Our duties did his welcome pay.

  (*Music. The Witches dance, and vanish.*)

Mac. Where are they? Gone?—Let this pernicious hour
Stand aye accursèd in the calendar!—
Come in, without there!

Enter LENOX.

Len.   What's your grace's will?
Mac. Saw you the weird sisters?
Len.   No, my lord.
Mac. Came they not by you?
Len.   No, indeed, my lord.
Mac. Infected be the air whereon they ride;
And damn'd all those that trust them!—I did hear
The galloping of horse; who was't came by?
Len. 'Tis two or three, my lord, that bring you word,
Macduff is fled to England.
Mac.   Fled to England!
Len. Ay, my good lord.
Mac. Time, thou anticipat'st my dread exploits:
The flighty purpose never is o'ertook,
Unless the deed go with it: From this moment,
The very firstlings of my heart shall be
The firstlings of my hand. And even now .
To.crown my thoughts with acts, be it thought and done:
The castle of Macduff I will surprise;
Seize upon Fife; give to the edge o' the sword
His wife, his babes, and all unfortunate souls
That trace him in his line. No boasting like a fool;
This deed I'll do before this purpose cool;
But no more sights! (⁴)—Where are these gentlemen?
Come, bring me where they are.
                                          [*Exeunt.*

(³) *Apparition of a bloody Child.*

The idea of a " bloody *child*," and of his being more
potent than the armed head, and one of the *masters* of the
witches, is very dreadful. So is that of the child crowned,
with a tree in his hand. They impersonate, it is true,

certain results of the war, the destruction of Macduff's children, and the succession of Banquo's; but the imagination does not make these reflections at first; and the dreadfulness still remains, of potent demons speaking in the shapes of children.   .

(⁴) *But no more sights.*

What a world of horrors is in this little familiar phrase!

THE QUARREL OF OBERON AND TITANIA.

A FAIRY DRAMA.

I have ventured to give the extract this title, because it not only contains the whole story of the fairy part of the *Midsummer Night's Dream*, but by the omission of a few lines, and the transposition of one small passage (for which I beg the reader's indulgence), it actually forms a separate little play. It is nearly such in the greater play; and its isolation was easily, and not at all injuriously effected, by the separation of the Weaver from his brother mechanicals.

Enter OBERON *at one door with his train; and* TITANIA *at another with hers.*

Ober. Ill met by moonlight, proud Titania.
Tit. What, jealous Oberon! Fairies, skip hence;
I have forsworn his bed and company.
Ober. Tarry, rash wanton; am not I thy lord?
Tit. Then I must be thy lady; but I know
When thou hast stol'n away from fairy-land,

And in the shape of Corin sat all day
Playing on pipes of corn, and versing love
To amorous Phillida. Why art thou here,
Come from the furthest steep of India, (⁵)
But that, forsooth, the bouncing Amazon,
Your buskin'd mistress and your warrior love,
To Theseus must be wedded ; and you come
To give their bed joy and prosperity?
    Ober. How canst thou thus, for shame, Titania,
Glance at my credit with Hippolyta,
Knowing I know thy love to Theseus?
Didst thou not lead him through the glimmering night
From Perigenia, whom he ravished?
And make him with fair Æglé break his faith,
With Ariadne, and Antiopa?
    Tit. These are the forgeries of jealousy :
And never since the middle summer's spring,
Met we on hill, in dale, forest, or mead,
By pavèd fountain, or by rushy brook,
Or on the beachèd margent of the sea,
To dance our ringlets to the whistling wind,
But with thy brawls thou hast disturbed our sport.
Therefore the winds, piping to us in vain,
As in revenge, have suck'd up from the sea
Contagious fogs ; which falling on the land,
Have every pelting river made so proud,
That they have overborne their continents ;
The ox hath therefore stretch'd his yoke in vain,
The ploughman lost his sweat, and the green corn
Hath rotted, *ere his youth attain'd a beard :*
The fold stands empty in the drownèd field,
And crows are fatted with the murrain flock ;
The nine men's morris * is filled up with mud ;
And the quaint mazes in the wanton green,
For lack of tread, are undistinguishable ;
The *human mortals* want their winter here ;

---

* *Nine men's morris :* A rustic game, played with stones upon
lines cut in the ground.

No night is now with hymn or carol blest:
Therefore the moon, the governess of floods
Pale in her anger, washes all the air,
That rheumatic diseases do abound.—
And thorough this distemperature, we see
The seasons alter; *hoary-headed frosts*
Fall in the fresh lap of the crimson rose,
And on old Hyems' chin, and icy crown,
An odorous chaplet of sweet summer buds
Is, as in mockery, set. The spring, the summer,
The chilling autumn, angry winter, change
Their wonted liveries; and the mazèd world,
By their increase, now knows not which is which:
And this same progeny of evil comes
From our debate, from our dissension:
We are their parents and original.

 Ober. Do you amend it then: it lies in you:
Why should Titania cross her Oberon?
I do but beg a little changeling boy,
To be my henchman. *

 Tit.   Set your heart at rest;
The fairy land buys not the child of me.
His mother was a vot'ress of my order;
And, *in the spicèd Indian air,* by night,
Full often hath she gossip'd by my side;
And sat with me on Neptune's yellow sands,
Marking the embarkèd traders on the flood;
When we have laughed to see the sails conceive
And grow big-bellied with the wanton wind:
Which she, with pretty and with swimming gait,
Following (her womb then rich with my young squire)
Would imitate; and sail upon the land,
To fetch me trifles and return again,
As from a voyage, rich with merchandise.
But she, being mortal, of that boy did die;
And, for her sake, I do rear up her boy;
And, for her sake, I will not part with him.

 Ober. How long within this wood intend you stay?

---

* *Henchman:* Page.

Tit. Perchance till after Theseus' wedding-day.
If you will patiently dance in our round,
And see our moonlight revels, go with us ;
If not, shun me, and I will spare your haunts.
   Ober. Give me that boy, and I will go with thee.
   Tit. Not for thy fairy kingdom.—Fairies, away :
We shall chide downright, if I longer stay.
                [*Exeunt* TITANIA *and her train.*
   Ober. Well, go thy way: thou shalt not from this grove,
Till I torment thee for this injury.—
My gentle Puck, come hither. Thou remember'st
Since once I sat upon a promontory,
And heard a mermaid, on a dolphin's back,
Uttering such dulcet and harmonious breath,
That the rude sea grew civil at her song ;
And certain stars shot madly from their spheres,
To hear the sea-maid's music.
   Puck.   I remember.
   Ober. That very time I saw *(but thou couldst not),*
Flying between the cold moon and the earth,
Cupid all arm'd : a certain aim he took
At a fair vestal, thronèd by the west ; *
And loos'd his love-shaft smartly from his bow,
As it should pierce a hundred thousand hearts :
But I might see young Cupid's fiery shaft
Quench'd in the chaste beams of the wat'ry moon :
And the imperial votaress pass'd on
In maiden meditation, fancy free.
Yet mark'd I where the bolt of Cupid fell :
It fell upon a little western flower,—
Before, milk-white ; now purple with love's wound,
And maidens call it Love-in-idleness. †
Fetch me that flower : the herb I show'd thee once:

---

* *At a fair vestal thronèd by the west.*—An allusion to Queen
Elizabeth. See in the Rev. Mr. Halpin's remarks on this passage,
published by the Shakspeare Society, a most ingenious speculation
on the hidden meaning of it, as a bit of secret court history.

† *Love-in-idleness :* The heart's-ease.

The juice of it on sleeping eyelids laid,
Will make or man or woman madly dote
Upon the next live creature that it sees.
Fetch me this herb : and be thou here again,
Ere the leviathan can swim a league.
    *Puck. I'll put a girdle round about the earth
In forty minutes.*

                             [Exit PUCK.
    Ober.   Having once this juice,
I'll watch Titania when she is asleep,
And drop the liquor of it in her eyes :
The next thing then she waking looks upon.
(Be it on lion, bear, or wolf, or bull,
On meddling monkey, or on busy ape,)
She shall pursue it with *the soul of love.*
And ere I take this charm off from her sight,
(As I can take it with another herb,)
I'll make her render up her page to me.

                          [Exit OBERON.

Another part of the Wood.

Enter TITANIA *and her train.*

    Tit. Come, now a roundel, and a fairy song :
Then, *for the third part of a minute,* hence ;
*Some to kill cankers in the musk-rose buds ;
Some, war with reremice for their leathern wings,
To make my small elves' coats ;* and some, keep back
The clamorous owl, *that nightly hoots, and wonders
At our quaint spirits :* Sing me now asleep ;
Then to your offices, and let me rest.

SONG.

    1st Fai. You spotted snakes, with double tongue,
          Thorny hedge-hogs, be not seen.
      Newts and blind-worms, do no wrong ;
          Come not near our fairy queen.
    Chorus. Philomel, with melody,
          Sing in our sweet lullaby :
      Lulla, lulla, lullaby : lulla, lulla, lullaby ;

Never harm, nor spell, nor charm,
  Come our lovely lady nigh ;
  So, good night—with lullaby.
2nd Fai. Weaving spiders, come not here ;
  Hence, you long-legged spinners, hence ;
  Beetles black, approach not near ;
  Worm, nor snail, do no offence.
Chorus. Philomel, with melody, &c.
1st Fai. Hence, away ; now all is well :
  One, aloof, stand sentinel.
      [*Exeunt* FAIRIES. TITANIA *sleeps.*

Enter OBERON.

Ober. What thou seest when thou dost wake,
      [*Squeezes the flower on* TITANIA'S *eyelids.*
  Do it for thy true love take ;
  Love and languish for his sake ;
  Be it ounce, or cat, or bear,
  Pard, or boar with bristled hair,
  In thy eye that shall appear
  When thou wak'st, it is thy dear ;
  Wake, when some vile thing is near.
          [*Exit.*

Enter BOTTOM, *singing ;* PUCK *having clapt on him an ass's head.*

SONG.

Bot. The ousel-cock, so black of hue,
  With orange-tawny bill,
  The throstle with his note so true,
  The wren with little quill—

Tit. *What angel wakes me from my flowery bed ?*   [*Wakes.*
  I pray thee, gentle mortal, sing again ;
  Mine ear is much enamour'd of thy note ;
  So is mine eye enthrallèd to thy shape ;
  And thy *fair virtue's* force perforce doth move me,
  On the first view, to say, to swear, I love thee.
Bot. Methinks, mistress, you should have little reason for that;
and yet, to say the truth, reason and love keep little company together

now-a-days. The more the pity that some honest neighbours will not make them friends. Nay, I can gleek * upon occasion.

Tit. Thou art as wise as thou art beautiful.

Bot. Not so, neither; but if I had wit enough to get out of this wood, I have enough to serve mine own turn.

Tit. Out of this wood do not desire to go ;
Thou shalt remain here, whether thou wilt or no.
I am a spirit of no common rate ;
The summer still doth tend upon my state, ·
And I do love thee; therefore go with me;
I'll give thee fairies to attend on thee ;
And they shall fetch thee jewels from the deep,
And sing, while thou on pressèd flowers dost sleep:
And I will purge thy mortal grossness so,
That thou shalt like an airy spirit go.—
Peas-blossom! Cobweb! Moth! and Mustard-seed!

Enter four Fairies.

1st *Fai.* Ready.
2nd *Fai.*   And I.
3rd *Fai.*   And I.
4th *Fai.*   Where shall we go ?

Tit. Be kind and courteous to this gentleman ;
Hop in his walks, and gambol in his eyes :
Feed him with apricots and dewberries,
With purple grapes, green figs, and mulberries :
The honey-bags steal from the humble-bees,
And for night-tapers crop their waxen thighs,
And light them at the fiery glow-worm's eyes,
To have my love to bed, and to arise :
And pluck the wings from painted butterflies,
To fan the moonbeams from his sleeping eyes :
Nod to him, elves, and do him courtesies.

1st. *Fai.* Hail, mortal !
2nd *Fai.* Hail !
3rd *Fai.* Hail !
4th *Fai.* Hail !

---

* *Gleek :* Banter,

Bot. I cry your worship's mercy, heartily.—I beseech your worship's name.

Cob. Cobweb.

Bot. I shall desire you of more acquaintance, good Master Cobweb. *If I cut my finger I shall make bold with you.* Your name, honest gentleman?

Peas. Peas-blossom.

Bot. I pray you commend me to Mistress Squash, your mother, and to Master Peascod, your father. Good Master Peas-blossom, I shall desire you of more acquaintance too. Your name, I beseech you, sir?

Mus. Mustard-seed.

Bot. Good Master Mustard-seed, I know your patience well. *That same cowardly, giant-like ox-beef hath devoured many a gentleman of your house.* I promise you your kindred hath made my eyes water ere now. I desire you more acquaintance, good Master Mustard-seed.

OBERON *enters unseen.*

Tit. Come, sit thee down upon this flowery bed,
While I thy *amiable cheeks* do coy,
And stick musk-roses in thy sleek smooth head,
And kiss thy fair large ears, my gentle joy.

Bot. Where's Peas-blossom?

Peas. Ready.

Bot. Scratch my head, Peas-blossom. Where's Monsieur Cobweb?

Cob. Ready.

Bot. Monsieur Cobweb, good monsieur, get your weapons in your hand, and kill me *a red-hipped humble-bee on the top of a thistle;* and, good monsieur, bring me the honey-bag. *Do not fret yourself too much in the action, monsieur;* and, good monsieur, have a care the honey-bag break not; *I would be loth to have you overflown with a honey-bag,* signior.—Where's Monsieur Mustard-seed?

Must. Ready.

Bot. Give me your neif,* Monsieur Mustard-seed. Pray you, leave your courtesy, good monsieur.

Must. What's your will?

---

* *Neif:* Fist.

Bot. Nothing, good monsieur, but to help Cavalero Cobweb to scratch. I must to the barber's, monsieur; *for methinks I am marvellous hairy about the face;* and I am such a tender ass, if my hair do but tickle me I must scratch.

Tit. What, wilt thou hear some music, my sweet love?

Bot. I have a reasonable good ear in music: let us have *the tongs and the bones.*

Tit. Or say, sweet love, what thou desirest to eat.

Bot. Truly a peck of provender. I could munch your *good dry oats.* Methinks I have a great desire to a bottle of hay. Good hay, sweet hay, hath no fellow.

Tit. I have a venturous fairy, that shall seek the squirrel's hoard, and fetch thee new nuts.

Bot. I had rather have a handful or two of dried peas:—but, I pray you, let none of your people stir me; I have an exposition of sleep come upon me.

Tit. Sleep thou, and I will wind thee in my arms.
Fairies, begone, and be all ways away.
So doth the woodbine the sweet honeysuckle
Gently entwist;—the female ivy so
Enrings *the barky fingers* of the elm.
Oh, how I love thee! How I dote on thee!
[*They sleep.*

OBERON *advances. Enter* PUCK.

Ober. Welcome, good Robin. Seest thou this sweet sight?
Her dotage now I do begin to pity:
For meeting her of late behind the wood,
Seeking sweet savours for this hateful fool,
I did upbraid her, and fall out with her:
For she his hairy temples then had rounded
With coronet of fresh and fragrant flowers;
And that same dew, which sometime on the buds
Was wont to swell, like round and orient pearls,
Stood now within the pretty flowrets' eyes,
Like tears that did their own disgrace bewail.
When I had, at my pleasure, taunted her,
And she, in mild tones, begg'd my patience,
I then did ask of her her changeling child;
Which straight she gave me, and her fairy sent

To bear him to my bower in fairy land.
And now I have the boy, I will undo
This hateful imperfection of her eyes.
And, gentle Puck, take this transformèd scalp
From off the head of this Athenian swain;
That he awaking when the others do,
May all to Athens back again repair,
And think no more of this night's accidents,
*But as the fierce vexation of a dream.**
But first, I will release the fairy queen.
    Be as thou wert wont to be;
                    [Touching her eyes with an herb.
    See as thou wert wont to see;
    Dian's bud o'er Cupid's flower
    Hath such force and blessed power.
Now, my Titania; wake you, my sweet queen.
    Tit. My Oberon! what visions have I seen!
Methought I was enamoured of an ass.
    Ober. There lies your love.
    Tit.   How came these things to pass?
O, how mine eyes do loath his visage now!
    Ober. Silence a while. Robin, take off this head,—·
Titania, music call; and strike more dead
Than common sleep, of all these five the sense.
    Tit. Music! ho! music! such as charmeth sleep.
    Puck. Now, when thou wak'st, with thine own fool's eyes peep.
    Ober. Sound, music! [*Still music.*] Come, my queen, take
        hands with me,
And rock the ground whereon these sleepers be.
Now thou and I are new in amity,
And will, to-morrow midnight, solemnly
Dance in Duke Theseus' house triumphantly,
And bless it to all fair posterity:
There shall the pairs of faithful lovers be
Wedded, with Theseus, all in jollity.
    Puck. Fairy king, attend and mark;
        I do hear the morning lark.

---

* *But as the fierce vexation of a dream :* This fine stray verse
comes looking in among the rest like a stern face through flowers.

Ober. Then, my queen, in silence sad,*
Trip we after the night's shade.
We the globe can compass soon,
Swifter than the wandering moon.
  Tit. Come, my lord, and in our flight
Tell me how it came, this night,
That I sleeping here was found
With these mortals on the ground.   [*Exeunt.*
                                    [*Horns sound within.*]

────── ·

(⁵) *Come from the furthest steep of India.*

Shakspeare understood the charm of *remoteness* in
poetry, as he did everything else.   Oberon has been
dancing on the sunny steeps looking towards Cathay,
where the

────── Chineses drive
Their cany waggons light.

THE BRIDAL HOUSE BLESSED BY THE FAIRIES.

Enter PUCK.

Puck. Now the hungry lion roars, (⁶)
  And the wolf behowls the moon,
While the heavy ploughman snores,
  All with weary task fordone.
Now the wasted brands do glow,
  Whilst the scritch-owl, scritching loud,
Puts the wretch, that lies in woe,
In remembrance of a shroud.

─────────

* *Sad .* Grave, serious (not melancholy).

Now it is the time of night
That the graves, all gaping wide,
Every one lets forth his sprite,
In the churchway paths to glide;
And we fairies, that do run ·
By the triple Hecate's team,
From the presence of the sun,
Following darkness like a dream,
Now are frolic; not a mouse
Shall disturb this hallow'd house;
I am sent, with broom before,
To sweep the dust behind the door.

Enter OBERON *and* TITANIA, *with their train.*

Ober. Through this house give glimmering light,
By the dead and drowsy fire:
Every elf and fairy sprite,
Hop as light as birds from brier;
And this ditty after me
Sing and dance it trippingly.
Tita. First rehearse this song by rote:
To each word a warbling note,
Hand in hand, with fairy grace,
Will we sing and bless this place.

SONG AND DANCE.

Ober. Now, until the break of day,
Through this house each fairy stray,
To the best bride-bed will we,
Which by us shall blessed be;
And the issue there create
Ever shall be fortunate.
So shall all the couples three
Ever true in loving be;
And the blots of Nature's hand
Shall not in their issue stand:
Never mole, hare-lip, nor scar,
Nor mark prodigious, such as are
Despisèd in nativity,
Shall upon their children be.

11

With this field-dew consecrate,
Every fairy take his gait;
And each several chamber bless
Through this palace with sweet peace
E'er shall it in safety rest,
And the owner of it blest.
        Trip away;
        Make no stay;
Meet me all by break of day.

(⁶) *Now the hungry lion roars.*

Upon the songs of Puck and Oberon, Coleridge exclaims, "Very Anacreon in perfectness, proportion, and spotaneity! So far it is Greek; but then add, Oh! what wealth, what wild ranging, and yet what compression and condensation of English fancy! In truth, there is nothing in Anacreon more perfect than these thirty lines, or half so rich and imaginative. They form a speckless diamond." —*Literary Remains*, vol. ii. p. 114.

LOVERS AND MUSIC.

LORENZO *and* JESSICA, *awaiting the return home of* PORTIA *and* NERISSA, *discourse of music, and then welcome with it the bride and her attendant.*

Lor. The moon shines bright. *In such a night as this,* (⁷)
When the sweet wind did gently kiss the trees,
And they did make no noise—in such a night
Troilus, methinks, mounted the Trojan walls,
And sigh'd his soul towards the Grecian tents, (⁸)
Where Cressid lay that night.

Jes.   *In such a night*
Did Thisbe fearfully o'ertrip the dew,
And saw the lion's shadow ere himself, (⁹)
And ran dismay'd away.
    Lor.   *In such a night*
Stood Dido with a willow in her hand (¹⁰)
Upon the wild sea-banks, and wav'd her **love**
To come again to Carthage.
    Jes.   *In such a night*
Medea gather'd the enchanted herbs (¹¹)
That did renew old Æson.
    Lor.   *In such a night*
Did Jessica steal from the wealthy Jew;
And with an unthrift love did run from Venice,
As far as Belmont.
    Jes.   *And in such a night*
Did young Lorenzo swear he lov'd her well;
Stealing her soul with many vows of faith,
And ne'er a true one.
    Lor.   *And in such a night*
Did pretty Jessica, like a little shrew,
Slander her love, *and he forgave it her.*
    Jes. I would out-night you, did nobody come:
But, hark, I hear the footing of a man.

Enter STEPHANO.

    Lor. Who comes so fast in silence of the night?
    Steph. A friend.
    Lor. A friend! what friend? your name, I pray you, friend?
    Steph. Stephano is my name: and I bring word
My mistress will, before the break of day,
Be here at Belmont: she doth stray about
By holy crosses, where she kneels and prays
For happy wedlock hours.
    Lor. Who comes with her?
    Steph. None but a holy hermit and her maid.
    Lor. Sweet soul, let's in, and there expect their coming.
And yet no matter:—why should we go in?

My friend Stephàno, signify, I pray you,
Within the house, your mistress is at hand;
And bring your music forth into the air.—

       [*Exit* STEPHANO.

How sweet the moonlight sleeps upon this bank !
Here will we sit, and let the sounds of music
Creep into our ears; soft stillness, and the night,
Become the touches of sweet harmony.
Sit, Jessica: Look, how the floor of heaven
Is thick inlaid with patines * of bright gold ;
There's not the smallest orb which thou behold'st, (¹²)
But in his motion *like an angel sings,*
Still quiring to the young-eyed cherubims :
Such harmony is in immortal souls ;
But, whilst this muddy vesture of decay
Doth grossly close us in, we cannot hear it.

Enter MUSICIANS.

Come, ho ! and wake Diana with a hymn ;
With sweetest touches pierce your mistress' ear,
And draw her home with music.   [*Music.*
 Jes. I am never merry when I hear sweet music.
 Lor. The reason is, your spirits are attentive :
For do but note a wild and wanton herd,
A race of youthful and unhandled colts,
Fetching mad bounds,—bellowing and neighing loud,
Which is the hot condition of their blood ;
If they but hear, perchance, a trumpet sound,
Or any air of music touch their ears,
You shall perceive them make a mutual stand—
Their savage eyes turned to a modest gaze
By the sweet power of music. Therefore the poet
Did feign that Orpheus drew trees, stones, and floods,

---

 * *Patines* (Pátine, Paténe, *Ital.*) have been generally understood
to mean plates of gold or silver used in the Catholic service. A new
and interesting commentator, however (the Rev. Mr. Hunter), is of
opinion that the proper word is *patterns.*

Since nought so stockish, hard, and full of rage,
But music for the time doth change his nature.
The man that hath no music in himself,
Nor is not mov'd with concord of sweet sounds,
Is fit for treasons, stratagems, and spoils;
The motions of his spirit are dull as night,
And his affections dark as Erebus:
Let no such man be trusted.—Mark the music.

Enter PORTIA *and* NERISSA, *at a distance.*

Por. That light we see is burning in my hall;
How far that little candle throws its beams!
So shines a good deed in a naughty world.
Ner. When the moon shone, we did not see the candle.
Por. So doth the greater glory dim the less;
A substitute shines brightly as a king,
Until a king be by; *and then his state*
Empties itself, as doth an inland brook
Into the main of waters. Music! hark!
Ner. It is your music, madam, of the house.
Por. Nothing is good, I see, without respect;
Methinks it sounds much sweeter than by day.
Ner. Silence bestows that virtue on it, madam.
Por. The crow doth sing as sweetly as the lark,
When neither is attended; and, I think,
The nightingale, if she should sing by day,
When every goose is cackling, would be thought
No better a musician than the wren.
How many things by season season'd are
To their right praise, and true perfection!
Peace, hoa! the moon sleeps with Endymion,
And would not be awak'd!   [*Music ceases.*
Lor.   That is the voice,
Or I am much deceiv'd, of Portia.
Por. He knows me, as the blind man knows the cuckoo
By the bad voice.
Lor.   Dear lady, welcome home. ([13])

(⁷) *In such a night as this, &c.*

All the stories here alluded to,—Troilus and Cressida,
Pyramus and Thisbe, Dido and Æneas, Jason and Medea,
are in Chaucer's *Legends of Good Women.* It is pleasant
to see our great poet so full of his predecessor. He cannot
help, however, inventing particulars not to be found in his
original.

(⁸) *And sigh'd his soul, &c.*

" The day go'th fast, *and after that came eve,*
  And yet came not Troilus to Crescid :
  He looketh forth by hedge, by tree, by greve (grove),
  And far his head over the wall he laid."
  —Clarke's *Chaucer,* vol. ii. p. 151.

(⁹) *And saw the lion's shadow.*

Thisbe in Chaucer does not see the shadow before she
sees the beast (a fine idea !) ; nor does she in Ovid. In
both poets, it is a lioness seen by moonlight.

" With bloody mouth, of strangling of a beast."
Cæde leæna boum spumantes oblita rictus.
  —*Metam.* lib. iv. v. 97.

(¹⁰) *Stood Dido with a willow in her hand.*

The willow, a symbol of being forsaken, is not in
Chaucer. It looks as if Shakspeare had seen it in a
picture, where it would be more necessary than in a
poem.

(¹¹) *Medea gather'd the enchanted herbs.*

Shakspeare has here gone from Chaucer to Gower.
Warton, in his *Observations on the Faerie Queene,* vol. i.

p. 361, edit. 1807, has noticed a passage in Gower's story, full of imagination. The poet is speaking of Medea going out upon the business noticed by Shakspeare:

> Thus it fell upon a night,
> When there was nought but starrie light,
> She was vanish'd right as she list,
> That no wight but herself wist,
> And that was at midnight tide.—.
> *The world was still on every side.*
> *With open head and foot all bare ;*
> *Her hair too spread, she gan to fare ;*
> Upon her clothés girt she was,
> *And speechless, upon the grass,*
> *Shè glode* forth, as an adder doth.*

(¹²) *There's not the smallest orb.*

The " warbler of wood-notes wild " has here manifestly joined with Plato and other learned spirits to suggest to Milton his own account of the Music of the Spheres, which every reader of taste, I think, must agree with Mr. Knight in thinking "less perfect in sentiment and harmony."—*Pictorial Shakspeare*, vol. ii. p. 448. The best thing in it is what is observed by Warton : that the listening to the spheres is the recreation of the Genius of the Wood (the speaker) after his day's duty, " when the world is locked up in sleep and silence."

> Then listen I
> To the celestial Sirens' harmony,
> That sit upon the nine infolded spheres, .
> And sing to those that hold the vital shears,

---

* *Glode*, is glided. If Chaucer's contemporary had written often thus, his name would have been as famous.

And turn the adamantine spindle round,
On which the fates of gods and men is wound.
Such sweet compulsion doth in music lie
To lull the daughters of Necessity,
And keep unsteady Nature in her law,
And the low world in measur'd motion draw
After the heavenly tune, which none can hear
Of human mould, with gross unpurged ear.

Arcades, v. 62.

The best account I remember to have read of the Music of the Spheres is in the History of Music by Hawkins.

(¹³) *Dear lady, welcome home.*

Never was a sweeter or more fitting and bridal elegance than in the whole of this scene, in which gladness and seriousness prettily struggle, each alternately yielding predominance to the other. The lovers are at once in heaven and earth. The new bride is "drawn home" with the soul of love in the shape of music; and to keep her giddy spirits down, she preached that little womanly sermon upon a good deed shining in a "*naughty* world." The whole play is, in one sense of the word, the most picturesque in feeling of all Shakspeare's. The sharp and malignant beard of the Jew (himself not unreconciled to us by the affections) comes harmlessly against the soft cheek of love.

ANTONY AND THE CLOUDS.

Ant. Eros, thou yet behold'st me?
Eros. Ay, noble lord.
Ant. Sometimes we see a cloud that's dragonish :
A vapour sometime like a bear, or lion,
A tower'd citadel, a pendent rock,
A forked mountain, *or blue promontory,*
With trees upon't that nod unto the world,
And mock our eyes with air ; thou hast seen these signs;
They are *black Vesper's pageants.*
Eros. Ay, my lord.
Ant. That which is now a horse, even with a thought
The rack *dislimns ;* and makes it indistinct,
As water is in water.
Eros. It does, my lord.
Ant. My good knave, Eros, now thy captain is
Even such a body:—here I am,—Antony—
Yet cannot hold this visible shape.

YOUNG WARRIORS.

Hotspur. My cousin Vernon ! welcome, by my soul !
Sir Richard Vernon. Pray God, my news be worth a welcome,
    lord.
The Earl of Westmoreland, seven thousand strong,
Is marching hitherwards ; with him, Prince John.
Hot. No harm : What more?
Ver. And further, I have learn'd,–
The king himself in person is set forth,
Or hitherwards intended speedily,
With strong and mighty preparation.
Hot. He shall be welcome too. Where is his son,
The nimble-footed mad-cap Prince of Wales,
And his comrades, *that daff'd the world aside,*
And bid it pass ?

Ver. All furnish'd, all in arms,
All plum'd like estridges that wing the wind :
Bated like eagles having lately bath'd ;
Glittering in golden coats, like images ;
As full of spirit as the month of May
And gorgeous as the sun at Midsummer ;
Wanton as youthful goats, wild as young bulls.
I saw young Harry,—with his beaver on,
His cuisses on his thighs, gallantly arm'd,—
Rise from the ground like feather'd Mercury,
And vaulted with such ease into his seat,
As if an angel dropp'd down from the clouds,
To turn and wind a fiery Pegasus,
And witch the world with noble horsemanship.,

Hot. No more, no more ; worse than the sun in March,
This praise doth nourish agues.   Let them come ;
They come like sacrifices in their trim,
And to the fire-eyed maid of smoky war,
All hot, and bleeding, will we offer them ;
The mailèd Mars shall on his altar sit,
Up to the ears in blood.   I am on fire,
To hear this rich reprisal is so nigh,
And yet not ours :—Come, let me take my horse,
Who is to bear me, like a thunder-bolt,
Against the bosom of the Prince of Wales ;
Harry to Harry shall, hot (query not ?) horse to horse, ([14])
Meet, and ne'er part, till one drop down a corse.

––––––

([14]) *Harry to Harry shall, hot horse to horse.*

I cannot help thinking that the word *hot* in this line
ought to be *not*.   "*Hot* horse to horse" is not a very
obvious mode of speech, and it is too obvious an image.
The horses undoubtedly would be hot enough.   But does
not Hotspur mean to say that the usual shock of horses
will not be sufficient for the extremity of his encounter

with the Prince of Wales?—their own bodies are to be dashed together, and not merely the horses :

Harry to *Harry* shall, *not* horse to horse:

so closely does he intend that their combat shall *hug.*

IMOGEN IN BED.

(FROM CYMBELINE.)

(*Iachimo, dared by Imogen's husband to make trial of her fidelity, hides in her chamber in order to bring away pretended proofs against it.*)

Imo. (*reading in bed.*) Who's there? my woman Helen?
Lady. Please you, madam.
Imo. What hour is it?
Lady. Almost midnight, madam.
Imo. I have read three hours then : mine eyes are weak
Fold down the leaf where I have left :—to bed :
Take not away the taper; leave it burning;
And if thou canst awake by four o' the clock,
I prithee, call me.   Sleep hath seized me wholly.
                              [*Exit Lady.*
To your protection I commend me, gods !
*From fairies, and the tempters of the night,
Guard me, I beseech ye !*
                    [*Sleeps.* IACHIMO, *from the trunk.*
   Iach. The crickets sing, and man's o'er-labour'd sense
Repairs itself by rest: our Tarquin thus
Did softly press the rushes, ere he waken'd
The chastity he wounded.—*Cytherea,
How bravely thou becom'st thy bed ! fresh lily !*
And whiter than the sheets ! that I might touch!
But kiss ; one kiss !—Rubies unparagon'd,
How dearly they do't—*'Tis her breathing that*

Perfumes the chamber thus :—the flame o' the taper
Bows towards her ; and would under-peep her lids,
To see the enclosed lights, now canopied
Under those windows, white and azure, lac'd
With blue of heaven's own tint. But my design !
To note the chamber.—I will write all down;
Such and such pictures :—there the window : such
The adornment of her bed :—the arras, figures,
Why, such and such :—And the contents o' the story,—
Ah, but some natural notes about her body
Above ten thousand meaner moveables
Would testify, to enrich mine inventory.
O sleep, thou ape of Death, lie dull upon her !
And be her sense but as a monument,
Thus in a chapel lying !—Come off, come off:

                     [Takes off her bracelet.

As slippery as the Gordian knot was hard !
'Tis mine, and this will witness outwardly,
As strongly as the conscience does within,
To the madding of her lord. *On her left breast*
A mole cinque-spotted, like the crimson drops
I' the bottom of a cowslip. Here's a voucher,
Stronger than ever law could make : this secret
Will force him think I have pick'd the lock, and ta'en
The treasure of her honour. No more.—To what end ?
Why should I write this down that's riveted,
Screw'd, to my memory ? She hath been reading late
The tale of Tereus: here the leaf's turn'd down,
Where Philomel gave up.—I have enough :—
To the trunk again, and shut the spring of it.
Swift, swift, you dragons of the night, that dawning
May bare the raven's eye ! I lodge in fear;
Though this a heavenly angel, hell is here.

                     [Clock strikes.

One, two, three,—Time, time !

           [Goes into the trunk. The scene closes.

BEN JONSON.

BORN, 1574,—DIED, 1637.

IF Ben Jonson had not tried to do half what he did, he
would have had a greater fame. His will and ambition
hurt him, as they always hurt genius when set in front of
it. Lasting reputation of power is only to be obtained by
power itself; and this, in poetry, is the result not so
much, if at all, of the love of the power, as of the power
of love,—the love of truth and beauty,—great and potent
things they,—not the love of self, which is generally a
very little thing. The "supposed rugged old bard," not-
withstanding his huffing and arrogance, had elegance, feel-
ing, imagination, great fancy; but by straining to make
them all greater than they were, bringing in the ancients
to help him, and aiming to include the lowest farce (per-
haps by way of outdoing the universality of Shakspeare),
he became as gross in his pretensions as drink had made
him in person. His jealous irritability and assumption
tired out the gentlest and most generous of his contempo-
raries—men who otherwise really liked him (and he them),
—Decker for one; and he has ended in appearing to

posterity rather the usurper than the owner of a true renown. He made such a fuss with his learning, that he is now suspected to have had nothing else. Hazlitt himself cannot give him credit for comic genius, so grave and all-in-all does his pedantry appear to that critic,—an erroneous judgment, as it seems to me,—who cannot help thinking, that what altogether made Ben what he was projected his ultra-jovial person rather towards comedy than tragedy; and as a proof of this, his tragedies are all borrowed, but his comedies his own. *Twelfth Night* and other plays of Shakspeare preceded and surpassed him in his boasted " humour ; " but his *Alchemist,* and especially his *Volpone,* seem to me at the head of all severer English comedy. The latter is a masterpiece of plot and treatment. Ben's fancy, a power tending also rather to the comic than tragic, was in far greater measure than his imagination ; and their strongest united efforts, as in the *Witches' Meeting,* and the luxurious anticipations of Sir Epicure Mammon, produce a smiling as well as a serious admiration. The three happiest of all his short effusions (two of which are in this volume) are the *Epitaph on Lady Pembroke,* the address to *Cynthia* (both of which are serious indeed, but not tragic), and the *Catch of the Satyrs,* which is unique for its wild and melodious mixture of the comic and the poetic. His huge farces, to be sure (such as *Bartholomew Fair*), are execrable. They seem to talk for talking sake, like drunkards. And though his famous verses, beginning, " Still to be neat, still to be drest," are elegantly worded, I never could admire them. There is a coarseness implied in their very refinement.

After all, perhaps it is idle to wish a writer had been otherwise than he was, especially if he is an original in his way, and worthy of admiration. His faults he may have been unable to mend, and they may not have been without their use, even to his merits. If Ben had not been Ben, Sir Epicure Mammon might not have talked in so high a tone. We should have missed, perhaps, something of the excess and altitude of his expectations—of his

> Gums of Paradise and *eastern air.*

Let it not be omitted, that Milton went to the masques and odes of Ben Jonson for some of the elegancies even of his dignified muse. See Warton's edition of his Minor Poems, *passim.* Our extracts shall commence with one of these odes, combining classic elegance with a tone of modern feeling, and a music like a serenade.

TO CYNTHIA;—THE MOON.

Queen and Huntress, chaste and fair,
    Now the sun is laid asleep,
Seated in thy silver chair,
    State in wonted manner keep,
    Hesperus entreats thy light,
    Goddess, excellently bright.

Earth, let not thy envious shade
    Dare itself to interpose;
Cynthia's shining orb was made
    Heav'n to *clear,* when day did *close.*
    Bless us then with wishèd sight,
    Goddess, excellently bright.

Lay thy bow of pearl apart,
   And thy crystal shining quiver ,
Give unto the flying hart
   Space to breathe, how short soever :
   Thou, that mak'st *a day of night*,
Goddess, excellently bright.

THE LOVE-MAKING OF LUXURY.

Volpone makes love to Celia

Volp.   See, behold,
What thou art queen of; not in expectation,
As I feed others, but possess'd and crown'd.
See here, a rope of pearl; and each, more orient
Than that the brave Ægyptian queen caroused:
Dissolve and drink them.   See, a carbuncle,
May put out both the eyes of our St. Mark;
A diamond would have bought Lolia Paulina,
When she came in like star-light, hid with jewels,
That were the spoils of provinces ; take these
And wear and lose them; yet remains an ear-ring
To purchase them again, and this whole state.
A gem but worth a private patrimony,
Is nothing : we will eat such at a meal.
The heads of parrots, tongues of nightingales,
The brains of peacocks, and of estriches,
Shall be our food : and, *could we get the phœnix,*
Though nature lost her kind, she were our dish.
   Cel. Good sir, these things might move a mind affected
With such delights ; but I, whose innocence
Is all I can think wealthy, or worth th' enjoying,
And which, once lost, I have nought to lose beyond it,
Cannot be taken with these sensual baits :
If you have conscience——
   Volp.   'Tis the beggar's virtue:
If thou had wisdom, hear me, Celia.

Thy baths shall be the juice of July flowers,
Spirit of roses and of violets,
The milk of unicorns, and panthers' breath
Gather'd in bags, and mixt with Cretan wines.
Our drink shall be preparèd gold and amber ;
Which we will take until my roof whirl round
With the vertigo : and my dwarf shall dance,
My eunuch sing, my fool make up the antic ;
Whilst we, in changèd shapes, act Ovid's tales :
Thou, like Europa now, and I like Jove ;
Then I like Mars, and thou like Erycine ;
So of the rest, till we have quite run through
And wearied all the fables of the gods.

TOWERING SENSUALITY.

Sir Epicure Mammon, expecting to obtain the Philosopher's Stone,
riots in the anticipation of enjoyment. ·

Enter MAMMON *and* SURLY.

Mam. Come on, sir. Now, you set your foot on shore
In *Novo Orbe :* here's the rich Peru :
And there within, sir, are the golden mines,
Great Solomon's Ophir ! *he was sailing to 't*
Three years ; but we have reached it in ten months.
This is the day wherein, to all my friends,
I will pronounce the happy words, BE RICH.—
* * * *
Where is my Subtle there ? Within !

Enter FACE.

How now ?
Do we succeed ? Is our day come ? and holds it ?
Face. The evening will set red upon you, sir ;
You have colour for it, crimson : the red ferment
Has done his office : three hours hence prepare you
To see projection.

12

Mam. Pertinax, my Surly,
Again I say to thee, aloud, BE RICH.
This day thou shalt have ingots ; *and to-morrow*
Give lords the affront.—Is it, my Zephyrus, right?—
    *   *   *   *
Thou'rt sure thou saw'st it blood ?
    Face. Both blood and spirit, sir.
    Mam. I will have all my beds blown up, not stuff'd :
Down is too hard.
    *   *   *   *
           My mists
I'll have of perfume, vapoured 'bout the room
To lose ourselves in ; and my baths, like pits,
To fall into : from whence we will come forth
And roll us dry in gossamer and roses.
Is it arriv'd at ruby ?
    *   *   *   *
           And my flatterers
Shall be the pure and *gravest of divines.*—
    *   *   *   *
And they shall fan me with ten estrich tails
Apiece, made in a plume to gather wind.
We will be brave, Puffe, now we have the med'cine.
My meat shall all come in in Indian shells,
Dishes of agate, set in gold, and studded
With emeralds, sapphires, hyacinths, and rubies.
The tongues of carps, dormice, and camels' heels,
Boil'd in the spirit of sol *and dissolv'd pearl,*
Apicius' diet 'gainst the epilepsy.
And I will eat these broths with spoons of amber,
Headed with diamond and carbuncle.
My foot-boy shall eat pheasants, calver'd salmons,
Knots, godwits, lampreys : I myself will have
The beards of barbels serv'd instead of salads ;
Oil'd mushrooms ; and the swelling, unctuous paps
Of a fat pregnant sow, newly cut off,
Drest with an exquisite and poignant sauce,
For which I'll say unto my cook, " There's gold ;
Go forth, and be a knight."
    Face.   **Sir, I'll go look**
A little, how it heightens.   [*Exit* FACE.

Mam.   Do.—My shirts
I'll have of taffeta-sarsnet, soft and light
As cobwebs; and for all my other raiment,
It shall be such as might provoke the Persian,
Were he to teach the world riot anew:
My gloves of fishes and birds' skins, perfum'd
With gums of paradise and eastern air.
    Sur. And do you think to have the stone with this?
    Mam. No; I do think t' have all this with the stone !
    Sur. Why, I have heard he must be *homo frugi*,
A pious, holy, and religious man,
One free from mortal sin, a very virgin.
    Mam. That makes it, sir; he *is* so; BUT I BUY IT.

THE WITCH.

From the Pastoral Fragment, entitled " The Sad Shepherd."

    Alken.   Know ye the witch's dell ?
    Scathlock. No more than I do know the walks of hell.
    Alken. Within a gloomy dimble she doth dwell,
Down in a pit o'ergrown with brakes and briers,
Close by the ruins of a shaken abbey,
Torn with an earthquake down unto the ground,—
'Mongst graves and grots, near an old charnel-house,
Where you shall find her sitting in her form,
As fearful and melancholic as that
She is about; with caterpillars' kells,
And knotty cobwebs, rounded in with spells.
Then she steals forth to relief in the fogs,
And rotten mists, upon the fens and bogs,
Down to the drownèd lands of Lincolnshire.
To make ewes cast their lambs, swine eat their farrow,
And housewives' tun not work, nor the milk churn !
Writhe children's wrists, and suck their breath in sleep,
Get vials of their blood ! and where the sea

Casts up his slimy ooze, search for a weed
To open locks with, and to rivet charms,
Planted about her in the wicked feat
Of all her mischiefs ; which are manifold.

    John. I wonder such a story could be told
Of her dire deeds.

    George. I thought a witch's banks
Had inclosed nothing but the merry pranks
Of some old woman.

    Scarlet.   Yes, her malice more.

    Scath. ·As it would quickly appear had we the store
Of his collects.

    George.   Ay, this good learned man
Can speak her right.

    Scar. He knows her shifts and haunts——

    Alken. And all her wiles and turns. The venom'd plants
Wherewith she kills ! where the sad mandrake grows,
Whose groans are deathful ; and dead-numbing night-
    shade,
The stupefying hemlock, adder's tongue,
And martagan : the shrieks of luckless owls
We hear, *and croaking night-crows in the air !*
Green-bellied snakes, blue fire-drakes in the sky,
And giddy flitter-mice with leather wings !
The scaly beetles, with their habergeons,
That make a humming murmur as they fly !
There in the stocks of trees *white fairies dwell,*
And span-long elves that dance about a pool,
With each a little changeling in their arms !
The airy spirits play with falling stars,
And mount the spheres of fire to kiss the moon !
While she sits reading by the glow-worm's light,
Or rotten wood, o'er which the worm hath crept,
The baneful schedule of her nocent charms.

A MEETING OF WITCHES,

FOR THE PURPOSE OF DOING A MISCHIEF TO A JOYFUL HOUSE, AND
BRINGING AN EVIL SPIRIT INTO BIRTH IN THE MIDST OF IT.

From the Masque of Queens.

Charm.   *The owl is abroad, the bat and the toad,*
     And so is the cat-a-mountain ;
   The ant and the mole both sit in a hole,
     And the frog peeps out of the fountain .
   The dogs they do bay and the timbrels play,
     The spindle is now a-turning ;
   The moon it is red and the stars are fled,
     But all the sky is a-burning.

     *   *   *   *

1st Hag.   I have been all day looking after
   A raven feeding upon a quarter ;
   And soon as she turn'd her beak to the south,
   I snatch'd this morsel out of her mouth.

2nd Hag.   I have been gathering wolves' hairs,
   The mad dog's foam and the adder's ears !
   The spurging of a dead man's eyes,
   And all since the evening star did rise.

3rd Hag.   I, last night, *lay all alone*
   On the ground to hear the mandrake groan ;
   And pluck'd him up, though he grew full low,
   And as I had done, the cock did crow.

4th Hag.   And I have been choosing out this skull
   From charnel-houses that were full ;
   From private grots and public pits ;
   And frighted a sexton out of his wits.

5th Hag.   Under a cradle I did creep,
   By day ; and when the child was asleep
   At night, I suck'd the breath ; and rose,
   And pluck'd the nodding nurse by the nose.

6th Hag. I had a dagger: what did I with that?
    Kill'd an infant to have his fat.
    *   *   *   *
    I scratch'd out the eyes of the owl before,
    I tore the bat's wing; what would you have more!

Dame. Yes, I have brought to help our vows
    Hornèd poppy, cypress-boughs,
    The fig-tree wild that grows on tombs,
    And juice that from the larch-tree comes,
    The basilisk's blood and the viper's skin;
    And now our orgies let us begin.

    You fiends and fairies, if yet any be
    Worse than ourselves, you that have quak'd to see
    These knots untied (*she unties them*)
    *   *   *   *
    Exhale earth's rottenest vapours,
    And strike a blindness through these blazing tapers.
    *   *   *   *

Charm. Deep, O deep we lay thee to sleep;
    We leave thee drink by, if thou chance to be dry;
    Both milk and blood, the dew and the flood;
    We breathe in thy bed, at the foot and the head;
    And when thou dost wake, *Dame Earth shall quake*
    Such a birth to make, as is the Blue Drake.
    *   *   *   *

Dame. Stay! all our charms do nothing win
    Upon the night; our labour dies,
    Our magic feature will not rise,
    Nor yet the storm! We must repeat
    More direful voices far, *and beat*
    The ground with vipers, till it sweat.
    *   *   *   *

Charm. Blacker go in, and blacker come out:
    At thy going down, we give thee a shout.
        Hoo!
    At thy rising again thou shalt have two;
    And if thou dost what we'd have thee do,
    Thou shalt have three, thou shalt have four.
        Hoo! har! har! hoo!

A cloud of pitch, a spur and a switch,
To haste him away, and a whirlwind play,
Before and after, *with thunder for laughter*
And storms of joy, of the roaring boy,
His head of a drake, his tail of a snake.

(*A loud and beautiful music is heard, and the Witches vanish.*)

A CATCH OF SATYRS.

Silenus bids his Satyrs awaken a couple of Sylvans, who have fallen asleep while they should have kept watch.

> *Buz*, quoth the blue fly,
> *Hum*, quoth the bee ;
> Bŭz ănd hŭm they cry,
> And sò do we,
> In his eàr, in his nòse,
> Thùs, do you see?
> Hè ate the dormouse ;
> Elsè it was hè.

"It is impossible that anything could better express than this, either the wild and practical joking of the satyrs, or the action of the thing described, or the quaintness and fitness of the images, or the melody and even the harmony, the *intercourse*, of the musical words, one with another. None but a boon companion with a very musical ear could have written it. It was not for nothing that Ben lived in the time of the fine old English composers, Bull and Ford, or partook his canary with his 'lov'd Alphonso,' as he calls him, the Signor Ferrabosco."—*A Jar of Honey from Mount Hybla*, in *Ainsworth's Magazine*, No. xxx. p. 86.

BEAUMONT AND FLETCHER.

BEAUMONT, BORN 1586—DIED 1615.
FLETCHER, BORN 1576—DIED 1625.

POETRY of the highest order and of the loveliest character abounds in Beaumont and Fletcher, but so mixed up with inconsistent, and too often, alas! revolting matter, that, apart from passages which do not enter into the plan of this book, I had no alternative but either to confine the extracts to the small number which ensue, or to bring together a heap of the smallest quotations,—two or three lines at a time. I thought to have got a good deal more out of the *Faithful Shepherdess*, which I had not read for many years; but on renewing my acquaintance with it, I found that the same unaccountable fascination with the evil times which had spoilt these two fine poets in their other plays, had followed its author, beyond what I had supposed, even into the regions of Arcadia.

Mr. Hazlitt, who loved sometimes to relieve his mistrust by a fit of pastoral worship, pronounces the *Faithful Shepherdess* to be "a perpetual feast of nectar'd sweets, where no crude surfeit reigns." I wish I could think so.

There are both hot and cold dishes in it, which I would
quit at any time to go and dine with the honest lovers of
Allan Ramsay, whose *Gentle Shepherd*, though of another
and far inferior class of poetry, I take upon the whole to
be the completest pastoral drama that ever was written.

It is a pity that Beaumont and Fletcher had not been
born earlier, and in the neighbourhood of Shakspeare, and
become his playmates. The wholesome company of the
juvenile yeoman (like a greater Sandford) might have
rectified the refined spirits of the young gentlemen, and
saved their Hippocrene from becoming ditch-water. Even
as it is, they seem different men when writing in their own
persons, and following the taste of the town. Compare,
for example, Beaumont's exquisite verses on *Melancholy*
(here printed) with any one of their plays ; or Fletcher's
lines entitled *An Honest Man's Fortune* with the play of
the same name, to which it is appended. The difference
is so great, and indeed is discernible to such an equal
degree in the poetry which startles you in the plays them-
selves (as if two different souls were writing one passage),
that it appears unaccountable, except on some principle
anterior to their town life, and to education itself. Little
is known of either of their families, except that there were
numerous poets in both ; but Fletcher's father was that
Dean of Peterborough (afterwards Bishop of London) who
behaved with such unfeeling impertinence to the Queen of
Scots in her last moments, and who is said (as became
such a man) to have died of chagrin because Elizabeth
was angry at his marrying a second time. Was poetry
such a " drug " with " both their houses " that the friends

lost their respect for it? or was Fletcher's mother some angel of a woman—some sequestered Miranda of the day— with whose spirit the "earth" of the Dean her husband but ill accorded?

Every devout lover of poetry must have experienced the wish of Coleridge, that Beaumont and Fletcher had written "poems instead of tragedies." Imagine as voluminous a set of the one as they have given us of the other? It would have been to sequestered real life what Spenser was to the land of Faery,—a retreat beyond all groves and gardens, a region of medicinal sweets of thought and feel- ing. Nor would plenty of fable have been wanting. What a loss! And this,—their birthright with posterity—these extraordinary men sold for the mess of the loathsome pottage of the praise and profligacy of the court of James I.

But let us blush to find fault with them, even for such a descent from their height, while listening to their diviner moods.

MELANCHOLY.

BY BEAUMONT.

Hence, all you vain delights,
As short as are the nights
    Wherein you spend your folly;
There's nought in this life sweet,
Were men but wise to see 't,
    But only Melancholy;
O sweetest Melancholy!

Welcome, folded arms and fixèd eyes ;
A sigh that, piercing, mortifies ;
A look that's fasten'd to the ground ;
A tongue chain'd up without a sound.

Fountain-heads and pathless groves,
Places which pale passion loves ; (¹)
Moonlight walks, when all the fowls
Are warmly hous'd save bats and owls ;
A midnight bell, a parting groan,
These are the sounds we *feed upon :*
Then stretch our bones in a still gloomy valley :
Nothing so dainty sweet as lovely Melancholy. (²)

(¹) *Places which pale passion loves.*

Beaumont, while writing this verse, perhaps the finest in the poem, probably had in his memory that of Marlowe, in his description of Tamburlaine :

Pale of complexion, wrought in him with passion.

(²) *Lovely Melancholy.*

Tradition has given these verses to Beaumont, though they appeared for the first time in a play of Fletcher's after the death of his friend. In all probability Beaumont had partly sketched the play, and left the verses to be inserted.

I cannot help thinking that a couplet has been lost after the words "bats and owls." It is true the four verses ending with those words might be made to belong to the preceding four, as among the things " welcomed ; " but the junction would be forced, and the modulation injured. They may remain, too, where they are, as combining to suggest the " sounds " which the melancholy man feeds upon : "fountain-heads" being audible, "groves" whispering, and the "moonlight walks" being attended by the hooting "owl." They also modulate beautifully in this case. Yet these intimations themselves appear a little forced; whereas, supposing a couplet to be supplied, there would be a distinct reference to melancholy *sights*, as well as sounds.

The conclusion is divine. Indeed the whole poem, as Hazlitt says, is "the perfection of this kind of writing." Orpheus might have hung it, like a pearl, in the ear of Proserpina. It has naturally been thought to have suggested the *Penseroso* to Milton, and is more than worthy to have done so; for fine as that is, it is still finer. It is the concentration of a hundred melancholies. Sir Walter Scott, in one of his biographical works, hardly with the accustomed gallantry and good-nature of the great novelist, contrasted it with the "melo-dramatic" abstractions of Mrs. Radclyffe (then living). He might surely, with more justice, have opposed it to the diffuseness and conventional phraseology of "novels in verse."

A SATYR PRESENTS A BASKET OF FRUIT TO THE FAITHFUL SHEPHERDESS.

BY FLETCHER.

Here be grapes whose *lusty blood*
Is the learned poet's good;
Sweeter yet did never crown
The head of Bacchus; nuts more brown
Than the squirrel's teeth that crack them;
Deign, O fairest fair! to take them.

For these black-eyed Dryope
Hath oftentimes commanded me
With my *claspèd knee* to climb :
See how well the lusty time
Hath deck'd their rising cheeks in red,
Such as on your lips is spread.
Here be berries for a queen,
Some be red—some be green; (^{3})
These are of *that luscious meat*
The great god Pan himself doth eat!
All these, and what the woods can yield.
The hanging mountain or the field,
I freely offer ; and ere long
Will bring you more, more sweet and strong ;
Till when, humbly leave I take,
Lest the great Pan do awake,
That sleeping lies in a deep glade,
Under a broad beech's shade: (^{4})
I must go, I must run,
Swifter than the fiery sun.

(^{3}) *Some be red—some be green.*

This verse calls to mind a beautiful one of Chaucer, in his description of a grove in spring :—

In which were oakès great, straight as a line,
Under the which the grass, so fresh of hue,
Was newly sprung, and an eight foot or nine
Ev-e-ry tree well from his fellow grew,
With branches broad, laden with leavès new,
That sprangen out against the sunny sheen,
Some very red, and some a glad light green.
—*The Flower and the Leaf.*

Coleridge was fond of repeating it.

(⁴) *That sleeping lies,* &c.

Pan was not to be waked too soon with impunity.

Οὐ θέμις, ὦ ποιμάν, τὸ μεσαμβρινὸν, οὐ θέμις ἄμμιν
Συρίσδεν· τὸν Πᾶνα δεδοίκαμες· ἦ γὰρ ἀπ' ἄγρας
Τανίκα κεκμακὼς ἀμπαύεται· ἐντὶ δὲ πικρὸς
Καὶ οἱ ἀεὶ δριμεῖα χολὰ ποτὶ ῥινὶ κάθηται.
—Theocritus, *Idyll.* i. v. 15.

No, shepherd, no ; we must not pipe at noon :
We must fear Pan, who sleeps after the chase,
Ready to start in snappish bitterness
With quivering nostril.

What a true picture of the half-goat divinity!

———————

A SPOT FOR LOVE-TALES.

Here be all new delights, cool streams and wells ;
Arbours o'ergrown with woodbines ; caves and dells.
Choose where thou wilt, whilst I sit by and sing,
Or gather rushes, to make many a ring
For thy long fingers ; tell thee tales of love ;
How the pale Phœbe, hunting in a grove,
First saw the boy Endymion, *from whose eyes*
She took eternal fire that never dies ;
How she conveyed him softly in a sleep,
His temples bound with poppy, to the steep
Head of old Latmus, where she stoops each night,
Gilding the mountain with her brother's light,
To kiss her sweetest.

———————

MORNING.

See, the day begins to break,
And the light *shoots like a streak*
Of subtle fire.   The wind blows cold
While the morning doth unfold.

I have departed from my plan for once, to introduce this very small extract, partly for the sake of its beauty, partly to show the student that great poets do not confine their pleasant descriptions to images or feelings pleasing in the commoner sense of the word, but include such as, while seeming to contradict, harmonize with them, upon principles of truth, and of a genial and strenuous sympathy. The " subtle streak of fire " is obviously beautiful, but the addition of the cold wind is a truth welcome to those only who have strength as well as delicacy of apprehension,—or rather, that healthy delicacy which arises from the strength. Sweet and wholesome, and to be welcomed, is the chill breath of morning.   There is a fine epithet for this kind of dawn in the elder Marston's *Antonio and Melida :—*

Is not yon gleam *the shuddering morn*, that flakes
With silver tincture the east verge of heaven ?

THE POWER OF LOVE.

Hear, ye ladies that despise
    What the mighty Love has done ;
Fear examples and be wise :
    Fair Calisto was a nun ;

Leda, sailing on the stream
　　To deceive the hopes of man.
Love accounting but a dream,
　　Doted on a silver swan ;
Danaè, in a brazen tower,
Where no love was, loved a shower. (⁵)

Hear, ye ladies that are coy,
　　What the mighty Love can do.
Fear the fierceness of the boy :
　　The chaste moon he makes to woo :
Vesta, kindling holy fires,
　　Circled round about with spies,
Never dreaming loose desires,
　　Doting at the altar dies ;
Ilion in a short hour, higher
He can build, and once more fire.

———

(⁵) *Where no love was.*

See how extremes meet, and passion writes as conceit does, in these repetitions of a word :

Where no love was, lov'd a shower.

So, still more emphatically, in the instance afterwards :—

Fear the *fierceness* of the boy—

than which nothing can be finer.   Wonder and earnestness conspire to stamp the iteration of the sound.

INVOCATION TO SLEEP.

Sung to Music; the EMPEROR VALENTINIAN *sitting by, sick, in a chair,*

Care-charming Sleep, thou easer of all woes,—
Brother to Death, *sweetly thyself dispose*
On this afflicted prince ; fall like a cloud
In gentle showers ; give nothing that is loud
Or painful to his slumbers ;—easy, sweet, ([6])
And as a purling stream, thou son of night,
Pass by his troubled senses :—sing his pain,
Like hollow murmuring wind, or silver rain ;
Into this prince *gently, oh, gently slide,*
And kiss him into slumbers like a bride !

([6]) *Easy, sweet.*

In rhymes like *night* and *sweet,* the fine ears of oui
ancestors discerned a harmony to which we have been
unaccustomed. They perceived the double *e,* which is in
the vowel *i,*—night *nah-eet.* There is an instance in a
passage in the *Midsummer Night's Dream,* extracted at
page 156, where the word *bees,* as well as *mulberries* and
dewberries, is made to rhyme with *eyes, arise,* &c. Indeed,
in such words as *mulberries* the practice is still retained,
and *e* and *i* considered corresponding sounds in the
fainter terminations of polysyllables :—*free, company,*—
fly, company.

Was ever the last line of this invocation surpassed ?
But it is all in the finest tone of mingled softness and
earnestness. The verses are probably Fletcher's. He has

repeated a passage of it in his poem entitled *An Honest Man's Fortune* :—

> Oh, man! thou image of thy Maker's good,
> What canst thou fear, when breath'd into thy blood
> His Spirit is that built thee? What dull sense
> Makes thee suspect, in need, that Providence
> *Who made the morning*, and who plac'd the light
> Guide to thy labours; who call'd up the night,
> And bid her fall upon thee *like sweet showers*
> *In hollow murmurs* to lock up thy powers?

O si sic omnia !

MIDDLETON, DECKER, AND WEBSTER.

WHEN about to speak of these and other extraordinary men of the days of Shakspeare, the Marstons, Rowleys, Massingers, Draytons, &c., including those noticed already, I wasted a good deal of time in trying to find out how it was that, possessing, as most of them did, such a pure vein of poetry, and sometimes saying as fine things as himself, they wrote so much that is not worth reading, sometimes not fit to be read. I might have considered that, either from self-love, or necessity, or both, too much writing is the fault of all ages and of every author. Even Homer, says Horace, sometimes nods. How many odes might not Horace himself have spared us! How many of his latter books, Virgil! What theology, Dante and Milton! What romances, Cervantes! What comedies, Ariosto! What tragedies, Dryden! What heaps of words, Chaucer and Spenser! What *Iliads*, Pope!

Shakspeare's contemporaries, however, appear to have been a singularly careless race of men, compared with

himself. Could they have been rendered so by that very
superiority of birth and education which threw them upon
the town, in the first instance, with greater confidence, his
humbler prospects rendering him more cautious ?   Or did
their excess of wit and fancy require a counter-perfection
of judgment, such as he only possessed ?   Chapman and
Drayton, though their pens were among the profusest and
most unequal, seem to have been prudent men in conduct;
so in all probability were Ford and Webster; but none of
these had the animal spirits of the other.   Shakspeare
had animal spirits, wit, fancy, judgment, prudence in
money matters, understanding like Bacon, feeling like
Chaucer, mirth like Rabelais, dignity like Milton !   What
a man !   Has anybody discovered the reason why he never
noticed a living contemporary, and but one who was dead ?
and this too in an age of great men, and when they
were in the habit of acknowledging the pretensions of one
another.   It could not have been jealousy, or formality, or
inability to perceive merits which his own included; and
one can almost as little believe it possible to have been
owing to a fear of disconcerting his aristocratic friends, for
they too were among the eulogizers : neither can it be
attributed to his having so mooted all points, as to end in
caring for none; for in so great and wise a nature, *good*
nature must surely survive everything, both as a pleasure
and a duty.   I have made up my mind to think that his
theatrical *managership* was the cause.   It naturally pro-
duced a dislike of pronouncing judgments and incurring
responsibilities.   And yet he was not always a manager ;
nor were all his literary friends playwrights.   I think it

probable, from the style, that he wrote the sonnet in which
Spenser is eulogized :—

If music and sweet poetry agree, &c. ;

but this is doubtful ; and Spenser was not one of his
dramatic fellows. Did he see too many faults in them
all to praise them ! ! Certainly the one great difference
between him and them, next to superiority of genius, is
the prevailing relevancy of all he wrote ; its freedom, how-
ever superabundant, from inconsistency and caprice. But
could he find nothing to praise ? Nothing in the whole
contemporary drama ? Nothing in all the effusions of his
friends and brother clubbists of the " Mermaid " and the
" Triple Tun ? "

I take Webster and Decker to have been the two
greatest of the Shakspeare men, for unstudied genius,
next after Beaumont and Fletcher ; and in some respects
they surpassed them. Beaumont and Fletcher have no
such terror as Webster, nor any such piece of hearty,
good, affecting human clay as Decker's " Old Signior
Orlando Friscobaldo." Is there any such man even in
Shakspeare ?—any such exaltation of that most delightful
of all things, *bonhomie* ? Webster sometimes overdoes his
terror ; nay, often. He not only riots, he debauches in it ;
and Decker, full of heart and delicacy as he is, and
qualified to teach refinement to the refined, condescends to
an astounding coarseness. Beaumont and Fletcher's good
company saved them from that, in words. In spirit they
are full of it. But Decker never mixes up (at least not as
far as I can remember) any such revolting and impossible
contradictions in the same character as they do. Neither

does he bring a doubt on his virtues by exaggerating them.
He believes heartily in what he does believe, and you
love him in consequence.   It was he that wrote that
character, the piety of which has been pronounced equal to
its boldness :—

> The best of men
> That e'er wore earth about him was a sufferer;
> A soft, meek, patient, humble, tranquil spirit;
> The first true gentleman that ever breath'd.

His universal sympathy enabled him to strike out that
audacious and happy simile, " untameable as *flies*," which
Homer would have admired, though it is fit to make
poetasters shudder.   The poetaster, had Decker offered to
make him a present of it, would have been afraid of being
taken for a fly himself.   Images are either grand in them-
selves, or for the thought and feeling that accompany
them.   This has all the greatness of Nature's " equal eye."
You may see how truly Decker felt it to be of this kind,
by the company in which he has placed it ; and there is a
consummation of propriety in its wildness, for he is speak-
ing of lunatics :—

> There are of mad men, as there are of tame,
> All humour'd not alike.   We have here some
> So apish and fantastic, will play with a feather;
> And though 't would grieve a soul to see God's image
> So blemish'd and defaced, yet do they act
> Such antic and such pretty lunacies,
> That, spite of sorrow, they will make you smile.
> Others again we have *like hungry lions*,
> *Fierce as wild bulls*, untameable as flies.

Middleton partakes of the poetry and sweetness of
Decker, but not to the same height : and he talks more at
random.   You hardly know what to make of the dialogue

or stories of some of his plays. But he has more fancy:
and there is one character of his (De Flores in the
"*Changeling*") which, for effect at once tragical, probable,
and poetical, surpasses anything I know of in the drama
of domestic life. Middleton has the honour of having
furnished part of the witch poetry to Macbeth, and of being
conjoined with it also in the powerful and beautiful music
of Locke.

From Massinger, Ford, and the others (as far as I
have met with them, and apart from the connexion of
Massinger's *name* with Decker), I could find nothing to
extract of a nature to suit this particular volume, and of
equal height with its contents. It is proper to state, how-
ever, that I have only glanced through their works : for
though no easily daunted reader, I never read an entire
play either of Ford or Massinger. They repel me with the
conventional tendencies of their style, and their unnatural
plots and characters. Ford, however, is elegant and
thoughtful ; and Massinger has passion, though (as far as
I know) not in a generous shape. With these two writers
began that prosaical part of the corruption of dramatic
style (merging passionate language into conventional)
which came to its head in Shirley.

> *Donusa.* What magic hath *transform'd me from myself ?*
> *Where is my virgin pride ?* how have I *lost*
> *My boasted freedom !* what *new fire burns up*
> My scorch'd entrails !! what unknown desires
> *Invade,* and *take possession* of my soul ?
> —Massinger's *Renegado.*

> *Hialas.*   To this union
> The good of both the Church and Commonwealth
> *Invite* you.

> *Durham.* To this unity, a mystery
> Of Providence *points out* a greater blessing
> For both these nations, than our human wisdom
> *Can search into.* King Henry hath a daughter,
> The Princess Margaret. *I need not urge,* &c.
> —Ford's *Perkin Warbeck.*

Both these passages are the first I came to, on dipping into their works. One might fancy oneself reading *Cato* or the *Grecian Daughter*, instead of men who had breathed the air of the days of Shakspeare.

Massinger was joint author with Decker, of the play from which the scene of the lady and the angel is taken ; but nobody who knows the style of the two men can doubt for a moment to which it belongs. I have, therefore, without hesitation assigned it according to the opinion expressed by Mr. Lamb.

FLIGHT OF WITCHES.

Scene, a Field. Enter HECATE, STADLIN, HOPPO, *and other Witches* FIRESTONE *in the background.*

Hec. The moon's a gallant ; see how brisk she rides !
Stad. Here's a rich evening, Hecate.
Hec.   Ay, is 't not, wenches,
To take a journey of five thousand miles ?
Hec.   O 't will be precious !
Heard you the owl yet ?
Stad.   Briefly in the copse,
As we came through now.
Hec.   'T is high time for us then.
Stad. There was a bat hung at my lips three times,
As we came through the woods, and drank her fill :
Old Puckle saw her.

Hec.   You are *fortunate* still ;
The very screech-owl lights upon your shoulder,
And woos you like a pigeon.   Are you furnished ?
Have you your ointments ?
   Stad.   All.
   Hec.   Prepare to flight then ;
I 'll overtake you swiftly.
   Stad.   Hie thee, Hecate ;
We shall be up betimes.
   Hec.   I 'll reach you quickly.
                      [*Exeunt all the Witches except* HECATE.

Fire. They are all going a-birding to-night : they talk of fowls i'
th' air that fly by day ; I am sure they 'll be a company of foul sluts
there to-night : if we have not mortality after 't, I 'll be hanged, for
they are able to putrefy it, to infect a whole region.   She spies me
now.

Hec. What, Firestone, our sweet son ?

Fire. A little sweeter than some of you, or a dunghill were too
good for me.   [*Aside.*

Hec. How much hast here ?

Fire.   Nineteen, and all brave plump ones,
besides six lizards and three serpentine eggs.

Hec. Dear and sweet boy ! what herbs hast thou ?

Fire. I have some marmartin and mandragon.

Hec. Marmaritin and mandragora, thou wouldst say.

Fire. Here 's panax too—I thank thee—my pan aches I 'm sure,
with kneeling down to cut 'em.

   Hec.   And selago,
Hedge-hysop too : how near he goes my cuttings !
Were they all cropt by moonlight ?

   Fire.   Every blade of 'em,
Or I 'm a moon-calf, mother.

   Hec.   Hie thee home with them :
Look well to the house to-night ; I 'm for aloft.

Fire. Aloft, quoth you ?   I would you would break your neck
once, *that I might have all quickly !* [*Aside.*]   Hark, hark, mother !
they are above the steeple already, *flying over your head with a noise
of musicians.*

Hec. They're they indeed.   Help, help me ; I 'm too late
else.

SONG ABOVE.

Come away, come away,
Hecate, Hecate, come away.
Hec. I come, I come, I come, I come,
With all the speed I may.
Where 's Stadlin?
[*Voice above.*]   Here.
Hec. Where 's Puckle?
[*Voice above.*]   Here.
And Hoppo too, and Hellwain too ;
We lack but you, we lack but you ;
Come away, make up the count.
Hec. I will but 'noint and then I mount.
                              [*A spirit like a cat descends.*
[*Voice above.*] There 's one comes down to fetch his dues,
A kiss, a coll, a sip of blood ;
And why thou stay'st so long, I muse,
Since the air 's so sweet and good ?
Hec. O, art thou come ? what news, what news ?
Spirit. All goes still to our delight.
Either come or else refuse.
Hec. Now I 'm furnished for the flight.
Fire. Hark, hark, the cat rings a brave treble in her own
language !
Hec. [*going up.*] *Now I go, now I fly,*
Malkin my sweet spirit and I.
O what a dainty pleasure 't is
To ride in the air
When the moon shines fair,
And sing and dance, and toy and kiss !
Over woods, high rocks, and mountains,
Over seas, our mistress' fountains ;
Over steeples, towers, and turrets,
We fly by night, 'mongst troops of spirits :
No ring of bells to our ear sounds ;
No howls of wolves, no yelps of hounds ;

No, not the noise of water's breach,
Or cannon's throat our height can reach.
[*Voice above.*] No ring of bells, &c.
Fire. Well, mother, I thank your kindness : you must be gambol-
ling i' th' air, and leave me to walk here, like a fool and a mortal.
                                                                —MIDDLETON.

THE CHRISTIAN LADY AND THE ANGEL.

An ANGEL, *in the guise of a Page, attends on* DOROTHEA.

   Dor. My book and taper.
   Ang.   Here, most holy mistress.
   Dor. Thy voice sends forth such music, that I never
Was ravish'd with a more celestial sound.
Were every servant in the world like thee,
So full of goodness, angels would come down
To dwell with us : thy name is Angelo,
And like that name thou art.   Get thee to rest ;
Thy youth with too much watching is opprest.
   Ang. No, my dear lady ; I could weary stars,
And force the wakeful moon to lose her eyes,
By my late watching, but to wait on you.
When at your prayers you kneel before the altar,
Methinks I'm singing with some quire in heaven,
So blest I hold me in your company ;
Therefore, my most lov'd mistress, do not bid
Your boy, so serviceable, to get hence ;
For then you break his heart.
   Dor.   Be nigh me still then.
In golden letters down I 'll set that day
Which gave thee to me.   Little did I hope
To meet such worlds of comfort in thyself,
This little, pretty body, when I, coming
Forth of the temple, heard my beggar-boy,
My sweet-faced, godly beggar-boy, crave an alms,
Which with glad hand I gave, with lucky hand !—

And when I took thee home, my most chaste bosom
Methought was fill'd with no hot wanton fire,
But with a holy flame, mounting since higher,
On wings of cherubims, than it did before.
 Ang. Proud am I, that my lady's modest eye
So likes so poor a servant.
 Dor.   I have offer'd
Handfuls of gold but to behold thy parents.
I would leave kingdoms, were I queen of some,
To dwell with thy good father : for, the son
Bewitching me so deeply with his presence,
He that begot him must do it ten times more.
I pray thee, my sweet boy, show me thy parents ;
Be not asham'd.
 Ang.   I am not : I did never
Know who my mother was ; but by yon palace,
Fill'd with bright heavenly courts, I dare assure you,
And pawn these eyes upon it, and this hand,
My father is in heaven ; and, pretty mistress,
If your illustrious hour-glass spend his sand
No worse than yet it does, upon my life,
You and I both shall meet my father there,
And he shall bid you welcome !
 Dor.   O blessed day !
We all long to be there, but lose the way.

           [*Exeunt.*

DOROTHEA *is executed ; and the* ANGEL *visits* THEOPHILUS, *the Judge*
that condemned her.

 Theoph. (alone).   This Christian slut was well,
A pretty one ; but let such horror follow
The next I feed with torments, that when Rome
Shall hear it, her foundation at the sound
May feel an earthquake. How now ? (*Music.*)
 Ang.   Are you amazed, sir ?
So great a Roman spirit, and doth it tremble ?
 Theoph. How cam'st thou in ? to whom thy business ?
 Ang. To you.
I had a mistress, late sent hence by you

Upon a bloody errand; you entreated
That, when she came into that blessed garden
Whither she knew she went, and where, now happy,
She feeds upon all joy, she would send to you
Some of that garden fruit and flowers; which here,
To have her promise sav'd, are brought by me.

    Theoph. Cannot I see this garden?

    Ang.   Yes, if the master
Will give you entrance.   [*He vanishes.*

    Theoph.   'T is a tempting fruit,
And the most bright-cheek'd child I ever view'd;
Sweet-smelling, goodly fruit. What flowers are these?
In Dioclesian's gardens, the most beauteous
Compar'd with these are weeds: is it not February,
The second day she died? frost, ice, and snow
Hang on the beard of winter? where 's the sun
That gilds this summer? pretty, sweet boy, say,
In what country shall a man find this garden?—
My delicate boy,—gone! vanish'd! within there,
Julianus! Geta!

    Both. My lord.

    Theoph.   Are my gates shut?

    Geta.   And guarded.

    Theoph.   Saw you not
A boy?

    Jul. Where?

    Theoph.   Here he enter'd, a young lad;
A thousand blessings *danc'd upon his eyes;*
A smooth-fac'd glorious thing, that brought this basket.

    Geta. No, sir.

    Theoph. Away! but be in reach, if my voice calls you.
                          —DECKER.

LADIES DANCING.

A fine sweet earthquake, gently mov'd
By the soft wind of whispering silks.

                             —*Id.*

APRIL AND WOMEN'S TEARS.

Trust not a woman when she cries,
For she'll pump water from her eyes
With a wet finger, and in faster showers
Than April *when he rains down flowers.*

—Decker.

DEATH.

There 's a lean fellow beats all conquerors.

—*Id.*

PATIENCE.

Duke. What comfort do you find in being so calm?
Candido. That which green wounds receive from sovereign balm.
Patience, my lord! why, 't is the *soul of peace;*
Of all the virtues 't is nearest kin to heaven;
It makes men look like gods. The best of men
That e'er *wore earth about him* was a sufferer,
A soft, meek, patient, humble, tranquil spirit,
The first true gentleman that ever breath'd.
The stock of patience then cannot be poor;
All it desires, it has; what award more?
It is the greatest enemy to law
That can be, for it doth embrace all wrongs,
And so chains up lawyers and women's tongues:
'T *is the perpetual prisoner's liberty,*
His walks and orchards : 't is the bond-slave's freedom,
And makes him seem proud of his iron chain,
As though he wore it more for state than pain;

It is the beggars' music, and thus sings,—
Although their bodies beg, their souls are kings.
O my dread liege! it is the sap of bliss,
Bears us aloft, *makes men and angels kiss :*
And last of all, to end a household strife,
It is the honey 'gainst a waspish wife.

—DECKER.

I had a doubt whether to put this exquisite passage
into the present volume, or to reserve it for one of Contem-
plative poetry; but the imagination, which few will not
think predominant in it, together with a great admiration
of the sentiments, of the thoughtful, good-natured alterna-
tion of jest and earnest, and of the sweetness of the versifi-
cation, increased by a certain wild mixture of rhyme and
blank verse, determined me to indulge the impulse. Per-
haps Decker, who had experienced the worst troubles of
poverty, not excepting loss of liberty, drew his patient man
from himself, half jesting over the portrait, in order to
reconcile his praises of the virtue in the abstract with a
modest sense of it in his own person. To the strain in it
of a " higher mood," I cannot but append what Mr. Hazlitt
has said in his *Lectures on the Literature of the Age of
Elizabeth* (Templeman's edition, p. 21). " There have
been persons who, being sceptics as to the divine mission
of Christ, have taken an unaccountable prejudice to his
doctrines, and have been disposed to deny the merit of his
character ; but this was not the feeling of the great men in
the age of Elizabeth (whatever might be their belief), one
of whom says of him, with a boldness equal to its piety,
' The best of men,' " &c. (Here the lecturer quotes the
verses alluded to, and adds,) " This was honest old Decker ;

and the lines ought to embalm his memory to every one
who has a sense either of religion, or philosophy, or
humanity, or true genius."

<hr />

A WICKED DREAM.

Vittoria Corombona. To pass away the time I'll tell your grace
A dream I had last night.
  Brachiano.   Most wishedly.
  Vit. Cor. A foolish idle dream.
Methought I walk'd, about the mid of night,
Into a churchyard, where a goodly yew-tree
Spread her large root in ground. Under that yew,
As I sat sadly leaning on a grave
Checquer'd with cross-sticks, there came stealing in
Your duchess and my husband; one of them
A pickaxe bore, th' other a rusty spade,
And in rough terms they 'gan to challenge me
About this yew.
  Brach.   That tree?
  Vit. Cor.   This harmless yew.
They told me my intent was to root up
That well-known yew, and plant i' th' stead of it
A wither'd blackthorn : and for that they vow'd
To bury me alive. My husband straight
With pickaxe 'gan to dig; and your fell duchess
With shovel, like a fury, voided out
The earth, and scattered bones : Lord, how, methought,
I trembled, and yet for all this terror
I could not pray—
  Flamineo (aside). No; the devil was in your dream.
  Vit. Cor. When to my rescue there arose, methought,
A whirlwind, *which let fall a massy arm*
From that strong plant;

And both were struck dead by that sacred yew,
In that base shallow grave which was their due.
   Flamineo (aside). Excellent devil ! she hath taught him in a dream
To make away his duchess and her husband.

—W<small>EBSTER</small>

NATURAL DEATH.

O thou soft natural death, that art joint twin
To sweetest slumber ! *no rough-bearded comet*
Stares on thy mild departure ; the dull owl
Beats not against thy casement ; the hoarse wolf
Scents not thy carrion : *pity winds thy corse,*
Whilst horror waits on princes.

—*Id.*

FUNERAL DIRGE.

(*Sung by a Mother over her Son.*)

Call for the robin redbreast and the wren,
   Since o'er shady groves they hover,
   And with leaves of flowers do cover
The friendless bodies of unburied men.
   Call unto his funeral dole
   The ant, the field-mouse, and the mole,
To raise him hillocks *that shall keep him warm ;*
And when gay tombs are robb'd sustain no harm :
But keep the wolf far thence, that's foe to men,
For with his nails he 'll dig them up again.

—*Id.*

" I never saw," says Lamb, " anything like this dirge,
except the ditty which reminds Ferdinand of his drowned
father in the *Tempest.* That is of the water, watery ; so

14

this is of the earth, earthy. Both have that intenseness
of feeling which seems to resolve itself into the elements
which it contemplates."—*Dramatic Specimens*, Moxon's
edition, vol. i. p. 251.

DISSIMULATION.

Be not cunning ;
For those whose faces do belie their hearts
Are witches ere they arrive at twenty years,
And give the devil suck.

—WEBSTER.

BEAUTEOUS MORAL EXAMPLE.

Her I hold
My honourable pattern ; one whose mind
Appears more like a *ceremonious chapel*,
Full of sweet music, than a thronging presence.

—*Id.*

UNLOVELINESS OF FROWNING.

Cupid sets a crown
Upon those lovely tresses ;
O spoil not with a frown
What he so sweetly dresses !

—*Id.*

MILTON.

BORN, 1608,—DIED, 1674.

I⊤ is difficult to know what to do with some of the finest passages in Milton's great poem. To treat the objectionable points of their story as mythological, might be thought irreverent to opinion; and to look upon them in the light in which he at first wished us to regard them (for he is understood to have changed his own opinions of it), involves so much irreverence towards the greatest of beings, that it is painful to seem to give them countenance. The difficulty is increased in a volume of the present kind, which is intended to give the reader no perplexity, except to know what to admire most. I have, therefore, thought it best to confine the extracts from *Paradise Lost* to unconnected passages; and the entire ones to those poems which he wrote when a happy youth, undegenerated into superstition. The former will still include his noblest flights of imagination: the rest are ever fresh, true, and delightful.

Milton was a very great poet, second only (if second) to the very greatest, such as Dante and Shakspeare; and, like all great poets, equal to them in particular instances. He had no pretensions to Shakspeare's universality; his wit is dreary; and (in general) he had not the faith in things that Homer and Dante had, apart from the intervention of words. He could not let them speak for themselves without helping them with his learning. In all he did, after a certain period of youth (not to speak it irreverently), something of the schoolmaster is visible; and a gloomy religious creed removes him still farther from the universal gratitude and delight of mankind. He is understood, however, as I have just intimated, to have given this up before he died. He had then run the circle of his knowledge, and probably come round to the wiser, more cheerful, and more poetical beliefs of his childhood.

In this respect, *Allegro* and *Penseroso* are the happiest of his productions : and in none is the poetical habit of mind more abundantly visible. They ought to precede the *Lycidas* (not unhurt with theology) in the modern editions of his works, as they did in the collection of minor poems made by himself. *Paradise Lost* is a study for imagination and elaborate musical structure. Take almost any passage, and a lecture might be read from it on contrasts and pauses, and other parts of metrical harmony; while almost every word has its higher poetical meaning and intensity; but all is accompanied with a certain oppressiveness of ambitious and conscious power. In the *Allegro* and *Penseroso*, &c., he is in better spirits with all about him ; his eyes had not grown dim, nor his soul been forced inwards by disappointment into a proud self-esteem, which he narrowly escaped erecting into self-worship. He loves nature, not for the power he can get out of it, but for the pleasure it affords him; he is at peace with town as well as country, with courts and cathedral-windows; goes to the play and laughs; to the village-green and dances; and his study is placed, not in the Old Jewry, but in an airy tower, from whence he good-naturedly hopes that his candle—I beg pardon, his "lamp" (for he was a scholar from the first, though not a Puritan)—may be "seen" by others. His mirth, it is true, is not excessively merry. It is, as Warton says, the "dignity of mirth;" but it is happy, and that is all that is to be desired. The mode is not to be dictated by the mode of others; nor would it be so interesting if it were. The more a man is himself the better, provided he add a variation to the stock of comfort, and not of sullenness. Milton was born in a time of great changes; he was bred to be one of the changers; and in the order of events, and the working of good out of ill, we are bound to be grateful to what was of a mixed nature in himself, without arrogating for him that exemption from the mixture which belongs to no man. But upon the same principle on which nature herself loves joy better than grief, health than disease, and a general amount of welfare than the reverse (urging men towards it where it does not prevail, and making many a form of discontent itself but a mode of pleasure and self-esteem), so Milton's great poem never has been, and never can be popular (sectarianism apart) compared with his minor ones; nor does it, in the very highest sense of popularity, deserve to be. It does not work out the very piety it proposes; and the piety which it does propose wants the highest piety of an intelligible charity and reliance. Hence a secret preference for his minor poems among many of the truest and selectest admirers of *Paradise Lost*,—perhaps with all who do not admire power in any shape above truth in the best ; hence Warton's fond edition of them, delightful for its luxurious heap of notes and parallel passages ; and hence the pleasure of being able to extract the finest of them, without misgiving, into a volume like the present.

SATAN'S RECOVERY FROM HIS DOWNFALL.

He scarce had ceas'd, when the superior Fiend
Was moving toward the shore, his ponderous shield,
Ethereal temper, massy, large, and round,
Behind him cast ; *the broad circumference*
Hung on his shoulders like the moon, whose orb
Through optick glass the Tuscan artist views
At evening from the top of Fesolé.
Or in Valdarno, to discry new lands,
Rivers or mountains in her spotty globe.
His spear, to equal which the tallest pine
Hewn on Norwegian hills, *to be the mast*
Of some great ammiral, were but a wand,
He walk'd with, to support uneasy steps
Over the burning marle, not like those steps
On Heaven's azure ; and the torrid clime
Smote on him sore besides, *vaulted* with fire :
Nathless he so endur'd, till on the beach
Of that inflamèd sea he stood, and call'd
His legions, angel forms, who lay entranc'd
Thick as autumnal leaves that strow the brooks
In Vallombrosa, where the Etrurian shades,
High over-arch'd, embower ; or scatter'd sedge
Afloat, when with fierce winds Orion arm'd

Hath *vex'd* the Red-Sea coast, whose waves o'erthrew
Busiris and his Memphian chivalry,
While with perfidious hatred they pursued
The sojourners of Goshen, who beheld
From the safe shore their floating carcasses
And broken chariot wheels : so thick bestrown,
Abject and lost lay these, covering the flood
Under amazement of their hideous change.
He call'd so loud that all the hollow deep
Of Hell resounded. " Princes, Potentates,
Warriors, the flower of Heaven, once yours, now lost,
If such astonishment as this can seize
Eternal spirits ; or have ye chosen this place
After the toil of battle to repose
Your *wearied virtue*, for the ease you find
To slumber here, as in the vales of Heaven ?
Or in this abject posture have ye sworn
To adore the conqueror ? who now beholds
Cherub and Seraph rolling in the flood,
With scatter'd arms and ensigns ; till anon
His swift pursuers from heaven-gates discern
The advantage, and descending, tread us down,
Thus drooping, or with linkèd thunderbolts
Transfix us to the bottom of this gulf.
Awake ! arise ! or be for ever fallen ! "

THE FALLEN ANGELS GATHERED AGAIN TO WAR.

All these and more came flocking ; but with looks
Downcast and damp ; yet such wherein appear'd,
Obscure, some glimpse of joy, to have found their chief
Not in despair ; to have found themselves not lost
In loss itself ; which on his countenance cast
Like doubtful hue ; but he, his wonted pride
Soon recollecting, with high words, that bore
Semblance of worth, not substance, gently rais'd
Their fainting courage, and dispell'd their fears.

Then straight commands, that at the warlike sound
Of trumpets loud and clarions be uprear'd
His mighty standard: that proud honour claim'd
Azazel as his right, a cherub tall;
Who forthwith from the glittering staff unfurl'd
The imperial ensign; which, full high advanc'd,
Shone like a meteor streaming to the wind,
With gems and golden lustre rich emblaz'd,
Seraphic arms and trophies; *all the while*
Sonorous metal blowing martial sounds:
At which the universal host up-sent
A shout, that tore Hell's concave, and beyond
Frighted the reign of Chaos and old Night.
All in a moment *through the gloom* were seen
Ten thousand banners rise into the air
With orient colours waving: with them rose
A forest huge of spears; and thronging helms
Appear'd, and serried shields, in thick array
Of depth immeasurable: *anon they move*
In perfect phalanx to the Dorian mood
Of flutes and soft recorders; such as rais'd
To height of noblest temper heroes old
Arming to battle; and instead of rage
Deliberate valour breath'd, firm and unmov'd
With dread of death to flight or foul retreat;
Nor wanting power to mitigate and swage
With solemn touches troubled thoughts, and chase
Anguish, and dòubt, and fèar, and sòrrow, and pàin,
From mortal, *or immortal* minds. Thus they
Breathing united force, with fixèd thought,
Mov'd on in silence to soft pipes, that charm'd
Their painful steps o'er the burnt soil: and now
Advanc'd in view they stand, a horrid front
Of dreadful length and dazzling arms, in guise
Of warriors old with order'd spear and shield;
Awaiting what command their mighty chief
Had to impose: he through the armèd files
Darts his experienc'd eye, and soon traverse
The whole battalion views; their order due;
Their visages and stature as of gods;

Their number last he sums. And now his heart
Distends with pride, and hardening in his strength,
Glories : for never, since created man,
Met such embodied force, as nam'd with these
Could merit more than that small infantry
Warr'd on by cranes; though all the giant brood
Of Phlegra with the heroic race were join'd
That fought at Thebes and Ilium, on each side
Mixed with *auxiliar gods ;* and what resounds
In fable or romance of Uther's son
Begirt with British and Armorick knights ;
And all who since, *baptized or infidel,*
Jousted in Aspramont, or Montalban,
Damasco, or Morocco, or Trebisond,
Or whom Biserta sent from Africk shore,
When Charlemain with all his peerage fell
By Fontarabbia. Thus far these beyond
Compare of mortal prowess, yet observ'd
Their dread commander : he, above the rest
In shape and gesture proudly eminent,
Stood like a tower : his form had yet not lost
All her original brightness ; nor appear'd
Less than arch-angel ruin'd, and the excess
Of glory obscur'd : as when the sun, new risen,
Looks through the horizontal misty air
Shorn of his beams ; or from behind the moon,
In dim eclipse, disastrous twilight sheds
On half the nations, and with fear of change
Perplexes monarchs. Darken'd so, yet shone
Above them all the arch-angel : but his face
Deep scars of thunder had intrench'd ; and care
Sat on his faded cheek ; but under brows
Of dauntless courage, and considerate pride,
Waiting revenge.

VULCAN.

Nor was his name unheard, or unador'd
In ancient Greece ;—and in Ausonian land
Men call'd him *Mulciber ;* and how he fell
From heaven, they fabled, thrown by angry Jove
*Sheer o'er the crystal battlements.   From morn
To noon he fell ;—from noon to dewy eve,
A summer's day ; and with the setting sun
Dropt from the zenith like a falling star.*

THE FALLEN ANGELS HEARD RISING FROM COUNCIL.

Their rising all at once was as the sound
Of thunder heard remote.

SATAN ON THE WING FOR EARTH.

Meanwhile the adversary of God and man,
Satan, with thoughts inflam'd of highest design,
Puts on swift wings, and toward the gates of hell
Explores his solitary flight : sometimes
He scours the right-hand coast, sometimes the left ;
Now shaves with level wing the deep ; then soars
Up to the fiery concave towering high.
*As when far off at sea a fleet descried
Hangs in the clouds,* by equinoctial winds
Close sailing from Bengala, or the isles
Of Ternate and Tidore, whence merchants bring

Their spicy drugs; they, on the trading flood,
Through the wide Ethiopian to the Cape,
Ply stemming nightly towards the pole : So seem'd
Far off the flying Fiend.

THE MEETING OF SATAN AND DEATH.

The other shape,
If shape it might be call'd that shape had none
Distinguishable in member, joint, or limb ;
Or substance might be call'd that shadow seem'd,
For each seemed either : black it stood as Night,
Fierce as ten Furies, terrible as Hell,
And shook a dreadful dart ; what *seem'd* his head
The likeness of a kingly crown had on.
Satan was now at hand, and from his seat
The monster moving onward came as fast
With horrid strides ; Hell trembled as he strode.
The undaunted Fiend what this might be admir'd,
Admir'd, not fear'd ; God and his Son except,
Created thing nought valued he, nor shunn'd ;
And with disdainful look thus first began :—
" Whence and what art thou, *execrable shape !*
That dar'st, though grim and terrible, advance
Thy miscreated front athwart my way
To yonder gates ? through them I mean to pass,
That be assur'd, without leave asked of thee :
Retire, or taste thy folly ; and learn by proof,
Hell-born ! not to contend with Spirits of Heaven."
To whom *the Goblin,* full of wrath, replied :—
" Art thou that Traitor-angel : art thou he
Who first broke peace in Heaven, and faith, till then
Unbroken ; and in proud rebellious arms
Drew after him the third part of Heaven's sons
Conjur'd against the Highest ; for which both thou
And they, outcast from God, are here condemn'd
To waste eternal days in woe and pain !

And reckon'st thou thyself with Spirits of Heaven,
Hell-doomed! and breath'st defiance here and scorn,
Where I reign king, and to enrage thee more,
Thy king and lord?   Back to thy punishment,
False fugitive! and to thy speed add wings,
Lest with a whip of scorpions I pursue
Thy lingering, or with one stroke of this dart,
Strange horror seize thee, and pangs unfelt before "
     So spake *the grizly Terror*, and in shape
So speaking and so threatening, grew ten-fold
More dreadful and deform.   On the other side
Incens'd with indignation, Satan stood
Unterrified, *and like a comet burn'd,*
That fires the length of Ophiuchus huge
In the arctic sky, and from his horrid hair
Shakes pestilence and war.   Each at the head
Levelled his deadly aim; their fatal hands
No second stroke intend; and such a frown
Each cast at the other, *as when two black clouds*
With Heaven's artillery fraught, come rattling on
Over the Caspian, then stand front to front,
Hovering a space, till winds the signal blow
To join their dark encounter in mid air:
So frown'd the mighty combatants, that hell
Grew darker at their frown; so match'd they stood;
For never but once more was either like
To meet so great a foe: and now great deeds
Had been achiev'd, whereof all hell had rung,
Had not the snaky Sorceress that sat
Fast by hell-gate, and kept the fatal key,
Risen, and with hideous outcry rush'd between.

L'ALLEGRO.

Hence, loathed Melancholy,
Of Cerberus and blackest midnight born
In Stygian cave forlorn,
'Mongst horrid shapes, and shrieks, and sights unholy!
Find out some uncouth cell,
Where brooding Darkness spreads his jealous wings,
And the night-raven sings ;
There under *ebon shades*, and low brow'd rocks
As ragged as thy locks,
In dark Cimmerian desert ever dwell.

But come, thou goddess fair and free,
In heaven yclept Euphrosyne,
And by men, heart-easing Mirth ;
Whom lovely Venus at a birth,
With two sister Graces more,
To ivy-crownèd Bacchus bore :
Or whether (as some sager sing) (¹)
The frolic wind, that breathes the spring,
Zephyr with Aurora playing,
As he met her once a Maying,
There on beds of violets blue
And fresh-blown roses wash'd in dew,
Fill'd her with thee, a daughter fair,
So buxom, blithe and debonair,
Haste thee, Nymph, and bring with thee
Jest and youthful Jollity,
Quips and Cranks, and wanton Wiles, (²)
Nods and Becks and *wreathèd Smiles*
Such as hang on Hebe's cheek,
And love to live in dimple sleek ;
Sport that wrinkled Care derides,
And Laughter holding both his sides.

Come and trip it, as you go,
On the light fantastic toe ;
And in thy right hand lead with thee
The mountain-nymph, sweet Liberty ;
And, if I give thee honour due,
Mirth, admit me of thy crew,
To live with her, and live with thee,
In unreprovèd pleasures free ;
To hear the lark begin his flight,
And singing, *startle* the dull night,
From his watch-tower in the skies,
Till the dappled dawn doth rise ;
Then to come *in spite of sorrow,*
And at my window bid good morrow,
Through the sweetbrier, or the vine, (³)
Or the twisted eglantine ;
While the cock with lively din
Scatters the rear of *darkness thin,*
And to the stack or the barn-door
Stoutly struts his dames before :
Oft listening how the hounds and horn
Cheerly rouse the slumbering morn,
From the side of some hoar hill,
Through the high wood echoing shrill :
Sometimes walking, *not unseen,*
By hedgerow elms, on hillocks green,
Right against the eastern gate
Where the great Sun begins his state,
Robed in flames and amber light,
The clouds in thousand liveries dight ;
While the ploughman, near at hand
Whistles o'er the furrowed land,
And the milkmaid singeth blithe,
And the mower whets his scythe,
And every shepherd tells his tale (⁴)
Under the hawthorn in the dale.
Straight mine eye hath caught new pleasures,
Whilst the landskip round it measures ;
Russet lawns, and fallows gray,
Where the nibbling flocks do stray ;

Mountains, on whose barren breast
The labouring clouds do often rest :
Meadows trim with daisies pied,
Shallow brooks and rivers wide.
Towers and battlements it sees
Bosom'd high in tufted trees,
Where perhaps *some beauty lies,*
The cynosure of neighbouring eyes. ([b])
Hard by, *a cottage chimney smokes*
From betwixt two aged oaks ;
Where Corydon and Thyrsis, met,
Are at their savoury dinner set
Of herbs, and other country messes,
Which the neat-handed Phillis dresses ;
And then in haste her bower she leaves
With Thestylis to bind the sheaves ;
Or, if the earlier season lead,
To the tann'd haycock in the mead.
Sometimes, with secure delight,
The upland hamlets will invite,
When the merry bells ring round,
And the jocund rebecks sound
To mǎnÿ ǎ youth and mǎnÿ ǎ maid,
Dancing in the chequer'd shade ;
And young and old come forth to play
On a sunshine holiday,
Till the live-long day-light fail.
Then to the spicy nut-brown ale,
With stories told of many a feat,
How faery Mab the junkets eat ;
She was pinch'd, and pull'd, she said,
And he, by friars' lantern led ;
Tells how the drudging Goblin sweat,
To earn his cream-bowl duly set,
When in one night, ere glimpse of morn,
His shadowy flail had thrash'd the corn,
That ten day-labourers could not end ;
Then lies him down the lubber fiend,
And stretch'd out all the chimney's length
Basks at the fire his hairy strength ;

And crop-full out of doors he flings,
Ere the first cock his matin rings.
Thus done the tales, *to bed they creep,*
By whispering winds soon lull'd asleep
Tower'd cities please us then,
And the busy hum of men,
Where throngs of knights and barons bold,
In weeds of peace, high triumphs hold,
With store of ladies, whose bright eyes
Rain influence, (⁶) and judge the prize
Of wit, or arms, while both contend
To win her grace, whom all commend.
There let Hymen oft appear
In saffron robe, with taper clear;
And pomp, and feast, and revelry,
With masque and antique pageantry;
Such sights as youthful poets dream
On summer eves by haunted stream.
Then to the well-trod stage anon,
If Jonson's learned sock be on, (⁷)
Or sweetest Shakspeare, Fancy's child,
Warble his native wood-notes wild.
And ever against eating cares,
Lap me in soft Lydian airs,
Married to immortal verse,
Such as the meeting soul may pierce,
In notes with many a winding bout
Of linkèd sweetness long drawn out,
With wanton heed and giddy cunning,
The melting voice through mazes running,
Untwisting all the chains that tie
The hidden soul of harmony;
That Orpheus' self may heave his head
From golden slumbers on a bed
Of heap'd Elysian flowers and hear
Such strains as would have won the ear
Of Pluto, to have quite set free
His half regain'd Eurydice.
These delights if thou canst give,
Mirth, with thee I mean to live.

Milton shows his early fondness for the Italian language, by taking from it the titles of these poems. *L'Allegro* is the mirthful (man), and *Il Penseroso* the melancholy (pensive rather, or thoughtful). These two poems are supposed, with good reason, to have been written at Horton in Buckinghamshire, where his parents were residing at the time of their composition. I mention this circumstance, first because it is pleasant to know when poetry is written in poetical places, and next for the sake of such readers as may happen to know the spot.

(¹) (*Some sager sing.*)

Ben Jonson, in one of his Masks. "Because," says Warburton, "those who give to Mirth such gross companions as Eating and Drinking, are the less sage mythologists."

(²) *Quips and Cranks, and wanton Wiles.*

What a *Crank* is, the commentators are puzzled to say. They guess, from · analogy with "winding turns" (which the word originally appears to signify), that the poet means *cross purposes,* or some other such pastime. The witty author of *Hints to a Young Reviewer* (afterwards, I believe, no mean reviewer himself), who criticised these poems upon the pleasant assumption of their having "just come out," and expressed his astonishment at "Mr. Milton's amatory notions" (I quote from memory), takes occasion, from the obscurity of this word, to observe that the "phenomenon of a tripping crank" would be very

15

curious, and "doubtless attract numerous spectators."
He also, in references to passages a little further on,
wonders how "Mirth can be requested to *come* and *go*
at the same instant;" and protests at the confident
immorality of the "young gentleman who takes himself
for a poet," in proposing to live with Mirth and Liberty
both together.

> To live with her, and live with thee,
> In unreproved pleasures free.

How delightful is wit, when bantering in *behalf* of
excellence!

(²) *Through the sweetbrier*, &c.

' Sweetbrier and eglantine," says Warton, "are the
same plant: by the *twisted* eglantine he therefore means
the honeysuckle: all three are plants often growing against
the side or walls of a house." This is true ; yet the
deduction is hardly certain. The same name sometimes
means different flowers, in different counties ; as may be
seen from passages in Shakspeare. *Eglantine,* however,
is the French word for the flower of the sweetbrier
(*églantier*) ; and hence it came to mean, in English, the
brier itself. Perhaps, if Milton had been asked why he
used it in this place, he would have made Johnson's noble
answer to the lady, when she inquired why he defined
pastern, in his Dictionary, to be a horse's *knee ;* —
"Ignorance, madam, ignorance." Poets are often fonder
of flowers than learned in their names ; and Milton, like
his illustrious brethren, Chaucer and Spenser, was born
within the sound of Bow bell.

(⁴) *And every shepherd tells his tale.*

It used to be thought, till Mr. Headley informed Warton otherwise, that *telling his tale* meant telling a *love-tale*, or *story*. The correction of this fancy is now admitted; namely, that *tale* is a technical word for *numbering* sheep, and is so used by several poets, — Dryden for one. Warton, like a proper Arcadian, was loth to give up the fancy; but he afterwards found the new interpretation to be much the better one. *Every* shepherd telling his *story* or *love-tale*, under a *hawthorn*, at one and the same instant, all over a district, would resemble indeed those pastoral groups upon bed-curtains, in which, and in no other place, such marvels are to be met with. Yet, in common perhaps with most young readers, I remember the time when I believed it, and was as sorry as Warton to be undeceived.

(⁵) *The cynosure of neighbouring eyes.*

Cynosure (dog's-tail) for *load-star*, must have been a term a little hazardous, as well as over-learned, when it first appeared; though Milton, thinking of the nymph who was changed into the star so called (since known as Ursa minor), was probably of opinion that it gave his image a peculiar fitness and beauty. That enjoying and truly poetical commentator, Thomas Warton, quotes a passage from Browne's *Britannia's Pastorals*, that may have been in Milton's recollection :—

Yond palace, whose pale turret-tops
Over the stately wood survey the copse,

and then he indulges in pleasing memories of the old style
of building, and in regrets for the new, which was less
picturesque and less given to concealment. " This was
the great mansion-house," says he, " in Milton's early
days. With respect to their rural residences, there was a
coyness in our Gothic ancestors. Modern seats are seldom
so deeply ambushed." Warton would have been pleased
at the present revival of the old taste, which indeed is far
superior to the bald and barrack-like insipidities of his
day ; though as to the leafy accessories, I am afraid the
poetic pleasure of living "embosom'd" in trees is not
thought the most conducive to health.

(⁶) *Rain influence.*

Da begli *occhi* un piacer si caldo *piove.*

Such fervent pleasure *rains* from her sweet *eyes.*

—*Petrarch*, Son. cxxxi.

(⁷) *Jonson's learned sock.*

"Milton has more frequently and openly copied the
plays of Beaumont and Fletcher than of Shakspeare. One
is therefore surprised, that in his panegyric on the stage
he did not mention the twin bards, when he celebrated
the learned sock of Jonson and the wood-notes wild of
Shakspeare. But he concealed his love."—WARTON.

Perhaps he was afraid of avowing it, on account of the
licence of their muse.

IL PENSEROSO.

Hence, vain deluding Joys,
The brood of Folly *without Father* bred!
How little you bested,
Or fill the fixèd mind with all your toys!
Dwell in some idle brain,
And fancies fond with gaudy shapes possess,
As thick and numberless
As the gay motes that *people* the sunbeams; (⁸)
Or likest hovering dreams,
The fickle pensioners of Morpheus' train.

But hail, thou Goddess, sage and holy,
Hail, divinest Melancholy!
Whose saintly visage is too bright
To hit the sense of human sight,
And therefore, to our weaker view,
O'erlaid with black, staid Wisdom's hue;
Black, but such as in esteem
Prince Memnon's sister might beseem, (⁹)
Or that starr'd Ethiop queen that strove
To set her beauty's praise above
The sea-nymphs, and their powers offended:
Yet thou art higher far descended:
Thee bright-haired Vesta, long of yore,
To solitary Saturn bore;
His daughter she; in Saturn's reign
Such mixture was not held a stain:
Oft in glimmering bowers and glades
He met her, and in secret shades
Of woody Ida's inmost grove,
Whilst yet there was no fear of Jove.
Come, pensive nun, devout and pure,
Sober, stedfast, and demure,
All in a robe of darkest grain,
Flowing with majestic train,

And sable stole of Cypress lawn
Over thy decent shoulders drawn.
Come, but keep thy wonted state,
With even step and musing gait,
And looks commèrcing with the skies,
Thy rapt soul sitting in thine eyes;
There held in holy passion still,
Forget thyself to marble, till,
With a sad leaden downward cast,
Thou fix them on the earth as fast.—
And join with thee calm Peace and Quiet,
Spare Fast, *that oft with gods doth diet,*
And hears the Muses in a ring
Aye round about Jove's altar sing :
And add to these retired Leisure,
That in trim gardens takes his pleasure :
But first, and chiefest, with thee bring
Him that yon soars on golden wing,
Guiding the fiery-wheeled throne,
The cherub Contemplation ; ([10])
And the mute Silence *hist along,*
Less Philomel will deign a song,
In her sweetest saddest plight,
Smoothing the rugged brow of night,
While Cynthia checks her dragon yoke
Gently o'er the accustom'd oak.
Sweet bird, that shunn'st the noise of folly,
Most musical, most melancholy ! ([11])
Thee, chauntress, oft the woods among
I woo to hear thy even-song;
And missing thee, I walk *unseen*
On the dry smooth-shaven green,
To behold the wandering moon
Riding near her highest noon,
Like one that hath been led astray ([12])
Through the heaven's wide pathless way :
And oft, as if her head she bow'd,
Stooping through a fleecy cloud.
Oft, on a plot of rising ground,
I hear the far-off curfew sound

Over some wide-water'd shore,
Swinging slow with sullen roar ;
Or, if the air will not permit,
Some *still removed place* will fit,
Where glowing embers through the room ([13])
Teach light to counterfeit a gloom ;
Far from all resort of mirth,
Save the cricket on the hearth,
Or the bellman's drowsy charm,
· To bless the doors from nightly harm.
Or let my lamp, at midnight hour,
Be *seen* in some *high lonely tower,* ([14])
Where I may oft out-watch the Bear
With thrice-great Hermes, or unsphere
The spirit of Plato, to unfold
What worlds, or what vast regions, hold
The immortal mind, that hath forsook
Her mansion in this fleshly nook :
And of those demons that are found
In fire, air, flood, or under ground,
Whose power hath a true consent
With planet or with element.
Sometime let gorgeous Tragedy
In *sceptred pall* come sweeping by,
Presenting Thebes or Pelops' line,
Or the tale of Troy divine ;
Or what (though rare) of later age
Ennobled hath the buskin'd stage.
But O, sad virgin, that thy power
Might raise Musæus from his bower !
Or bid the soul of Orpheus sing
Such notes as, warbled to the string,
Drew *iron* tears down Pluto's cheek,
And made Hell grant what love did seek !
Or call up him that left half told ([15])
The story of Cambuscan bold,
Of Camball, and of Algarsife,
And who had Canace to wife,
That own'd the virtuous ring and glass:
And of the wondrous horse of brass,

On which the Tartar king did ride:
And if aught else great bards beside
In sage and solemn tunes have sung,
Of turneys and of trophies hung,
Of forests and enchantments drear,
Where more is meant than meets the ear.
Thus, Night, oft see me in thy pale career,
Till civil-suited morn appear;
Not trick'd and flounc'd as she was wont
With the Attic boy to hunt,
But kercheft in a comely cloud,
While rocking winds are piping loud,
Or usher'd with a shower still
When the gust hath blown his fill,
Ending on the rustling leaves
With minute-drops from off the eaves ,
And when the sun begins to fling
His flaring beams, me, Goddess, bring
To arched walks of twilight groves,
And shadows brown, that Sylvan loves,
Of pine, or monumental oak,
Where the rude axe, with heavèd stroke,
Was never heard the nymphs to daunt,
Or fright them from their hallow'd haunt.
There in close covert by some brook,
Where no profaner eye may look,
Hide me from day's *garish* eye,
While the bee with honied thigh,
That at her flowery work doth sing,
And the waters murmuring,
With such consort as they keep,
Entice the dewy-feather'd Sleep;
And let some strange mysterious dream
Wave at his wings in airy stream
Of lively portraiture display'd,
Softly on my eyelids laid;
And, as I wake, sweet music breathe
Above, about, or underneath,
Sent by some spirit to mortals good,
Or the unseen Genius of the wood,

But let my due feet never fail
To walk the *studious cloisters pale*,
And love the high embowèd roof,
With antick pillars, massy proof,
And storied windows richly dight,
Casting a dim religious light :
There let the pealing organ blow
To the full-voic'd quire below ;
In service high and anthems clear,
As may with sweetness, through mine ear,
Dissolve me into ecstacies,
And bring all heaven before mine eyes.
And may at last my weary age
Find out the peaceful hermitage,
The hairy gown and mossy cell,
Where I may sit and rightly spell
Of every star that heaven doth shew,
And every herb that sips the dew ;
Till old experience do attain
To something like prophetic strain.
These pleasures, Melancholy, give,
And I with thee will choose to live.

He puts the *Penseroso* last, as a climax ; because he prefers the pensive mood to the mirthful. I do not know why he spells the word in this manner. I have never seen it without the *i*,—*Pensieroso*. In Florio's *Dictionary* the *ie* varies into an *o*,—*Pensoroso ;* whence apparently the abbreviated form,—*Pensoso*.

(⁸) *As thick as motes in the sunne beams.*—CHAUCER.

But see how by one word, *people*, a great poet improves what he borrows.

(⁹) *Prince Memnon's sister.*

It does not appear, by the ancient authors, that Memnon had a sister; but Milton wished him to have one; so here she is. It has been idly objected to Spenser, who dealt much in this kind of creation, that he had no right to add to persons and circumstances in old mythology. As if the same poetry which saw what it did might not see more!

(¹⁰) *The cherub Contemplation.*

Learnedly called cherub, not seraph; because the cherubs were the angels of knowledge, the seraphs of love. In the celestial hierarchy, by a noble sentiment, the seraphs rank higher than the cherubs.

(¹¹) *Most musical, most melancholy.*

A question has been started of late years, whether the song of the nightingale is really melancholy; whether it ought not rather to be called merry, as, in fact, Chaucer does call it. But *merry*, in Chaucer's time, did not mean solely what it does now; but any kind of hasty or strenuous prevalence, as " merry *men*," meaning men in their heartiest and manliest condition. He speaks even of the " merry organ," meaning the church organ—the " merry organ of the mass." Coleridge, in some beautiful lines, thought fit to take the merry side, out of a notion, real or supposed, of the necessity of vindicating nature from sadness. But the question is surely very simple,—one of pure association of ideas. The nightingale's song is not in itself melancholy, that is, no result of sadness on the part of the bird; but coming, as it does, in the nigh time, and making us reflect, and reminding us by its very beauty of the mystery and fleetingness of all sweet things, it becomes melancholy in the finer sense of the word, by the combined overshadowing of the hour and of thought.

(^{12}) *Like one that hath been led astray.*

This calls to mind a beautiful passage about the moon, in Spenser's *Epithalamium* :—

> Who is the same that at my window peeps?
> Or who is that fair face that shines so bright?
> Is it not Cynthia, she that never sleeps,
> *But walks about high heaven all the night?*

(^{13}) *Where glowing embers.*

Here, also, the reader is reminded of Spenser.—See p. 114 :—

> A little glooming light, much like a shade.

(^{14}) *Or let my lamp, at midnight hour,*
> *Be seen.*

The picturesque of the " be seen " has been much admired. Its good-nature seems to deserve no less approbation. The light is seen afar by the traveller, giving him a sense of home comfort, and perhaps helping to guide his way.

(^{15}) *Call up him that left half told*
> *The story of Cambuscan bold.*

Chaucer, with his *Squire's Tale*. But why did Milton turn Càmbuscàn, that is, Cambus the Khan, into Cambùscan? The accent in Chaucer is never thrown on the middle syllable.

LYCIDAS.

The poet bewails the death of his young friend and fellow-student, Edward King, of Christ's College, Cambridge, who was drowned at sea, on his way to visit his friends in Ireland. The vessel, which was in bad condition, went suddenly to the bottom, in calm weather, not far from the English coast; and all on board perished. Milton was then in his twenty-ninth year, and his friend in his twenty-fifth. The poem, with good reason, is supposed to have been written, like the preceding ones, at Horton, in Buckinghamshire :—

Yet once more, O ye laurels, and once more,
Ye myrtles brown, with ivy never sere.
I come to pluck your berries harsh and crude,
And with forc'd fingers rude
Shatter your leaves before the mellowing year.
Bitter constraint, and sad occasion dear,
Compels me to disturb your season due :
For Lycidas is dead, dead ere his prime,
Young Lycidas, and hath not left his peer.
Who would not sing for Lycidas ? he knew
Himself to sing, and build the lofty rhyme.
He must not float upon his watery bier
Unwept, and welter to the parching wind,
Without the meed of *some melodious tear*. ([16])
  Begin, then, sisters of the sacred well,
That from beneath the seat of Jove doth spring,
Begin, and somewhat loudly sweep the string. ([17])
Hence with denial vain, and coy excuse,
So may some gentle Muse
With lucky words favour my destin'd urn,
And, as he passes, turn,
And bid fair peace be to my sable shroud.
  For we were nurst upon the self-same hill,
Fed the same flock by fountain, shade, and rill :

Together both, e'er the high lawns appear'd
Under the opening eyelids of the Morn,
We drove a-field, and both together heard
What time the grey-fly winds her *sultry* horn,
Batt'ning our flocks with the fresh dews of night
Oft till the star, that rose, at evening, bright,
Tow'rd heav'n's descent had slop'd his west'ring wheel.
Meanwhile the rural ditties were not mute,
Temper'd to the oaten flute;
Rough Satyrs danc'd; and Fauns with cloven heel
From the glad sound would not be absent long,
And old Damætas lov'd to hear our song.
    But, O the heavy change, *now thou art gone,*
Now thou art gone, and never must return!
Thee, Shepherd, thee the woods and desert caves
With wild thyme and the *gadding* vine o'ergrown,
And all their echoes mourn.
The willows, and the hazel copses green,
Shall now no more be seen
Fanning their joyous leaves to thy soft lays.
As killing as the canker to the rose,
Or taint worm to the weanling herds that graze,
Or frost to flowers, that their gay wardrobe wear,
When first the white thorn blows;
Such, Lycidas, thy loss to shepherd's ear.
    Where were ye, Nymphs, when the remorseless deep
Clos'd o'er the head of your lov'd Lycidas? ([18])
For neither were ye playing on the steep,
Where your old bards, the famous Druids, lie,
Nor on the shaggy top of Mona high,
Nor yet where Deva spreads her *wizard* stream: ([19])
Ay me! I fondly dream,
Had ye been there—for what could that have done?
What could the Muse herself that Orpheus bore,
The Muse herself, for her enchanting son,
Whom universal Nature did lament,
When, by the rout that made the hideous roar,
His *gory visage* down the stream was sent,
Down the swift Hebrus to the Lesbian shore?

Alas! what boots it with incessant care
To tend the homely, slighted, shepherd's trade,
And strictly meditate the thankless Muse?
Were it not better done, as others use,
To sport with Amaryllis in the shade,
Or with the tangles of Neæra's hair?
Fame is the spur that the clear spirit doth raise
(*That last infirmity of noble mind*)
To scorn delights, and live laborious days;
But the fair guerdon when we hope to find,
And think to burst out into sudden blaze,
Comes the blind Fury with th' abhorred shears,
And slits the thin-spun life.—" *But not the praise,*"
Phœbus reply'd, *and touch'd my trembling ears;*
" Fame is no plant that grows on mortal soil.
Nor in the glistering foil
Set off to the world, nor in broad rumour lies,
But lives, *and spreads aloft by those pure eyes,*
And perfect witness of all-judging Jove;
As he pronounces lastly on each deed,
Of so much fame in heaven expect thy meed."
    O fountain Arethuse, and thou honour'd flood,
Smooth-sliding Mincius, crown'd with vocal reeds,
That strain I heard was of a higher mood:
But now my oat proceeds,
And listens to the herald of the sea
That came in Neptune's plea;
He ask'd the waves, and ask'd the felon winds,
What hard mishap hath doom'd this gentle swain?
And question'd *every gust of rugged wings*
That blows from off each beaked promontory:
They knew not of his story;
And sage Hippotades their answer brings,
That not a blast was from his dungeon stray'd;
The air was calm, *and on the level brine
Sleek Panope with all her sisters play'd.*
It was that fatal and perfidious bark,
Built in the eclipse, and rigg'd with curses dark,
That sunk so low that sacred head of thine.

Next Camus, reverend sire, went footing slow,
His mantle hairy, and his bonnet sedge,
Inwrought with figures dim, and on the edge
Like to that sanguine flower inscrib'd with woe. ([20])
" Ah ! who hath reft," quoth he, " my dearest pledge ? "
Last came, and last did go, ([21])
The pilot of the Galilean lake ;
Two massy keys he bore of metals twain,
(The golden opes, the iron shuts amain,)
He shook his mitred locks, and stern bespake :
" How well could I have spar'd for thee, young swain, ([22])
Enow of such, as for their bellies' sake
Creep, and intrude, and climb into the fold ?
Of other care they little reckoning make,
Than how to scramble at the shearers' feast,
And shove away the worthy bidden guest ;
Blind mouths ! that scarce themselves know how to hold
A sheep-hook, or have learn'd aught else the least
That to the faithful herdman's art belongs !
What recks it them ? What need they ? They are sped ;
And, when they list, their lean and flashy songs
Grate on their scrannel pipes of wretched straw ;
The hungry sheep look up, and are not fed,
But swoln with wind and the rank mist they draw,
Rot inwardly, and foul contagion spread :
Besides what the grim wolf with privy paw
Daily devours apace, and nothing said :
But that two-handed engine at the door
Stands ready to smite once, and smite no more."
Return, Alpheus, the dread voice is past, ([23])
That shrunk thy streams ; return, *Sicilian Muse,*
And call the vales, and bid them hither cast
Their bells, and flowerets, of a thousand hues ;
Ye valleys low, where the mild whispers use
Of shades, and wanton winds, and gushing brooks,
On whose fresh lap the swart-star sparely looks—
Throw hither all your *quaint enamell'd eyes,*
That on the green turf *suck the honied showers,* ([24])
And purple all the ground with vernal flowers :
Bring the rathe primrose that forsaken dies,

The tufted crow-toe, and pale jessamine,
The white pink, and the pansy *freak'd* with jet,
The glowing violet, (²⁵)
The musk-rose, and the well attir'd woodbine,
With cowslips wan that hang the pensive head,
And every flower that sad embroidery wears:
Bid amaranthus all his beauty shed,
And daffodillies fill their cups with tears,
To strew the laureat hearse where Lycid lies;
For, so to interpose a little ease,
Let our frail thoughts dally with false surmise.—
Ah me! whilst thee the shores and sounding seas
Wash far away, where'er thy bones are hurl'd,
Whether beyond the stormy Hebrides,
Where thou perhaps, under the whelming tide,
Visit'st the bottom of the monstrous world;
Or whether thou, to our moist vows denied,
Sleep'st by the fable of Bellarus old,
Where the great vision of the guarded Mount (²⁶)
Looks towards Namancos and Bayona's hold;
Look homeward, Angel, now. and melt with ruth:
And, O ye dolphins! waft the hapless youth.
   Weep no more, woful Shepherds, weep no more,
For Lycidas, your sorrow, is not dead,
Sunk though he be beneath the watèry floor;
So sinks the day-star in the ocean bed,
And yet anon repairs his drooping head,
And tricks his beams, and with new-spangled ore
Flames in the forehead of the morning sky;
So Lycidas sunk low, but mounted high,
Through the dear might of Him that walk'd the waves:
Where, other groves and other streams along,
With nectar pure his oozy locks he laves,
And hears the unexpressive nuptial song
In the blest kingdoms meek of joy and love.
There entertain him all the saints above,
In solemn troops and sweet societies,
That sing, and, singing, in their glory move,
And wipe the tears for ever from his eyes.
Now Lycidas, the shepherds weep no more

Henceforth thou art the genius of the shore,
In thy large recompence, and shalt be good
To all that wander in that perilous flood.
 Thus sang the uncouth swain to the oaks and rills,
While the still morn went out with sandals gray ;
He touch'd the tender stops of various quills,
With eager thought warbling his Doric lay :
And now the sun had *stretch'd out all the hills,*
And now was dropt into the western bay :
At last he rose, and twitch'd his mantle blue :
To-morrow to fresh woods and pastures new.

(¹⁶) *Without the meed of some melodious tear.*

Catullus uses the word in a like sense, when alluding to the elegies of Simonides in his touching expostulation with his friend Cornificius, whom he requests to come and see him during a time of depression :—

Paulum quid lubet allocutionis
Mæstius lacrymis Simonideis.

Prithee a little talk for ease, for ease,
Sad as the tears of poor Simonides.

(¹⁷) *Begin, and somewhat loudly sweep the string.*
Hence with denial vain, &c.

The first of these lines has a poor, prosaic effect, like one of the inane mixtures of familiarity and assumed importance in the " Pindaric " writers of the age. And " hence with denial vain " is a very unnecessary piece of harshness towards the poor Muses, who surely were not disposed to ill-treat the young poet.

16

(¹⁸) *Clos'd o'er the head*, &c.

The very best image of drowning he could have chosen, especially during calm weather, both as regards sufferer and spectator. The combined sensations of darkness, of liquid enclosure, and of the final interposition of a heap of waters between life and the light of day, are those which most absorb the faculties of a drowning person. *Haud insubmersus loquor.*

(¹⁹) *Nor yet where Deva spreads her wizard stream.*

The river Dee, in Spenser's and Drayton's poetry, and old British history, is celebrated for its ominous character and its magicians.

(²⁰) *Sanguine flow'r inscribed with woe.*

The ancient poetical hyacinth, proved, I think, by Professor Martyn, in his Virgil's *Georgics*, to be the turk's-cap lily, the only flower on which characters like the Greek exclamation of woe, AI, AI, are to be found. The idea in Milton is from Moschus's *Elegy on the Death of Bion* :—

> Νῦν, ὑάκινθε, λάλει τά σὰ γράμματα, καὶ πλέον αἲ αἲ
> Βάμβαλε σοῖς πετάλοισι.

> Now more than ever say, O hyacinth!
> "Ai ai," and babble of your written sorrows.

(²¹) *Last came, and last did go.*

"This passage," says Hazlitt, "which alludes to the clerical character of Lycidas, has been found fault with, as combining the truths of the Christian religion with the fiction of the Heathen mythology. I conceive there is very little foundation for this objection, either in reason or good taste. I will not go so far as to defend Camoens, who, in his *Lusiad*, makes Jupiter send Mercury with a dream to propagate the Catholic religion; nor do I know that it is generally proper to introduce the two things in the same poem, though I see no objection to it here; but of this I am quite sure, that there is no inconsistency or natural repugnance between this poetical and religious faith in the same mind. To the understanding, the belief of the one is incompatible with that of the other, but, in the imagination, they not only may, but do constantly, co-exist. I will venture to go farther, and maintain that every classical scholar, however orthodox a Christian he may be, is an honest Heathen at heart. This requires explanation. Whoever, then, attaches a reality to any idea beyond the mere name, has to a certain extent (though not an abstract) an habitual and practical belief in it. Now, to any one familiar with the names of the personages of the heathen mythology, they convey a positive identity beyond the mere name. We refer them to something out of ourselves. It is only by an effort of abstraction that we divest ourselves of the idea of their reality; all our involuntary prejudices are on their side. This is enough for the poet. They impose on the imagination by the attractions of beauty and grandeur. They come down to us in sculpture and in song. We have the same associations with them as if they had really been: for the belief of the fiction in ancient times has produced all the same effects as the reality could have done. It was a reality to the minds of the ancient Greeks and Romans, and through them it is reflected to us."—*Lectures on the English Poets* (Templeman's edition), p. 328.

(²²) "*How well could I have spar'd,*" &c.

"He here animadverts," says Warton, "to the endowments of the church, at the same time insinuating that they were shared by those only who sought the emoluments of the sacred office, to the exclusion of a learned and conscientious clergy." An old complaint! Meantime the church has continued mild and peaceful. An incalculable blessing!

(²³) *Return, Alpheus,* &c.

How much more sweet and Christian Paganism itself sounds, after those threats of religious violence! The "two-handed engine" is supposed to mean the axe preparing for poor, weak, violent Laud! Milton was now beginning to feel the sectarian influence of his father; one, unfortunately, of a sullen and unpoetical sort.

(²⁴) *Honied showers.*

There is an awkwardness of construction between this and the preceding line which hurts the beautiful idea of the *flowers* "sucking the honied showers," by seeming to attribute the suction to their "eyes." There might, indeed, be learned allowance for such an ellipsis; and we hardly know where to find the proper noun substantive or predicate for the verb, if it be not so; but the image is terribly spoilt by it.

(²⁵) *Glowing violet.*

Why " glowing ? " The pansy (heart's-ease) " freak'd with jet " is exquisite ; equally true to letter and spirit.

(²⁶) *The great Vision of the guarded Mount.*

This is the Archangel Michael, the guardian of seamen, sitting on the Mount off the coast of Cornwall known by his name, and looking towards the coast of Gallicia. It is rather surprising that Milton, with his angelical tendencies, did not take the opportunity of saying more of him. But the line is a grand one.

COMUS THE SORCERER.

THYRSIS *tells the Brothers of a Lady, that their Sister has fallen into the hands of the Sorcerer* COMUS, *dwelling in a wood.*

Within the navel of this hideous wood,
Immur'd in cypress shades, a sorcerer dwells,
Of Bacchus and of Circe born,—great Comus,
Deep skill'd in all his mother's witcheries ;
And here to every thirsty wanderer
By sly enticement gives his baneful cup,
With many murmurs mix'd, whose pleasing poison
The visage quite transforms of him that drinks,
And the inglorious likeness of a beast
Fixes instead, *unmoulding reason's mintage*
Character'd in the face. This have I learnt,
Tending my flocks hard by i' the hilly crofts,
That brow this bottom-glade ; whence, night by night,
He and his monstrous rout are heard to howl,
Like stabled wolves, or tigers at their prey,

Doing abhorrèd rites to Hecatè
In their obscurèd haunts of inmost bowers ;
Yet have they many baits and guileful spells,
To inveigle and invite the unwary sense
Of them that pass unweeting by the way.
This evening late, by then the chewing flocks (27)
Had ta'en their supper on the savoury herb
Of knot-grass dew-besprent, and were in fold,
I sat me down to watch upon a bank
With ivy canopied, and interwove
With *flaunting* honey-suckle, and began,
Wrapt in a pleasing fit of melancholy,
To meditate my rural minstrelsy,
Till fäncy had her fill ; but, ere a close,
The wonted roar was up amidst the woods,
And fill'd the air with barbarous dissonance ;
At which I ceas'd, and listen'd them awhile,
Till an unusual stop of sudden silence
Gave respite to the drowsy frighted steeds,
That draw the litter of close-curtained Sleep ;
At last *a soft and solemn-breathing sound*
Rose like a steam of rich distill'd perfumes,
And stole upon the air, that even Silence
Was took ere she was ware, and wish'd she might
Deny her nature, and be never more
Still to be so displac'd.   I was all ear,
And took in strains that might create a soul
Under the ribs of Death : but O ! ere long,
Too well did I perceive it was the voice
Of my most honour'd lady, your dear sister.
Amaz'd I stood, harrow'd with grief and fear,
And, O poor hapless nightingale, thought I,
How sweet thou sing'st, how near the deadly snare !
Then down the lawns I ran with headlong haste,
Through paths and turnings often trod by day ;
Till, guided by mine ear, I found the place,
Where that damn'd wizard, hid in sly disguise,
(For so by certain signs I knew,) had met
Already, ere my best speed could prevent,
The aidless innocent lady, his wish'd prey ;

Who gently ask'd if he had seen such two,
Supposing him some neighbour villager.
Longer I durst not stay, but soon I guess'd
Ye were the two she meant; with that I sprung
Into swift flight, till I had found you here ;
But further know I not.
 Sec. Br.   O night, and shades !
How are ye join'd with hell in triple knot
Against the unarmed weakness of one virgin,
Alone and helpless ! Is this the confidence
You gave me, Brother ?
 Eld. Br.   Yes, and keep it still :
Lean on it safely ; not a period
Shall be unsaid for me : against the threats
Of malice, or of sorcery, or that power
Which erring men call chance, this I hold firm ;—
Virtue may be assail'd, but never hurt,—
Surpris'd by unjust force, but not enthrall'd ;
Yea, even that, which mischief meant most harm,
Shall in the happy trial prove most glory ;
But evil on itself shall back recoil,
And mix no more with goodness ; when at last,
Gather'd like scum, and settled to itself,
It shall be in eternal restless change,
Self-fed and self-consumèd ; if this fail,
The pillar'd firmament is rottenness,
And earth's base built on stubble.

(²⁷) *The chewing flocks,* &c.

" The supper of the sheep," says Warton, " is from a beautiful comparison in Spenser,—

> As gentle shepherd, in sweet eventide,
> When ruddy Phœbus gins to welk (decline) in west,
> High on a hill, his flock to viewen wide,
> Marks which do *bite their hasty supper best.*
>   *Faerie Queene,* i. s. 23."

" Chewing flocks " is good, but not equal to " biting their hasty supper." It is hardly dramatical, too, in the speaker to stop to notice the sweetness and dewiness of the sheep's grass, while he had a story to tell, and one of agitating interest to his hearers.

COLERIDGE.

BORN, 1773—DIED, 1834.

COLERIDGE lived in the most extraordinary and agitated period of modern history; and to a certain extent he was so mixed up with its controversies, that he was at one time taken for nothing but an apostate republican, and at another for a dreaming theosophist. The truth is, that both his politics and theosophy were at the mercy of a discursive genius, intellectually bold but educationally timid, which, anxious, or rather willing, to bring conviction and speculation together, mooting all points as it went, and throwing the subtlest-glancing lights on many, ended in satisfying nobody, and concluding nothing. Charles Lamb said of him, that he had "the art of making the unintelligible appear intelligible." He was the finest dreamer, the most eloquent talker, and the most original thinker of his day; but for want of complexional energy, did nothing with all the vast *prose* part of his mind but help the Germans to give a subtler tone to criticism, and sow a few valuable seeds of thought in minds worthy to receive them. Nine-tenths of his theology would apply equally well to their own creeds in the mouths of a Brahmin or a Mussulman.

His poetry is another matter. It is so beautiful, and was so quietly content with its beauty, making no call on the critics, and receiving hardly any notice, that people are but now beginning to awake to a full sense of its merits. Of pure poetry, strictly so called, that is to say, consisting of nothing but its essential self, without conventional and perishing helps, he was the greatest master of his time. If you could see it in a phial, like a distillation of roses (taking it, I mean, at its best), it would be found without a speck. The poet is happy with so good a gift, and the reader is "happy in his happiness." Yet so little, sometimes, are a man's contemporaries and personal acquaintances able or disposed to estimate him properly, that while Coleridge, unlike Shakspeare, lavished praises on his poetic friends, he had all the merit of the generosity to himself; and even Hazlitt, owing perhaps to causes of political alienation, could see nothing to admire in the exquisite poem of *Christabel*, but the description of the quarrel between the friends! After speaking, too, of the *Ancient Mariner* as the only one of his poems that he could point out to any one as giving an adequate idea of his great natural powers, he adds, "It is High German, however, and in it he seems to conceive of poetry but as a drunken dream, reckless, careless, and heedless of past, present, and to come." This is said of a poem, with which fault has been found for the exceeding conscientiousness of its moral! O ye critics, the best of ye, what havoc does personal difference play with your judgments! It was not Mr. Hazlitt's only or most unwarrantable censure, or one which friendship found hardest to forgive. But peace, and honour too, be with his memory! If he was a splenetic and sometimes jealous man, he was a disinterested politician and an admirable critic : and lucky were those whose natures gave them the right and the power to pardon him.

Coleridge, though a born poet, was in his style and general musical feeling the disciple partly of Spenser, and partly of the fine old English ballad-writers in the collection of Bishop Percy. But if he could not improve on them in some things, how he did in others, especially in the art of being thoroughly musical! Of all our writers of the briefer narrative poetry, Coleridge is the finest since Chaucer ; and assuredly he is the sweetest of all our poets. Waller's music is but a court-flourish in comparison ; and though Beaumont and Fletcher, Collins, Gray, Keats, Shelley, and others, have several as sweet passages, and Spenser is in a certain sense musical throughout, yet no man has written whole poems, of equal length, so perfect in the sentiment of music, so varied with it, and yet leaving on the ear so unbroken and single an effect.

> *A damsel with a dulcimer*
> *In a vision once I saw ;*
> *It was an Abyssinian maid,*
> *And on her dulcimer she play'd,*
> *Singing of Mount Abora.*

That is but one note of a music ever sweet, yet never cloying.

> It ceas'd; yet still the sails made on
> A pleasant noise till noon—
> A noise like of a hidden brook
> In the leafy month of June,
> *That to the sleeping woods all niyht*
> *Singeth' a quiet tune.*

The stanzas of the poem from which this extract is made (*The Ancient Mariner*) generally consist of four lines only; but see how the " brook " has carried him on with it through the silence of the night.

I have said a good deal of the versification of *Christabel*, in the Essay prefixed to this volume, but I cannot help giving a further quotation :—

> It was a lovely sight to see
> The lady Christabel, when she
> Was praying at the old oak tree.
> *Amid the jagged shadows*
> *Of mossy leafless boughs,*
> *Kneeling in the moonlight*
> *To make her gentle vows ;*
> Her slender palms together press'd,
> *Heaving sometimes on her breast ;*
> *Her face resigned to bliss or bale—*
> *Her face, O call it fair, not pale !*
> And both blue eyes more bright than clear,
> *Each about to have a tear.*

All the weeping eyes of Guido were nothing to that. But I shall be quoting the whole poem. I wish I could; but I fear to trespass upon the bookseller's property. One more passage, however, I cannot resist. The good Christabel has been undergoing a trance in the arms of the wicked witch Geraldine :—

A star hath set, a star hath risen,
  O Geraldine! since arms of thine
Have been the lovely lady's prison.
  O Geraldine! one hour was thine—
Thou hast thy will! *By tarn and rill*
The night-birds all that hour were still,

(An appalling fancy)

But now they are *jubilant* anew,
From cliff and tower tu-whoo! tu-whoo!
Tu-whoo! tu-whoo! from wood and fell.

And see! the lady Christabel

(This, observe, begins a new paragraph, with a break
the rhyme)

Gathers herself from out her trance;
Her limbs relax, her countenance
Grows sad and soft; the smooth thin lids
Close o'er her eyes; and tears she sheds—
Large tears that leave the lashes bright!
And oft the while she seems to smile,
As infants at a sudden light.

Yea, she doth smile, and she doth weep,
Like a youthful hermitess
Beauteous in a wilderness,
Who praying always, prays in sleep.
And, if she move unquietly,
Perchance 't is but the blood so free
Comes back and tingles in her feet.
No doubt she hath a vision sweet:
What if her guardian spirit 't were?
What if she knew her mother near?
But this she knows in joys and woes,
That saints will aid, if men will call,
For the blue sky bends over all.

We see how such a poet obtains his music. Such
forms of melody can proceed only from the most beautiful

inner spirit of sympathy and imagination. He sympathizes, in his universality, with antipathy itself. If Regan or Goneril had been a young and handsome witch of the times of chivalry, and attuned her violence to craft, or betrayed it in venomous looks, she could not have beaten the soft-voiced, appalling spells, or sudden, snake-eyed glances of the Lady Geraldine,—looks which the innocent Christabel, in her fascination, feels compelled to "imitate."

> A snake's small eye blinks dull and shy,
> And the lady's eyes they shrank in her head,
> Each shrank up to a serpent's eye ;
> And with somewhat of malice and more of dread,
> At Christabel she look'd askance.
>   *   *   *   *   *
> The maid devoid of guile and sin,
> I know not how, in fearful wise,
> So deeply had she drunken in
> That look, those *shrunken serpent eyes,*
> That all her features were resign'd
> To this sole image in her mind,
> *And passively did imitate*
> *That look of dull and treacherous hate.*

This is as exquisite in its knowledge of the fascinating tendencies of fear as it is in its description. And what can surpass a line quoted already in the Essay (but I must quote it again !) for very perfection of grace and sentiment ? —the line in the passage where Christabel is going to bed, before she is aware that her visitor is a witch.

> Quoth Christabel,—So let it be !
> And as the lady bade, did she.
> Her gentle limbs did she undress,
> *And lay down in her loveliness.*

Oh! it is too late now; and habit and self-love
·blinded me at the time, and I did not know (much as I
admired him) how great a poet lived in that grove at
Highgate ; or I would have cultivated its walks more, as I
might have done, and endeavoured to return him, with my
gratitude, a small portion of the delight his verses have
given me.

I must add, that I do not think Coleridge's earlier
poems at all equal to the rest. Many, indeed, I do not
care to read a second time ; but there are some ten or a
dozen, of which I never tire, and which will one day make
a small and precious volume to put in the pockets of all
enthusiasts in poetry, and endure with the language.
Five of these are *The Ancient Mariner, Christabel, Kubla
Khan, Genevieve,* and *Youth and Age.* Some, that more
personally relate to the poet, will be added for the love of
him, not omitting the *Visit of the Gods,* from Schiller,
and the famous passage on the Heathen Mythology, also
from Schiller. A short life, a portrait, and some other
engravings perhaps, will complete the book, after the good
old fashion of Cooke's and Bell's editions of the Poets ;
and then, like the contents of the Jew of Malta's casket,
there will be

Infinite riches in a little room.

LOVE: OR, GENEVIEVE.

All thoughts, *all* passions, *all* delights.
Whatever stirs this mortal frame,
Are *all* but ministers of Love,
And feed his sacred flame.

Oft in my waking dreams do I
Live o'er again that happy hour,
When midway on the mount I lay,
Beside the ruin'd tower.

The moonlight stealing o'er the scene
Had blended with the lights of eve ;
And she was there, my hope, my joy,
My own dear Genevieve !

She leant against the armèd man,
The statue of the armèd knight ;
She stood and listen'd to my lay,
Amid the lingering light.

Few sorrows hath she of her own,
My hope ! my joy ! my Genevieve !
She loves me best whene'er I sing
The songs that make her grieve.

I play'd a soft and doleful air,
I sang an old and moving story—
An old rude song, that suited well
That ruin wild and hoary.

She listen'd with a flitting blush,
With downcast eyes and modest grace,
For well she knew I could not choose
But gaze upon her face.

I told her of the knight that wore
  Upon his shield a burning brand;
And that for ten long years he woo'd
  The lady of the land.

I told her how he pin'd, and—ah!
  The deep, the low, the pleading tone
With which I sang another's love,
  Interpreted my own.

She listened with a flitting blush,
  With downcast eyes and modest grace,
And she *forgave* me, that I gaz'd
  Too fondly on her face!

But when I told the cruel scorn
  That crazed that bold and lovely knight,
And that he cross'd the mountain-woods,
  Nor rested day nor night:

That sometimes from the savage den,
  And sometimes from the darksome shade,
And sometimes starting up at once
  In green and sunny glade,

There came and look'd him in the face
  An angel beautiful and bright;
And that he knew it was a fiend,
  This miserable knight!

And that, unknowing what he did,
  He leap'd amid a murderous band,
And sav'd from outrage worse than death
  The lady of the land!

And how she wept and claspt his knees;
  And how she tended him in vain—
And ever strove to expiate
  The scorn that crazed his brain;

17

And that she nurs'd him in a cave:
   And how his madness went away,
When on the yellow forest leaves
   A dying man he lay.

His dying words—but when I reach'd
   That tenderest strain of all the ditty,
My faltering voice and pausing harp
   Disturb'd her soul with pity.

All impulses of soul and sense
   Had thrill'd my guileless Genevieve;
The music and the doleful tale,
   The rich and balmy eve;

And hopes, and fears that kindle hope,
   An undistinguishable throng,
And gentle wishes long subdued,
   Subdued and cherished long.

She wept with pity and delight,
   She blush'd with love and virgin-shame;
And like the murmur of a dream,
   I heard her breathe my name.

Her bosom heav'd—she stept aside,
   As conscious of my look she stept—
Then suddenly, with timorous eye,
   She fled to me and wept.

She half enclos'd me in her arms,
   She press'd me with a meek embrace;
And bending back her head, look'd up,
   And gazed upon my face.

'Twas partly love and partly fear,
   And partly 'twas a bashful art
That I might rather feel, than see
   The swelling of her heart.

I calm'd her fears, and she was calm,
    And told her love with virgin pride,
    And so I won my Genevieve,
    My own, my beauteous bride!

I can hardly say a word upon this poem for very admiration. I must observe, however, that one of the charms of it consists in the numerous repetitions and revolvings of the words, one on the other, as if taking delight in their own beauty.

KUBLA KHAN.

SUGGESTED TO THE AUTHOR BY A PASSAGE IN PURCHAS'S
PILGRIMAGE.

In Xanadu did Kubla Khan (¹)
    A stately pleasure-dome decree,
Where Alph, the sacred river, ran,
    Through caverns measureless to man,
    Down to a sunless sea.

So twice five miles of fertile ground
With walls and towers were girdled round;
And here were gardens bright with sinuous rills,
Where blossom'd many an incense-bearing tree;
And here were forests ancient as the hills,
Enfolding sunny spots of greenery.

But oh, that deep romantic chasm which slanted
Down the green hill, athwart a cedarn cover!
A savage place! as holy and enchanted
As e'er beneath a waning moon was haunted
By woman wailing for her demon-lover;

And from this chasm, with ceaseless turmoil seething,
As if this earth in fast thick pants were breathing,
A mighty fountain momently was forc'd ;
Amid whose swift half-intermitted burst
Huge fragments vaulted like rebounding hail,
Or chaffy grain beneath the thrasher's flail :
And mid these dancing rocks, at once and ever
It flung up momently the sacred river.
Five miles meandering with a mazy motion,
Through wood and dale the sacred river ran,
Then reach'd *the caverns measureless to man,*
And sank in tumult to a lifeless ocean ;
And mid this tumult Kubla heard from far
Ancestral voices prophesying war. (²)
The shadow of the dome of pleasure
Floated midway on the waves ;
Where was heard the mingled measure
From the fountain and the caves.
It was a miracle of rare device,
A sunny pleasure-dome with caves of ice !
  A damsel with a dulcimer
  In a vision once I saw :
  It was an Abyssinian maid,
  And on her dulcimer she play'd,
  Singing of Mount Abora.
  Could I revive within me
  Her symphony and song,
  To such a deep delight 'twould win me,
  That with music loud and long,
  I would build that dome in air,
  That sunny dome ; those caves of ice ;
  And all who heard should see them there,
  And all should cry, Beware ! Beware !
  His flashing eyes, his floating hair ;
  Weave a circle round him thrice,
  And close your eyes with holy dread,
  For he on honey-dew hath fed,
  And drunk the milk of Paradise.

(¹) *In Xanadu.*

I think I recollect a variation of this stanza, as follows :—

> In Xanadu did Kubla Khan
> A stately *pleasure-house ordain,*
> Where Alph, the sacred river, ran,
> Through caverns measureless to man,
> Down to a sunless *main.*

The nice-eared poet probably thought there were too many *n*'s in these rhymes; and *man* and *main* are certainly not the best neighbours : yet there is such an open-sounding and stately intonation in the words *pleasure-house ordain,* and it is so superior to *pleasure-dome decree,* that I am not sure I would not give up the correctness of the other terminations to retain it.

But what a grand flood is this, flowing down through measureless caverns to a sea without a sun ! I know no other sea equal to it, except Keats's, in his *Ode to a Nightingale ;* and none can surpass that.

(²) *Ancestral voices prophesying war.*

Was ever anything more wild, and remote, and majestic, than this fiction of the " ancestral voices ? " Methinks I hear them, out of the blackness of the past.

YOUTH AND AGE.

Verse, a breeze mid blossoms straying,
Where hope clung feeding like a bee—
Both were mine! Life went a-Maying
With Nature, Hope, and Poesy,
    When I was young!

When I was young? Ah woful *when !*
Ah, for the change 'twixt now and then !
This breathing house not built with hands,
This body that does me grievous wrong,
O'er aery cliffs and glittering sands,
How lightly then it flash'd along !—
Like those trim skiffs, unknown of yore,
On winding lakes and rivers wide
That ask no aid of sail or oar,
That fear no spite of wind or tide !
Nought cared this body for wind or weather,
When Youth and I lived in 't together.

Flowers are lovely ; Love is flower-like :
Friendship is a sheltering tree ;
Oh, the joys that came down shower-like,
Of Friendship, Love, and Liberty,
    Ere I was old !
Ere I was old ? Ah woful *ere !*
Which tells me Youth's no longer here !
O Youth ! for years so many and sweet,
'T is known, that thou and I were one ;
I'll think it but a fond deceit—
It cannot be, that thou art gone !
Thy vesper-bell hath not yet toll'd,
And thou wert aye a masker bold !
What strange disguise hast now put on,
To make believe that thou art gone ?

I see these locks in silvery slips,
This drooping gait; this alter'd size ,
But springtide blossoms on thy lips,
And tears take sunshine from thine eyes !
Life is but thought; so think I will,
That Youth and I are house-mates still.

This is one of the most perfect poems, for style, feeling, and everything, that ever were written.

THE HEATHEN DIVINITIES MERGED INTO ASTROLOGY.

FROM THE TRANSLATION OF SCHILLER'S PICCOLOMINI.

—Fable is Love's world, his home, his birthplace:
Delightedly dwells he 'mong fays and talismans.
And spirits : *and delightedly believes*
Divinities, being himself divine.
The intelligible forms of ancient poets,
The fair humanities of old religion,
The power, the beauty, and the majesty,
That had her haunts in dale, or piny mountain,
Or forest by slow stream, or pebbly spring,
Or chasms and wat'ry depths; all these have vanish'd ;
They live no longer in the faith of reason ;
But still the heart doth need a language ; still
Doth the old instinct bring back the old names ;
And to yon starry world they now are gone,
Spirits or gods, that used to share this earth
With man as with their friend ; and to the lover
Yonder they move ; from yonder visible sky
Shoot influence down ; and even at this day
'T is Jupiter who brings whate'er is great,
And Venus who brings everything that 's fair.

WORK WITHOUT HOPE.

LINES COMPOSED 21ST FEBRUARY, 1827.

All Nature seems at work. Stags leave their lair—
   The bees are stirring—birds are on the wing—
And Winter, slumbering in the open air,
   Wears on his smiling face a dream of Spring !
And I, the while, the sole unbusy thing,
Nor honey make, nor pair, nor build, nor sing.
Yet well I ken the banks where amaranths blow,
Have traced the fount whence streams of nectar flow.
Bloom, O ye amaranths ! bloom for whom ye may ;
For me ye bloom not ! Glide, rich streams, away !
With lips unbrighten'd, wreathless brow, I stroll :
And would you learn the spells that drowse my soul ?
Work without hope draws nectar in a sieve,
   And hope without an object cannot live.

I insert this poem on account of the exquisite imagina-
tive picture in the third and fourth lines, and the terseness
and melody of the whole. Here we have a specimen of a
perfect style,—unsuperfluous, straightforward, suggestive,
impulsive, and serene. But how the writer of such
verses could talk of "work without hope," I cannot say.
What work had he better to do than to write more ? and
what hope but to write more still, and delight himself and
the world ? But the truth is, his mind was too active
and self-involved to need the diversion of work; and
his body, the case that contained it, too sluggish with
sedentary living to like it ; and so he persuaded himself
that if his writings did not sell, they were of no use. Are
we to disrespect these self-delusions in such a man ? No ;
but to draw from them salutary cautions for ourselves,—
his inferiors.

SHELLEY.

BORN, 1792—DIED, 1822.

AMONG the many reasons which his friends had to deplore
the premature death of this splendid poet and noble-
hearted man, the greatest was his not being able to repeat,
to a more attentive public, his own protest, not only
against some of his earlier effusions (which he did in the
newspapers), but against all which he had written in a
wailing and angry, instead of an invariably calm, loving,
and therefore thoroughly helping spirit. His works, in
justice to himself, require either to be winnowed from
what he disliked, or to be read with the remembrance of
that dislike. He had sensibility almost unique, seemingly
fitter for a planet of a different sort, or in more final
condition, than ours: he has said of himself,—so delicate
was his organization,—that he could

> hardly bear
> The weight of the superincumbent hour ;

and the impatience which he vented for some years against
that rough working towards good, called evil, and which

he carried out into conduct too hasty, subjected one of the most naturally pious of men to charges which hurt his name, and thwarted his philanthropy. Had he lived, he would have done away all mistake on these points, and made everybody know him for what he was,—a man idolized by his friends,—studious, temperate, of the gentlest life and conversation, and willing to have died to do the world a service. For my part, I never can mention his name without a transport of love and gratitude. I rejoice to have partaken of his cares, and to be both suffering and benefiting from him at this moment; and whenever I think of a future state, and of the great and good Spirit that must pervade it, one of the first faces I humbly hope to see there, is that of the kind and impassioned man, whose intercourse conferred on me the title of the Friend of Shelley.

The finest poetry of Shelley is so mixed up with moral and political speculation, that I found it impossible to give more than the following extracts, in accordance with the purely poetical design of the present volume. Of the poetry of reflection and tragic pathos, he has abundance; but even such fanciful productions as the *Sensitive Plant* and the *Witch of Atlas* are full of metaphysics, and would require a commentary of explanation. The short pieces and passages, however, before us, are so beautiful, that they may well stand as the representatives of the whole powers of his mind in the region of pure poetry. In sweetness (and not even there in passages) the *Ode to the Skylark* is inferior only to Coleridge,—in rapturous passion to no man. It is like the bird it sings,—enthusiastic, enchanting, profuse, continuous, and alone,—small, but filling the heavens. One of the triumphs of poetry is to associate its remembrance with the beauties of nature. There are probably no lovers of Homer and Shakspeare, who, when looking at the moon, do not often call to mind the descriptions in the eighth book of the *Iliad* and the fifth act of the *Merchant of Venice*. The nightingale (in England) may be said to have belonged exclusively to Milton (see page 230), till a dying young poet of our own day partook of the honour by the production of his exquisite ode : and notwithstanding Shakspeare's lark singing " at heaven's gate," the longer effusion of Shelley will be identified with thoughts of the bird hereafter, in the minds of all who are susceptible of its beauty. What a pity he did not live to produce a hundred such ! or to mingle briefer lyrics, as beautiful as Shakspeare's, with tragedies which Shakspeare himself might have welcomed ! for assuredly, had he lived, he would have been the greatest dramatic writer since the days of Elizabeth, if indeed he has not abundantly proved himself such in his tragedy of the *Cenci*. Unfortunately, in his indignation against every conceivable form of oppression, he took a subject for that play too much resembling one which Shakspeare had taken in his youth, and still more unsuitable to the stage ; otherwise, besides grandeur and terror, there are things in it lovely as heart can worship ; and the author showed himself able to draw both men and women, whose names would have become " familiar in our mouths as household words." The utmost might of gentleness, and of the sweet habitudes of domestic affection, was

never more balmily impressed through the tears of the
reader, than in the unique and divine close of that
dreadful tragedy. Its loveliness, being that of the
highest reason, is superior to the madness of all the
crime that has preceded it, and leaves nature in a state
of reconcilement with her ordinary course. The daughter,
who is going forth with her mother to execution, utters
these final words :—

> Give yourself *no unnecessary pain,*
> My dear Lord Cardinal. Here, mother, tie
> My girdle for me, and bind up this hair
> In any simple knot. Ay, that does well ;
> *And yours, I see, is coming down. How often*
> *Have we done this for one another ! now*
> *We shall not do it any more.* My Lord,
> We are quite ready. *Well,—'t is very well.*

The force of simplicity and moral sweetness cannot go
further than this. But in general, if Coleridge is the
sweetest of our poets, Shelley is at once the most ethereal
and most gorgeous ; the one who has clothed his thoughts
in draperies of the most evanescent and most magnificent
words and imagery. Not Milton himself is more learned
in Grecisms, or nicer in etymological propriety ; and
nobody, throughout, has a style so Orphic and primæval.
His poetry is as full of mountains, seas, and skies, of light,
and darkness, and the seasons, and all the elements of our
being, as if Nature herself had written it, with the creation
and its hopes newly cast around her ; not, it must be con-
fessed, without too indiscriminate a mixture of great and
small, and a want of sufficient shade,—a certain chaotic

brilliancy, "dark with excess of light." Shelley (in the verses to a Lady with a Guitar) might well call himself Ariel. All the more enjoying part of his poetry is Ariel,— the "delicate" yet powerful "spirit," jealous of restraint, yet able to serve; living in the elements and the flowers; treading the "ooze of the salt deep," and running "on the sharp wind of the north;" feeling for creatures unlike himself; "flaming amazement" on them too, and singing exquisitest songs. Alas! and he suffered for years, as Ariel did in the cloven pine: but now he is out of it, and serving the purposes of Beneficence with a calmness befitting his knowledge and his love.

TO A SKYLARK.

I.

Hail to thee, blithe spirit!
Bird thou never wert,
That from heaven, or near it,
Pourest thy full heart
In profuse strains of unpremeditated art. (˙)

II.

Higher still and higher
From the earth thou springest;
Like a cloud of fire,
The blue deep thou wingest,
And singing, still dost soar; and soaring, ever singest.

III.

In the golden lightning
  Of the sunken sun,
O'er which clouds are brightening,
  Thou dost float and run ;
Like an embodied joy, whose race has just begun.

IV.

The pale purple even
  Melts round thy flight;
Like a star of heaven
  In the broad daylight,
Thou art unseen, but yet I hear thy shrill delight.

V.

Keen as are the arrows
  Of that silver sphere
Whose intense lamp narrows
  In the white dawn clear,
Until we hardly see, we feel that it is there.

VI.

All the earth and air
  With thy voice is loud,
As, when night is bare,
  From one lonely cloud
The moon rains out her beams, and heaven is overflow'd.

VII.

What thou art, we know not.
  What is most like thee?
From rainbow clouds there flow not
  Drops so bright to see,
As from thy presence showers a rain of melody.

VIII.

Like a poet hidden
  In the light of thought,
Singing hymns unbidden,
  Till the world is wrought
To sympathy with hopes and fears it heeded not.

IX.

Like a high-born maiden (²)
In a palace tower,
Soothing her love-laden
Soul in secret hour
With music sweet as love, which overflows her bower.

X.

Like a glow-worm golden
In a dell of dew,
Scattering unbeholden
Its aërial hue
Among the flowers and grass, which screen it from the view.

XI.

Like a rose embowered
In its own green leaves,
By warm winds deflowered
Till the scent it gives
Makes faint with too much sweet these heavy-winged thieves.

XII.

Sound of vernal showers
On the twinkling grass,
Rain-awakened flowers,
All that ever was
Joyous, and clear, and fresh, thy music doth surpass.

XIII.

Teach me, sprite or bird,
What sweet thoughts are thine :
I have never heard
Praise of love or wine
That *panted* forth a flood of rapture so divine.

XIV.

Chorus hymeneal,
Or triumphal chaunt,
Match'd with thine would be all
But an empty vaunt—
A thing wherein we feel there is some hidden want.

XV.

What objects are the fountains
   Of thy happy strain ?
What fields, or waves, or mountains,
   What shapes of sky or plain ?
What love of thine own kind ?   What ignorance of pain !

XVI.

With thy clear keen joyance
   Languor cannot be :
Shadow of annoyance
   Never came near thee :
Thou lovest ; but ne'er knew love's sad satiety.

XVII.

Waking or asleep,
   Thou of death must deem
Things more true and deep
   Than we mortals dream,
Or how could thy note flow in such a crystal stream ?

XVIII.

We look before and after,
   And pine for what is not ;
Our sincerest laughter
   With some pain is fraught ;
Our sweetest songs are those which tell of saddest thought.

XIX.

Yet if we could scorn
   Hate and pride and fear :
If we were things born
   Not to shed a tear,
I know not how thy joy we ever should come near.

XX.

Better than all measures
   Of delightful sound,
Better than all treasures
   That in books are found,
Thy skill to poet were, *thou scorner of the ground* ! (³)

xxi.

Teach me half the gladness
That thy brain must know .
Such harmonious madness
From my lips would flow,
The world should listen then, as I am listening now.

"In the spring of 1820," says Mrs. Shelley, "we spent a week or two near Leghorn, borrowing the house of some friends, who were absent on a journey to England. It was on a beautiful summer evening, while wandering among the lanes where myrtle hedges were the bowers of the fire-flies, that we heard the carolling of the skylark, which inspired one of the most beautiful of his poems."— Moxon's edition of 1840, p. 278.

Shelley chose the measure of this poem with great felicity. The earnest hurry of the four short lines, followed by the long effusiveness of the Alexandrine, expresses the eagerness and continuity of the lark. There is a luxury of the latter kind in Shakspeare's song, produced by the reduplication of the rhymes :—

> Hark! hark! the lark at heaven's gate sings,
> And Phœbus 'gins *arise*
> His steeds to water at those springs
> On chalic'd flowers that *lies ,*
> And winking mary-buds begin
> To ope their golden *eyes :*
> With everything that pretty bin,
> My lady sweet, *arise.*

"Chalic'd flowers that *lies* " is an ungrammatical licence in use with the most scholarly writers of the time ; and, to say the truth, it was a slovenly one; though there

18

is all the difference in the world between the licence of power and that of poverty.

(¹) *In profuse strains of unpremeditated art.*

During the prevalence of the unimaginative and un-musical poetry of the last century, it was thought that an Alexandrine should always be cut in halves, for the greater sweetness; that is to say, monotony. The truth is, the pause may be thrown anywhere, or even entirely omitted, as in the unhesitating and characteristic instance before us. See also the eighth stanza. The Alexandrines through-out the poem evince the nicest musical feeling.

(²) *Like a high-born maiden*
In a palace tower.

Mark the accents on the word "love-laden," so beauti-fully carrying on the stress into the next line—

Soothing her *love-làden*
Sòul in secret hour.

The music of the whole stanza is of the loveliest sweetness; of energy in the midst of softness; of dulcitude and variety. Not a sound of a vowel in the quatrain resembles that of another, except in the rhymes; while the very sameness or repetition of the sounds in the Alexandrine intimates the revolvement and continuity of the music which the lady is playing. Observe, for instance (for nothing is too minute to dwell upon in such beauty), the contrast of the *i* and *o* in "high-born;" the difference of the *a* in "maiden" from that in "palace;" the strong opposition of *maiden* to *tower* (making the rhyme more vigorous in proportion to the general softness); then the new differences in *soothing*, *love*-laden, *soul*, and *secret*, all diverse from one another, and from the whole strain; and finally, the strain itself, winding up in the Alexandrine with a cadence of particular repetitions, which constitutes nevertheless a new difference on that account, and by the prolongation of the tone

> It gives a very echo to the seat
> Where love is throned.

There is another passage of Shakspeare which it more particularly calls to mind;—the

> Ditties highly penn'd, ·
> Sung by a fair queen in a summer bower
> With ravishing division to her lute.

But as Shakspeare was not writing lyrically in this passage, nor desirous to fill it with so much love and sentiment, it is no irreverence to say that the modern excels it. The music is carried on into the first two lines of the next stanza :—

> Like a glow-worm golden
> In a dell of dew:

a melody as happy in its alliteration as in what may be termed its counterpoint. And the colouring of this stanza is as beautiful as the music.

(³) *Thou scorner of the ground.*

A most noble and emphatic close of the stanza. Not that the lark, in any vulgar sense of the word, "scorns" the ground, for he dwells upon it : but that, like the poet, nobody can take leave of commonplaces with more heavenly triumph.

A GARISH DAY.

(SAID BY A POTENT RUFFIAN.)

The all-beholding sun yet shines ; I hear
A busy stir of men about the streets ;
I see the bright sky through the window-panes :
It is a garish, broad, and peering day ;
Loud, light, suspicious, full of eyes and ears :
And every little corner, nook, and hole,
Is penetrated with the *insolent* light.
Come, darkness !

CONTEMPLATION OF VIOLENCE.

(BY A MAN NOT BAD.)

Spare me now.
I am as one lost in a midnight wood,
Who dares not ask some harmless passenger
The path across the wilderness, *lest he,*
As my thoughts are, should be a murderer.

A ROCK AND A CHASM.

I remember,
Two miles on this side of the fort, the road
Crosses a deep ravine : 't is rough and narrow,
And winds with short turns down the precipice
And in its depth there is a mighty rock,
Which has, from unimaginable years,
Sustained itself with terror and with toil
Over a gulf, and with the agony
With which it clings seems slowly coming down ;
Even as a wretched soul, hour after hour,
Clings to the mass of life ; yet clinging leans,
And, leaning, makes more dark the dread abyss
In which it fears to fall. Beneath this crag,
Huge as despair, as if in weariness,
The melancholy mountain yawns. Below
You hear, but see not, an impetuous torrent
Raging among the caverns ; and a bridge
Crosses the chasm ; and high above these grow,
With intersecting trunks, from crag to crag,
Cedars, and yews, and pines ; whose tangled hair
Is matted in one solid roof of shade
By the dark ivy's twine. *At noon-day here*
'T is twilight, and at sunset blackest night.

LOVELINESS INEXPRESSIBLE.

Sweet lamp ! my moth-like muse has burnt its wings ,
Or, like a dying swan who soars and sings,
Young Love should teach Time in his own gray style
All that thou art. Art thou not void of guile ;
A lovely soul form'd to be blest and bless ?
A well of seal'd and secret happiness,

Whose waters like blithe light and music are,
*Vanquishing dissonance and gloom ?—*a star
Which moves not in the moving heavens, alone !
A smile amid dark frowns ?—a gentle tone
Amid rude voices ?—a beloved sight ?
A Solitude, a Refuge, a Delight ?
A lute, *which those whom love has taught to play,*
Make music on, to soothe the roughest day,
And lull fond grief asleep ?—a buried treasure ?
A cradle of young thoughts of wingless pleasure ?
A violet-shrouded grave of woe ?   I measure
The world of fancies, seeking one like thee,
And find—alas ! mine own infirmity.

EXISTENCE IN SPACE.

Life, like a dome of many-coloured glass,
Stains the white radiance of eternity.

DEVOTEDNESS UNREQUIRING

One word is too often profaned
    For me to profane it ;
One feeling too falsely disdain'd
    For thee to disdain it.
One hope is too like despair
    For prudence to smother,
And pity from thee more dear
    Than that from another.

I can give not what men call love ;
    But wilt thou accept not
The worship the heart lifts above,
    And the Heavens reject not ?
The desire of the moth for the star ;
    Of the night for the morrow ;
The devotion to something afar
    From the sphere of our sorrow.

TO A LADY WITH A GUITAR.

Ariel to Miranda :—Take
This slave of music, for the sake
Of him who is the slave of thee ;
And teach it all the harmony
In which thou canst, and only thou,
Make the delighted spirit glow,
Till joy denies itself again,
And, too intense, is turned to pain.
For by permission and command
Of thine own Prince Ferdinand,
Poor Ariel sends this silent token
Of more than ever can be spoken ;
Your guardian spirit, Ariel, who
From life to life must still pursue
Your happiness, for thus alone
Can Ariel ever find his own :
From Prospero's enchanted cell,
As the mighty verses tell,
To the throne of Naples he
Lit you o'er the trackless sea,
Flitting on, your prow before,
Like a living meteor :
When you die, the silent moon,
In her *interlunar swoon,*
Is not sadder in her cell
Than deserted Ariel :

When you live again on earth,
Like an unseen star of birth,
Ariel guides you o'er the sea
Of life from your nativity.
Many changes have been run,
Since Ferdinand and you begun
Your course of love, and Ariel still
Has track'd your steps and serv'd your will.
Now in humbler, happier lot,
This is all remembered not;
And now, alas! the poor sprite is
Imprisoned for some fault of his
In a body like a grave.
From you, he only dares to crave,
For his service and his sorrow,
A smile to-day—a song to-morrow.

The artist who this idol wrought,
To echo all harmonious thought,
Fell'd a tree, while on the steep
The woods were in their winter sleep,
Rock'd in that repose divine
On the wind-swept Apennine:
And dreaming, some of autumn past,
And some of spring approaching fast,
And some of April buds and showers,
And some of songs in July bowers,
And all of love; and so this tree—
O that such our death may be!—
Died in sleep, and felt no pain,
To live in happier form again:
From which, beneath Heaven's fairest star,
The artist wrought this lov'd Guitar,
And taught it justly to reply
To all who question skilfully,
In language gentle as thine own;
Whispering in enamour'd tone
Sweet oracles of woods and dells,
And summer winds in sylvan cells;
For it had learnt all harmonies
Of the plains and of the skies,

Of the forest and the mountains,
And the *many-voicèd fountains*,
The clearest echoes of the hills,
The softest notes of falling rills,
The melodies of birds and bees,
The murmuring of summer seas,
And pattering rain, and breathing dew,
And airs of evening ; and it knew
That seldom-heard mysterious sound,
Which, driv'n on its diurnal round,
As it floats through boundless day,
Our world *enkindles* on its way :—
All this it knows, but will not tell
To those who cannot question well
The spirit that inhabits it ;
*It talks according to the wit
Of its companions ; and no more
Is heard than has been felt before,*
By those who tempt it to betray
These secrets of an elder day.
But, sweetly as its answers will
Flatter hands of perfect skill,
It keeps its highest, holiest tone
For our beloved friend alone.

This is a Catullian melody of the first water. The transformation of the dreaming wood of the tree into a guitar was probably suggested by Catullus's Dedication of the Galley,—a poem with which I know he was conversant, and which was particularly calculated to please him ; for it records the consecration of a favourite old sea-boat to the Dioscuri. The modern poet's imagination beats the ancient ; but Catullus equals him in graceful flow ; and there is one very Shelleian passage in the original :—

> Ubi iste, post phaselus, antea fuit
> Comata silva : nam Cytorio in jugo
> Loquente sæpe sibilum edidit comâ.

For of old, what now you see
A galley, was a leafy tree
On the Cytorian heights, and there
Talk'd to the wind with whistling hair.

MUSIC, MEMORY, AND LOVE.

TO ————.

Music, when soft voices die, ([1])
Vibrates in the memory ;
Odours, *when sweet violets sicken,*
Live within the sense they quicken;
Rose-leaves, when the rose is dead,
Are heap'd for the beloved's bed ;
And so thy thoughts, when thou art gone,
Love itself shall slumber on.

([1]) *Music, when soft voices die.*

This song is a great favourite with musicians : and no
wonder. Beaumont and Fletcher never wrote anything of
the kind more lovely.

KEATS.

BORN, 1796,—DIED, 1821.

KEATS was born a poet of the most poetical kind. All his
feelings came to him through a poetical medium, or were
speedily coloured by it. He enjoyed a jest as heartily as
any one, and sympathized with the lowliest commonplace;
but the next minute his thoughts were in a garden of
enchantment, with nymphs, and fauns, and shapes of
exalted humanity:

> Elysian beauty, melancholy grace.

It might be said of him, that he never beheld an oak-tree
without seeing the Dryad. His fame may now forgive the
critics who disliked his politics, and did not understand
his poetry. Repeated editions of him in England, France,
and America, attest its triumphant survival of all obloquy;
and there can be no doubt that he has taken a permanent
station among the British Poets, of a very high, if not
thoroughly mature, description.

Keats's early poetry, indeed, partook plentifully of the
exuberance of youth; and even in most of his later, his

sensibility, sharpened by mortal illness, tended to a morbid excess. His region is " a wilderness of sweets,"—flowers of all hue, and " weeds of glorious feature,"—where, as he says, the luxuriant soil brings

> The pipy hemlock to strange overgrowth.

But there also is the " rain-scented eglantine," and bushes of May-flowers, with bees, and myrtle, and bay,—and endless paths into forests haunted with the loveliest as well as gentlest beings; and the gods live in the distance, amid notes of majestic thunder. I do not say that no " surfeit " is ever there; but I do, that there is no end of the " nectared sweets." In what other English poet (however superior to him in other respects) are you so *certain* of never opening a page without lighting upon the loveliest imagery and the most eloquent expressions ? Name one. Compare any succession of their pages at random, and see if the young poet is not sure to present his stock of beauty ; crude it may be, in many instances; too indiscriminate in general ; never, perhaps, thoroughly perfect in cultivation ; but there it is, exquisite of its kind, and filling envy with despair. He died at five-and-twenty ; he had not revised his earlier works, nor given his genius its last pruning. His *Endymion,* in resolving to be free from all critical trammels, had no versification ; and his last noble fragment, *Hyperion,* is not faultless,—but it is nearly so. The *Eve of St. Agnes* betrays morbidity only in one instance (noticed in the comment). Even in his earliest productions, which are to be considered as those of youth just emerging from boyhood, are to be found passages of

as masculine a beauty as ever were written. Witness the
Sonnet on reading Chapman's Homer,—epical in the
splendour and dignity of its images, and terminating with
the noblest Greek simplicity. Among his finished pro-
ductions, however, of any length, the *Eve of Saint Agnes*
still appears to me the most delightful and complete
specimen of his genius. It stands mid-way between his
most sensitive ones (which, though of rare beauty, occa-
sionally sink into feebleness) and the. less generally
characteristic majesty of the fragment of *Hyperion.*
Doubtless his greatest poetry is to be found in *Hyperion ;*
and had he lived, there is as little doubt he would have
written chiefly in that strain ; rising superior to those
languishments of love which made the critics so angry, and
which they might so easily have pardoned at his time of
life. But the *Eve of St. Agnes* had already bid most of
them adieu,—exquisitely loving as it is. It is young, but
full-grown poetry of the rarest description ; graceful as the
beardless Apollo ; glowing and gorgeous with the colours of
romance. I have therefore reprinted the whole of it in the
present volume, together with the comment alluded to in
the Preface ; especially as, in addition to felicity of treat-
ment, its subject is in every respect a happy one, and helps
to "paint" this our bower of "poetry with delight."
Melancholy, it is true, will "break in" when the reader
thinks of the early death of such a writer ; but it is one of
the benevolent provisions of nature, that all good things
tend to pleasure in the recollection ; when the bitterness of
their loss is past, their own sweetness embalms them.

A thing of beauty is a joy for ever.

While writing this paragraph, a hand-organ out-of-doors has been playing one of the mournfullest and loveliest of the airs of Bellini—another genius who died young. The sound of music always gives a feeling either of triumph or tenderness to the state of mind in which it is heard : in this instance it seemed like one departed spirit come to bear testimony to another, and to say how true indeed may be the union of sorrrowful and sweet recollections.

Keats knew the youthful faults of his poetry as well as any man, as the reader may see by the preface to *Endymion,* and its touching though manly acknowledgment of them to critical candour. I have this moment read it again, after a lapse of years, and have been astonished to think how anybody could answer such an appeal to the mercy of strength, with the cruelty of weakness. All the good for which Mr. Gifford pretended to be zealous, he might have effected with pain to no one, and glory to himself ; and therefore all the evil he mixed with it was of his own making. But the secret at the bottom of such unprovoked censure is exasperated inferiority. Young poets, upon the whole,—at least very young poets, —had better not publish at all. They are pretty sure to have faults ; and jealousy and envy are as sure to find them out, and wreak upon them their own disappointments. The critic is often an unsuccessful author, almost always an inferior one to a man of genius, and possesses his sensibility neither to beauty nor to pain. If he does, —if by any chance he is a man of genius himself (and such things have been), sure and certain will be his regret, some day, for having given pains which he might. have turned into noble pleasures; and nothing will console him but that very charity towards himself, the grace of which can only be secured to us by our having denied it. to no one.*

Let the student of poetry observe, that in all the luxury of the *Eve of Saint Agnes* there is nothing of the conventional craft of artificial writers; no heaping up of words or similes for their own sakes or the rhyme's sake; no gaudy commonplaces; no borrowed airs of earnestness; no tricks of inversion; no substitution of reading or of ingenious thoughts for feeling or spontaneity; no irrelevancy or unfitness of any sort. All flows out of sincerity and passion. The writer is as much in love with the heroine as his hero is; his description of the painted window, however gorgeous, has not an untrue or superfluous word; and the only speck of a fault in the whole poem arises from an excess of emotion.

---

* Allusion, of course, is not here made to *all* the critics of the time, but only to such reigning reviewers as took earliest and most frequent notice of Keats. The *Edinburgh Review*, though not quick to speak of him, did so before he died, with a fervour of eulogy at least equal to its objections; and I think I may add, that its then distinguished Editor (who became a revered ornament of the Scottish bench) has since felt his admiration of the young poet increase, instead of diminish.

THE EVE OF SAINT AGNES. (¹)

I.

St. Agnes' Eve—Ah! bitter chill it was ;
The owl, for all his feathers, was a-cold ; (²)
The hare limp'd trembling through the frozen grass,
And silent was the flock in woolly fold ;
Numb were the beadsman's fingers while he told
His rosary, and while his frosted breath,
Like pious incense from a censer old,
Seem'd taking flight for heaven without a death
Past the sweet Virgin's picture, while his prayer he saith.(³)

II.

His prayer he saith, this patient, holy man,
Then takes his lamp, and riseth from his knees,
And back returneth, meagre, barefoot, wan,
Along the chapel aisle by slow degrees :
The sculptur'd dead on each side seem'd to freeze,
Imprison'd in black purgatorial rails :
Knights, ladies, praying in dumb orat'ries,
He passeth by ; and his weak spirit fails
To think how they may ache in icy hoods and mails. (⁴)

III.

Northward he turneth through a little door,
And scarce three steps, ere music's golden tongue
Flatter'd to tears this aged man and poor : (⁵)
But no : already had his death-bell rung ;
The joys of all his life were said and sung :
His was harsh penance on St. Agnes' Eve :
Another way he went, and soon among
Rough ashes sat he, for his soul's reprieve ;
And all night kept awake, for sinner's sake to grieve.

IV.

That ancient beadsman heard the prelude soft ;
And so it chanc'd (for many a door was wide,
From hurry to and fro) soon up aloft
The silver-snarling trumpets 'gan to chide ;
The level chambers, ready with their pride,
Were glowing to receive a thousand guests :
And carvèd angels, ever eager-eyed,
Stared, where upon their heads the cornice rests,
With hair blown back, and wings put cross-wise on their breasts.

V.

At length burst in the argent revelry
With plume, tiara, and all rich array,
Numerous as shadows haunting fairily
The brain, new stuff'd in youth with triumphs gay
Of old romance. These let us wish away,
And turn, sole-thoughted, to one lady there,
Whose heart had brooded all that wintry day
On love, and wing'd St. Agnes' saintly care,
As she had heard old dames full many times declare.

VI.

They told her how, upon St. Agnes' Eve,
Young virgins might have visions of delight ;
And soft adorings from their loves receive
Upon the honey'd middle of the night,
If ceremonies due they did aright ;
As, supperless to bed they must retire,
And couch supine their beauties, lily white ;
Nor look behind nor sideways, but require
Of heaven with upward eyes for all that they desire.

VII.

Full of this whim was youthful Madeline ;
The music, yearning, like a god in pain,
She scarcely heard ; her maiden eyes divine,
Fix'd on the floor, saw many a sweeping train

19

Pass by, she heeded not at all; in vain
Came many a tip-toe amorous cavalier,
And back retired, not cool'd by high disdain,
But she saw not; her heart was otherwhere;
She sigh'd for Agnes' dreams, the sweetest of the year.

VIII.

She danc'd along with vague, regardless eyes,
Anxious her lips, her breathing quick and short;
The hallow'd hour was near at hand; she sighs
Amid the timbrels and the throng'd resort
Of whisperers in anger or in sport;
Mid looks of love, defiance, hate, and scorn;
Hoodwink'd with faery fancy; all amort,
Save to St. Agnes and her lambs unshorn,
And all the bliss to be before to-morrow morn.

IX.

So, purposing each moment to retire,
She linger'd still. Meantime across the moors
Had come young Porphyro, with heart on fire
For Madeline. Beside the portal doors
Buttress'd from moonlight, stands he, and implores
All saints to give him sight of Madeline,
But for one moment in the tedious hours,
That he might gaze and worship all unseen,
Perchance speak, kneel, touch, kiss;—in sooth such things
    have been.

X.

He ventures in, let no buzz'd whisper tell;
All eyes be muffled, or a hundred swords
Will storm his heart, Love's feverous citadel.
For him those chambers held barbarian hordes,
Hyæna foemen, and hot-blooded lords,
Whose very dogs would execrations howl
Against his lineage. Not one breast affords
Him any mercy, in that mansion foul,
Save one old beldame, weak in body and in soul.

XI.

Ah ! happy chance ! the aged creature came
Shuffling along with ivory-headed wand,
To where he stood, hid from the torches' light,
Behind a broad hall pillar, far beyond
The sound of merriment and chorus bland.
He startled her ; but soon she knew his face,
And grasp'd his fingers in her palsied hand :
Saying, " Mercy, Porphyro ! hie thee from this place ;
They are all here to-night, the whole blood-thirsty race.

XII.

" Get hence ! get hence ! there 's dwarfish Hildebrand,
He had a fever late, and in the fit
He cursèd thee and thine, both house and land :
Then there 's that old Lord Maurice, *not a whit*
More tame for his grey hairs—Alas, me ! flit ;
Flit like a ghost away."—" Ah, gossip dear,
We 're safe enough ; here in this arm-chair sit,
And tell me how—"—" Good saints ! not here ! not here !
Follow me, child, or else these stones will be thy bier."

XIII.

He follow'd through a lowly, archèd way,
Brushing the cobwebs with his lofty plume ;
And as she mutter'd, " Well-a-well-a-day ! "
He found him *in a little moonlight room,* (⁶)
Pale, latticed, chill, and silent as a tomb.
" Now tell me where is Madeline," said he ;
" Oh, tell me, Angela, by the holy loom
Which none but secret sisterhood may see,
When they St. Agnes' wool are weaving piously."

XIV.

" St. Agnes ! Ah ! it is St. Agnes' Eve—
Yet men will murder upon holidays ;
Thou must hold water in a witch's sieve,
And be the liege lord of all elves and fays,

To venture so : it fills me with amaze
To see thee, Porphyro!—St. Agnes' Eve !
God's help! my lady fair the conjuror plays
This very night: good angels her deceive !
But let me laugh awhile ; I 've mickle time to grieve."

XV.

Feebly she laugheth in the languid moon,
While Porphyro upon her face doth look,
Like puzzled urchin on an aged crone,
Who keepeth clos'd a wond'rous riddle-book,
As spectacled she sits in chimney nook;
But soon his eyes grow brilliant, when she told
His lady's purpose ; and he scarce could brook
Tears, at the thought of those enchantments cold, (⁷)
And Madeline asleep in lap of legends old.

XVI.

Sudden a thought came, *like a full-blown rose,*
Flushing his brow, and in his painèd heart
Made purple riot; then doth he propose
A stratagem, that makes the beldame start.
" A cruel man and impious thou art;   ·
Sweet lady! let her pray, and sleep and dream,
Alone with her good angels far apart
From wicked men like thee. Go! go! I deem
Thou canst not, surely, be the same that thou dost seem."

XVII.

" I will not harm her, by all saints, I swear ! "
Quoth Porphyro. " Oh, may I ne'er find grace,
When my weak voice shall whisper its last prayer
If one of her soft ringlets I displace,
Or look with *ruffian passion* in her face !
Good Angela, believe me, by these tears,
Or I will, even in a moment's space,
Awake with horrid shout my foemen's ears,
And beard them, though they be more fang'd than wolves and
    bears."

XVIII.

" Ah ! why wilt thou affright a feeble soul ?
A poor, weak, palsy-stricken, *churchyard* thing,
Whose passing bell may ere the midnight toll;
Whose prayers for thee, each morn and evening,
Were never miss'd ? " Thus plaining, doth she bring
A gentler speech from burning Porphyro,
So woeful and of such deep sorrowing,
That Angela gives promise she will do
Whatever he shall wish, betide or weal or woe:

XIX.

Which was to lead him in close secrecy
Even to Madeline's chamber, and there hide
Him in a closet, of such privacy
That he might see her beauty unespied,
And win perhaps that night a peerless bride,
While legion'd fairies paced the coverlet,
And pale enchantment held her sleepy-eyed.
Never on such a night have lovers met,
Since Merlin paid his demon all the monstrous debt. (*)

XX.

" It shall be as thou wishest," said the dame ;
" All cates and dainties shall be storèd there,
Quickly on this feast-night ; by the tambour-frame
Her own lute thou wilt see : no time to spare,
For I am slow and feeble, and scarce dare,
On such a catering, trust my dizzy head.
Wait here, my child, with patience ; kneel in prayer
The while ; ah ! thou must needs the lady wed ;
Or may I never leave my grave among the dead ! "

XXI.

So saying, she hobbled off with busy fear ;
The lover's endless minute slowly pass'd,
The dame return'd, and whisper'd in his ear
To follow her, with aged eyes aghast

From fright of dim espial.   Safe at last,
Through many a dusky gallery, they gain
The maiden's chamber, *silken, hush'd, and chaste,*
Where Porphyro took covert, pleas'd amain :
His poor guide hurried back with agues in her brain.

XXII.

Her faltering hand upon the bulustrade,
Old Angela was feeling for the stair,
When Madeline, St. Agnes' charmed maid,
Rose, like a mission'd spirit, unaware ;
With silver taper-light, and pious care
She turn'd, and down the aged gossip led
To a safe level matting.   Now prepare,
Young Porphyro, for gazing on that bed ;
She comes, she comes again, like ring-dove fray'd and fled.

XXIII.

Out went the taper as she hurried in ;
Its little smoke in pallid moonshine died : ([9])
She clos'd the door, she panteth all akin
To spirits of the air and visions wide ;
Nor utter'd syllable, or " Woe betide ! ".
But to her heart her heart was voluble,
Paining with eloquence her balmy side :
As though a tongueless nightingale should swell
Her throat in vain, and die heart-stifled in her dell.

XXIV.

A casement high and triple-arch'd there was,
All garlanded with carven images
Of fruits, and flowers, and bunches of knot-grass,
And diamonded with panes of quaint device,
Innumerable of stains and splendid dyes,
As are the tiger-moth's deep damask'd wings ,
And in the midst, 'mong thousand heraldries,
And twilight saints, and dim emblazonings,
A shielded scutcheon blush'd with blood of queens and kings. ([10])

XXV.

Full on this casement shone the wintry moon,
And threw warm *gules* on Madeline's fair breast,
As down she knelt for heaven's grace and boon:
Rose-bloom fell on her hands together prest,
And on her silver cross soft amethyst,
And on her hair a glory like a saint;
She seemed a *splendid angel, newly drest,*
Save wings, for heaven :—Porphyro grew faint—(")
She knelt, so pure a thing, so free from mortal taint.

XXVI.

Anon his heart revives: her vespers done,
Of all its wreathèd pearls her hair she frees;
Unclasps her *warmèd* jewels one by one; (¹²)
Loosens her fragrant bodice : *by degrees*
Her rich attire creeps rustling to her knees :
Half hidden, *likè a mermaid in seaweed,*
Pensive awhile she dreams awake, and sees
In fancy fair St. Agnes in her bed,
But dares not look behind, or all the charm is fled.

XXVII.

Soon, trembling in her soft and chilly nest,
In sort of wakeful swoon, perplex'd she lay,
Until the poppied warmth of sleep oppress'd
Her smoothèd limbs, and soul, fatigued away,
Flown, like a thought, until the morrow day ;
Blissfully haven'd both from joy and pain ;
Clasp'd like a missal, where swart Paynims pray ;
Blinded alike from sunshine and from rain,
As though a rose should shut, and be a bud again. (¹³)

XXVIII.

Stol'n to this paradise and so entranc'd,
Porphyro gaz'd upon her empty dress,
And listen'd to her breathing if it chanc'd
To wake unto a slumb'rous tenderness ;

Which when he heard, that minute did he bless,
And breath'd himself; then from the closet crept,
Noiseless as fear in a wide wilderness,
And over the hush'd carpet silent stept,
And 'tween the curtains peep'd, where lo! how fast she slept.

XXIX.

Then, by the bedside, *where the faded moon*
Made a dim silver twilight,—soft he set
A table, and, half-anguish'd, threw thereon
A cloth of *woven crimson, gold, and jet :*—
Oh, for some drowsy Morphean amulet!
The boist'rous, midnight, festive clarion,
The kettle-drum and far-heard clarionet,
Affray his ears, though but in dying tone :—
The hall-door shuts again, and all the noise is gone.

XXX.

And still she slept *an azure-lidded sleep*
In blanchéd linen, smooth and lavender'd,
While he from forth the closet brought a heap
Of candied apple, quince, and plum, and gourd,
With jellies soother than the creamy curd,
And lucent syrups tinct with cinnamon : ([14])
Manna and dates, in argosy transferr'd
From Fez; and spicéd dainties every one,
From silken Samarcand to cedar'd Lebanon.

XXXI.

These delicates he helped with glowing hand
On golden dishes and in baskets bright
Of wreathéd silver; sumptuously they stand
In the retiréd quiet of the night,
Filling the chilly room with perfume light.
" And now, my love, my seraph fair, awake!
Thou art my heaven, and I thine eremite.
Open thine eyes for meek St. Agnes' sake,
Or I shall drowse beside thee, so my soul doth ache."

XXXII.

Thus whispering, his warm, unnervèd arm
Sank in her pillow.   Shaded was her dream
By the dusk curtains ;—'t was a midnight charm
· Impossible to melt as icèd stream :
The lustrous salvers in the moonlight gleam·,
Broad golden fringe upon the carpet lies ;
It seem'd he never, never could redeem
From such a stedfast spell his lady's eyes ;
So mus'd awhile, entail'd in woofèd fantasies.

XXXIII.

Awakening up, he took her hollow lute,—
Tumultuous,—and, in chords that tenderest be,
He play'd an ancient ditty, long since mute,
In Provence call'd " La belle dame sans mercy : "
Close to her ear touching the melody ;—
Wherewith disturb'd she utter'd a soft moan :
He ceas'd—she panted quick—and suddenly
Her blue affrayèd eyes wide open shone :
Upon his knees he sank, pale as smooth sculptured stone.

XXXIV.

Her eyes were open, but she still beheld,
Now wide awake, the vision of her sleep :
There was a painful change that nigh expell'd
The blisses of her dream, so pure and deep,
At which fair Madeline began to weep,   ·
And moan forth witless words with many a sigh ;
While still her gaze on Porphyro would keep ;
Who knelt, with joinèd hands and piteous eye,
Fearing to move or speak, she look'd so dreamingly.

XXXV.

" Ah, Porphyro !" said she, " but even now
Thy voice was a sweet tremble in mine ear,
Made tunable with every sweetest vow ;
And those sad eyes were spiritual and clear ;

How chang'd thou art ! how pallid, chill, and drear !—
Give me that voice again, my Porphyro,
Those looks immortal, those complainings dear ;
Oh ! leave me not in this eternal woe,
For if thou diest, my love, I know not where to go."

XXXVI.

Beyond a mortal man impassion'd far (¹⁵)
At these voluptuous accents he arose,
Ethereal, flush'd, and like a throbbing star
Seen mid the sapphire heaven's deep repose ;
Into her dream he melted, as the rose
Blendeth its odours with the violet,—
Solution sweet. Meantime the frost wind blows
Like love's alarum, pattering the sharp sleet
Against the window-panes : St. Agnes' moon hath set.

XXXVII.

'T is dark; quick pattereth the flaw-blown sleet :
" This is no dream ; my bride, my Madeline ! "
'T is dark : the icèd gusts still rave and beat.
" No dream, alas ! alas ! and woe is mine ;
Porphyro will leave me here to rave and pine ;
Cruel ! what traitor could thee hither bring !
I curse not, for my heart is lost in thine,
Though thou forsakest a deceivèd thing ;—
A dove, forlorn and lost, with sick unprunèd wing."

XXXVIII.

" My Madeline ! sweet dreamer ! lovely bride
Say, may I be for aye thy vassal blest ?
Thy beauty's shield, heart-shap'd, and vermeil-dyed ? (¹⁶)
Ah ! silver shrine, here will I take my rest,
After so many hours of toil and quest—
A famish'd pilgrim, saved by miracle :
Though I have found, I will not rob thy nest,
Saving of thy sweet self ; if thou think'st well
To trust, fair Madeline, to no rude infidel.

XXXIX.

" Hark ! 't is an elfin storm from faery land,
Of haggard seeming, but a boon indeed.
Arise,—arise !—the morning is at hand ;
The bloated wassailers will never heed ;—
Let us away, my love, with happy speed ;
There are no ears to hear, nor eyes to see,—
Drown'd all in Rhenish and the sleepy mead :
Awake ! arise ! my love, and fearless be ;
For o'er the southern moors I have a home for thee."

XL.

She hurried at his words, beset with fears,
For there were sleeping dragons all around
At glaring watch, perhaps with ready spears.
Down the wide stairs a darkling way they found,—
In all the house was heard no human sound.
A chain-droop'd lamp was flickering by each door ;
The arras, rife with horseman, hawk and hound,
Flutter'd in the besieging wind's uproar ;
And the long carpets rose along the gusty floor. (¹⁷)

XLI.

They glide like phantoms into the wide hall ;
Like phantoms to the inner porch they glide,
Where lay the porter, in uneasy sprawl,
With a huge empty flagon by his side ;
The watchful blood-hound rose, and shook his hide,
But his sagacious eye an inmate owns ;
By one, and one, the bolts full easy slide :
The chains lie silent on the foot-worn stones ;
The key turns, and the door upon its hinges groans.

XLII.

And they are gone ; ay, ages long ago,
These lovers fled away *into the storm.*
That night the Baron dreamt of many a woe,
And all his warrior-guests, with shade and form

Of witch, and demon, and large coffin-worm,
Were long benightmared. Angela the old
Died palsy-twitch'd, with meagre face deform :
The beadsman, after thousand aves told,
For aye unsought-for slept among his ashes cold.

(¹) *The Eve of St. Agnes.*

St. Agnes was a Roman virgin, who suffered martyr-
dom in the reign of Dioclesian. Her parents, a few days
after her decease, are said to have had a vision of her,
surrounded by angels and attended by a white lamb, which
afterwards became sacred to her. In the Catholic Church,
formerly, the nuns used to bring a couple of lambs to her
altar during mass. . The superstition is (for I believe it is
still to be found), that, by taking certain measures of
divination, damsels may get a sight of their future hus-
bands in a dream. The ordinary process seems to have
been by fasting. Aubrey (as quoted in Brand's *Popular
Antiquities*) mentions another, which is, to take a row of
pins, and pull them out one by one, saying a Paternoster ;
after which, upon going to bed, the dream is sure to ensue.
Brand quotes Ben Jonson :—

> And on sweet St. Agnes' night,
> Pleas'd you with the promis'd sight,
> Some of husbands, some of lovers,
> Which an empty dream discovers.

(²) *The owl, for all his feathers, was a-cold.*

Could he have selected an image more warm and
comfortable in itself, and, therefore, better contradicted

by the season ? We feel the plump, feathery bird, in his nook, shivering in spite of his natural household warmth, and staring out at the strange weather. The hare cringing through the chill grass is very piteous, and the "silent flock" very patient; and how quiet and gentle, as well as wintry, are all these circumstances, and fit to open a quiet and gentle poem! The breath of the pilgrim, likened to "pious incense," completes them, and is a simile in admirable "keeping," as the painters call it; that is to say, is thoroughly harmonious with itself and all that is going on. The breath of the pilgrim is visible, so is that of a censer; the censer, after its fashion, may be said to pray; and its breath, like the pilgrim's, ascends to heaven. Young students of poetry may, in this image alone, see what imagination is, under one of its most poetical forms, and how thoroughly it "tells." There is no part of it unfitting. It is not applicable in one point, and the reverse in another.

(³) *Past the sweet Virgin's picture*, &c.

What a complete feeling of winter-time is in this stanza, together with an intimation of those Catholic elegances, of which we are to have more in the poem!

(⁴) *To think how they may ache*, &c.

The germ of the thought, or something like it, is in Dante, where he speaks of the figures that perform the part of sustaining columns in architecture. Keats had read Dante in Mr. Cary's translation, for which he had a great respect. He began to read him afterwards in

Italian, which language he was mastering with surprising
quickness. A friend of ours has a copy of Ariosto con-
taining admiring marks of his pen. But the same thought
may have struck one poet as well as another. Perhaps
there are few that have not felt something like it on
seeing the figures upon tombs. Here, however, for the
first time, we believe, in English poetry, it is expressed,
and with what feeling and elegance! Most wintry as well
as penitential is the word "aching" in "icy hoods and
mails;" and most felicitous the introduction of the
Catholic idea in the word "purgatorial." The very colour
of the rails is made to assume a meaning, and to shadow
forth the gloom of the punishment—

Imprisoned in black purgatorial rails.

(⁵) *Flattered to tears.*

This "flattered" is exquisite. A true poet is by
nature a metaphysician; far greater in general than meta-
physicians professed. He feels instinctively what the
others get at by long searching. In this word "flattered"
is the whole theory of the secret of tears; which are the
tributes, more or less worthy, of self-pity to self-love.
Whenever we shed tears, we take pity on ourselves; and
we feel, if we do not consciously say so, that we deserve to
have the pity taken. In many cases, the pity is just, and
the self-love not to be construed unhandsomely. In many
others it is the reverse; and this is the reason why selfish
people are so often found among the tear-shedders, and
why they seem never to shed them for others. They
imagine themselves in the situation of others, as indeed

the most generous must, before they can sympathize; but the generous console as well as weep. Selfish tears are niggardly of everything but themselves.

"Flattered to tears." Yes, the poor old man was moved, by the sweet music, to think that so sweet a thing was intended for his comfort, as well as for others. He felt that the mysterious kindness of heaven did not omit even his poor, old, sorry case, in its numerous workings and visitations; and, as he wished to live longer, he began to think that his wish was to be attended to. He began to consider how much he had suffered—how much he had suffered wrongly and mysteriously—and how much better a man he was, with all his sins, than fate seemed to have taken him for. Hence he found himself deserving of tears and self-pity, and he shed them, and felt soothed by his poor, old, loving self. Not undeservedly either; for he was a painstaking pilgrim, aged, patient, and humble, and willingly suffered cold and toil for the sake of something better than he could otherwise deserve; and so the pity is not exclusively on his own side: we pity him, too, and would fain see him out of that cold chapel, gathered into a warmer place than a grave. But it was not to be. We must therefore console ourselves in knowing, that this icy endurance of his was the last, and that he soon found himself at the sunny gate of heaven.

(6) *A little moonlight room.*

The poet does not make his "little moonlight room" comfortable, observe. The high taste of the exordium is kept up. All is still wintry. There is to be no comfort

in the poem, but what is given by love.   All else may be
left to the cold walls.

(⁷) *Tears*, &c.

He almost shed tears of sympathy, to think how his
treasure is exposed to the cold ; and of delight and pride,
to think of her sleeping beauty, and her love for himself.
This passage, " asleep in lap of legends old," is in the
highest imaginative taste, fusing together the imaginative
and the spiritual, the remote and the near.   Madeline is
asleep in her bed; but she is also asleep in accordance
with the legends of the season ; and therefore the bed
becomes *their* lap as well as sleep's.   The poet does
not critically think of all this; he feels it : and thus
should other young poets draw upon the prominent points
of their feelings on a subject, sucking the essence out
of them into analogous words, instead of beating about
the bush for *thoughts*, and, perhaps, getting clever ones,
but not thoroughly pertinent, not wanted, not the best.
Such, at least, is the difference between the truest poetry
and the degrees beneath it.

(⁸) *Since Merlin paid his demon all the monstrous debt.*

What he means by Merlin's "monstrous debt," I
cannot say.   Merlin, the famous enchanter, obtained King
Arthur his interview with the fair Iogerne ; but though
the son of a devil, and conversant with the race, I am
aware of no debt that he owed them.   Did Keats suppose
that he had sold himself, like " Faustus ?"

(⁹) *Its little smoke in pallid moonshine died.*

This is a verse in the taste of Chaucer, full of minute grace and truth. The smoke of the wax-taper seems almost as ethereal and fair as the moonlight, and both suit each other and the heroine. But what a lovely line is the seventh about the heart,

> Paining with eloquence her balmy side!

And the nightingale! how touching the simile! the heart a " tongueless nightingale," dying in the bed of the bosom. What thorough sweetness, and perfection of lovely imagery! How one delicacy is heaped upon another! But for a burst of richness, noiseless, coloured, suddenly enriching the moonlight, as if a door of heaven were opened, read the stanza that follows.

(¹⁰) *A shielded scutcheon blush'd with blood of queens and kings.*

Could all the pomp and graces of aristocracy, with Titian's and Raphael's aid to boot, go beyond the rich religion of this picture, with its " twilight saints " and its scutcheons " *blushing* with the blood of queens ? "

(¹¹) *Save wings for heaven.*

The lovely and innocent creature, thus praying under the gorgeous painted window, completes the exceeding and unique beauty of this picture,—one that will for ever stand by itself in poetry, as an addition to the stock. It would have struck a glow on the face of Shakspeare himself. He might have put Imogen or Ophelia under such a shrine. How proper as well as pretty the heraldic term

20

gules, considering the occasion. " Red " would not have
been a fiftieth part as good. And with what elegant
luxury he touches the " silver cross " with " amethyst,"
and the fair human hand with " rose-colour," the kin of
their carnation ! The lover's growing " faint " is one
of the few inequalities which are to be found in the latter
productions of this great but young and over-sensitive
poet. He had, at the time of his writing this poem, the
seeds of a mortal illness in him, and he, doubtless, wrote
as he had felt, for he was also deeply in love ; and
extreme sensibility struggled in him with a great under-
standing.

(¹²) Unclasps her warmèd jewels.

How true and cordial the *warmed* jewels, and what
matter of fact also, made elegant, in the rustling down-
ward of the attire ; and the mixture of dress and undress,
and of the dishevelled hair, likened to a " mermaid in
seaweed ! " But the next stanza is perhaps the most
exquisite in the poem.

(¹³) As though a rose should shut.

Can the beautiful go beyond this ! I never saw it.
And how the imagery rises ! flown like a *thought*—bliss-
fully *haven'd*—clasp'd like a missal in a land of *Pagans :*
that is to say, where Christian prayer-books must not be
seen, and are, therefore, doubly cherished for the danger.
And then, although nothing can surpass the preciousness
of this idea, is the idea of the beautiful, crowning all—

> *Blinded* alike from sunshine and from rain,
> *As though a rose should shut, and be a bud again.*

Thus it is that poetry, in its intense sympathy with creation, may be said to create anew, rendering its words more impressive than the objects they speak of, and individually more lasting; the spiritual perpetuity putting them on a level (not to speak it profanely) with the fugitive compound.

([14]) *Lucent syrups tinct with cinnamon.*

Here is delicate modulation, and super-refined epicurean nicety!

Lucent syrups tinct with cinnamon,

make us read the line delicately, and at the tip-end, as it were, of one's tongue.

([15]) *Beyond a mortal man.*

Madeline is half awake, and Porphyro reassures her with loving, kind looks, and an affectionate embrace.

([16]) *Heart-shap'd and vermeil dyed.*

With what a pretty wilful conceit the costume of the poem is kept up in this line about the shield! The poet knew when to introduce apparent trifles forbidden to those who are void of real passion, and who, feeling nothing intensely, can intensify nothing.

([17]) *Carpets rose.*

This is a slip of the memory, for there were hardly carpets in those days. But the truth of the painting makes amends, as in the unchronological pictures of old masters.

LONELY SOUNDS.

Undescribed sounds,
That come *a-swooning* over hollow grounds,
And wither drearily on barren moors.

ORION.

At this, with madden'd stare,
And lifted hands, and trembling lips he stood
Like old Deucalion mountain'd o'er the flood,
Or blind Orion hungry for the morn.

CIRCE AND HER VICTIMS.

Fierce, wan,
And tyrannizing was the lady's look,
As over them a gnarlèd staff she shook.
Ofttimes upon the sudden she laugh'd out,
And from a basket emptied to the rout
Clusters of grapes, the which they raven'd quick
And roar'd for more, with many a hungry lick
About their shaggy jaws.   Avenging, slow,
Anon she took a branch of mistletoe,
And emptied on 't *a black dull gurgling phial :*
Groan'd one and all, as if some piercing trial
Were sharpening for their pitiable bones.
She lifted up the charm : appealing groans
From their poor breasts went suing to her ear
In vain : *remorseless as an infant's bier,*

She whisk'd against their eyes the sooty oil ;
Whereat was heard a noise of *painful toil*,
Increasing gradual to a tempest rage,
Shrieks, yells, and groans, of torture-pilgrimage.

A BETTER ENCHANTRESS IMPRISONED IN THE SHAPE OF A SERPENT.

She was a gordian shape of dazzling hue,
Vermilion-spotted, golden, green, and blue,
Striped like a zebra, speckled like a pard,
Eyed like a peacock, *and all crimson-barr'd*,
And full of silver moons, that as she breath'd
Dissolv'd or brighter shone, or interwreath'd
Their lustres with the gloomier tapestries.
So *rainbow-sided, full of miseries*,
She seem'd, at once, some penanc'd lady elf,
Some demon's mistress, or the demon's self.
Upon her crest she wore *a wannish fire*
Sprinkled with stars, like Ariadne's tiar ;
Her head was serpent; *but, ah bitter sweet !*
She had a woman's mouth, with all its pearls complete.

SATURN DETHRONED.

Deep in the shady sadness of a vale,
Far sunken from the healthy breath of morn,
Far from the fiery noon, *and eve's one star*,
Sat grey-hair'd Saturn, quiet as a stone,
Still as the silence round about his lair ;
Forest on forest hung about his head,
Like cloud on cloud. No stir of air was there,
Not so much life as on a summer's day

Robs not one light seed from the feather'd grass,
But where the dead leaf fell, there did it rest.
A stream went voiceless by, still deaden'd more
By reason of his fallen divinity
Spreading a shade : the Naiad mid her reeds
Press'd her cold finger closer to her lips.
Along the margin sand large footmarks went,
No further than to where his feet had stray'd,
And slept there since. Upon the sodden ground
His old right hand lay nerveless, listless, dead,
Unsceptred ; and his *realmless eyes* were closed.

THE VOICE OF A MELANCHOLY GODDESS SPEAKING TO SATURN.

As when upon a trancèd summer-night
Those green-robed senators of mighty woods,
Tall oaks, branch-charmèd by the earnest stars,
Dream, and so dream all night without a stir,
Save from one gradual solitary gust,
Which comes upon the silence, and dies off,
As if the ebbing air had but one wave :
So came these words, and went.

A FALLEN GOD.

—the bright Titan, frenzied with new woes,
Unus'd to bend, by hard compulsion, bent
His spirit to the sorrow of the time ;
And all along a dismal rack of clouds,
Upon the boundaries of day and night,
He stretch'd himself, in grief and radiance faint.

OTHER TITANS FALLEN.

Scarce images of life, one here, one there,
Lay vast and edgeways ; like a dismal cirque
Of Druid stones, upon a forlorn moor,
When the chill rain begins at shut of eve
In dull November, and their chancel vault,
The heaven itself, is blinded throughout night.

ODE TO A NIGHTINGALE. (¹ᵉ)

My heart aches, and a drowsy numbness pains
  My sense, as though of hemlock I had drunk,
Or emptied some dull opiate to the drains
  One minute past, and Lethe-wards had sunk.
'T is not through envy of thy happy lot,
  But being too happy in thy happiness,—
    That thou, *light-winged Dryad of the trees,*
      In some *melodious plot*
    Of beeches green, *and shadows numberless,*
      Singest of summer in full-throated ease.

Oh, for a draught of vintage, that hath been
  Cool'd a long age in the deep-delvèd earth,
Tasting of Flora and the country-green,
  Dance, and Provençal song, and sun-burnt mirth !
Oh, for a beaker full of the warm South,
  Full of the true, the blushful Hippocrene,
    With beaded bubbles winking at the brim,
      And purple-stainèd mouth ;
    That I might drink, and leave the world unseen,
      And with thee fade away into the forest dim :

Fade far away, dissolve, and quite forget
  What thou among the leaves hast never known,
The weariness, the fever, and the fret
  Here, where men sit, and hear each other groan ;

Where palsy shakes a few, sad, last grey hairs ;
   Where youth grows pale, and spectre-thin, and dies ;
Where but to think is to be full of sorrow
     And leaden-eyed despairs ;
  Where beauty cannot keep her lustrous. eyes,
    Or new love pine at them beyond to-morrow

Away ! away ! for I will fly to thee,
   Not charioted by Bacchus and his pards,
But on the viewless wings of Poesy,
   Though the dull brain perplexes and retards ;
Already with thee ! tender is the night,
   And haply the Queen-Moon is on her throne,
    Cluster'd around by all her starry Fays ;
     But here there is no light,
  Save what from heaven is with the breezes blown
   Through verdurous glooms and winding mossy wavs.

I cannot see what flowers are at my feet,
   Nor what soft incense hangs upon the boughs,
But, in embalmèd darkness, guess each sweet
   Wherewith the seasonable month endows
The grass, the thicket, and the fruit-tree wild ;
   White hawthorn, and the pastoral eglantine ,
    Fast-fading violets, cover'd up in leaves ;
     And mid-May's eldest child,
  The coming musk-rose, full of dewy wine,
   The murmurous haunt of flies on summer eves.

Darkling I listen ; and, for many a time,
   I have been *half in love with easeful Death,*
Call'd him soft names in many a musèd rhyme
   To take into the air my quiet breath ;
Now more than ever seems it *rich* to die,
   To cease upon the midnight with no pain,
    While thou art pouring forth thy soul abroad
     In such an ecstasy !
  Still wouldst thou sing, and I have ears in vain—
   To thy high requiem become a sod.

Thou wast not born for death, immortal bird!
No hungry generations tread thee down ;
The voice I hear this passing night was heard
In ancient days by emperor and clown;
Perhaps the self-same song that found a path
Through the sad heart of Ruth, *when, sick for home,*
She stood in tears amid the alien corn ;
The same that ofttimes hath
Charm'd magic casements, opening on the foam
Of perilous seas, in faery lands forlorn. ([19])

Forlorn! the very word is like a bell
To toll me back from thee to my sole self
Adieu! the fancy cannot cheat so well
As she is fam'd to do, deceiving elf.
Adieu! adieu! *thy plaintive anthem fades*
Past the near meadows, over the still stream,
Up the hill side ; and now 't is buried deep
In the next valley-glades!
Was it a vision, or a waking-dream?
Fled is that music? Do I wake or sleep?

([18]) *Ode to a Nightingale.*

This poem was written in a house at the foot of High-gate Hill, on the border of the fields looking towards Hampstead. The poet had then his mortal illness upon him, and knew it. Never was the voice of death sweeter.

([19]) *Charm'd magic casements,* &c.

This beats Claude's *Enchanted Castle,* and the story of *King Beder* in the *Arabian Nights.* You do not know what the house is, or where, nor who the bird. Perhaps a king himself. But you see the window open on the

perilous sea, and hear the voice from out the trees in which
it is nested, sending its warble over the foam.   The whole
is at once vague and particular, full of mysterious life.
You see nobody, though something is heard; and you
know not what of beauty or wickedness is to come over that
sea.   Perhaps it was suggested by some fairy tale.   I
remember nothing of it in the dream-like wildness of
things in *Palmerin of England*, a book which is full of
colour and home landscapes, ending with a noble and
affecting scene of war; and of which Keats was very fond.

ON FIRST LOOKING INTO CHAPMAN'S HOMER.

Much have I travell'd in the realms of gold,
    And many goodly states and kingdoms seen;
    Round many western islands have I been,
Which bards in fealty to Apollo hold:
Oft of one wide expanse had I been told,
    That deep-brow'd Homer ruled as his demesne ·
    Yet did I never breathe its pure serene,
Till I heard Chapman speak out loud and bold:
Then felt I like some watcher of the skies,
    When a new planet swims into his ken;
Or like stout Cortez, when with eagle eyes
    He star'd at the Pacific [20]*—and all his men*
Look'd at each other with a wild surmise—
    Silent, upon a peak in Darien. [21]

[20] *He star'd at the Pacific,* &c.

" Stared " has been thought by some too violent, but
it is precisely the word required by the occasion.   The

Spaniard was too original and ardent a man either to look, or to affect to look, coldly superior to it. His " eagle eyes " are from life, as may be seen by Titian's portrait of him.

The public are indebted to Mr. Charles Knight for a cheap reprint of the *Homer of Chapman.* ·

(²¹) *Silent, upon a peak in Darien.*

A most fit line to conclude our volume. We leave the reader standing upon it, with all the illimitable world of thought and feeling before him, to which his imagination will have been brought, while journeying through these " realms of gold."

Lightning Source UK Ltd.
Milton Keynes UK
UKHW030806221022
410882UK00001B/377